"Amid nature's beauty, hope survives an incredible bloodbath." *(Kirkus)*

"[A] simple but powerful story is given added poignance by Huỳnh's recollections of the family, the life and the land he had to leave." *(Publishers Weekly)*

"The end of his story is *this story* by the fine writer that Huỳnh has become." *(Elle Magazine)*

South Wind Changing is the powerful saga of an unimaginable life's adventure, filled with courage, perseverance, and vision. Jade Ngọc Quang Huỳnh brilliantly captures the suffering, the tenacity, and the hope of the South Vietnamese people in the face of personal and cultural devastation.

The story takes Jade through the wartime shattering of his family, the brutality of prison camp, his numerous attempts at escape, and his struggle to resettle in a new land. Ngọc Quang Huỳnh's story resonates with hope and displays a unique respect for his homeland and his resilience in adapting to the culture he encounters in the United States.

South Wind Changing

South Wind Changing

Jade Ngọc Quang Huỳnh

GRAYWOLF

PRESS

Publication of this volume is made possible in part by a grant provided by
the Minnesota State Arts Board through an appropriation by the Minnesota
State Legislature, and by a grant from the National Endowment for the Arts.
Substantial additional support has been provided by the Andrew W. Mellon
Foundation, the Lila Wallace-Reader's Digest Fund, and the McKnight Foundation; we have received many other generous contributions from foundations,
corporations, and individuals. Graywolf Press is a member agency of United Arts,
Saint Paul. To these organizations and individuals who make our work possible,
we offer heartfelt thanks.

Published by
GRAYWOLF PRESS
2402 University Avenue, Suite 203
Saint Paul, Minnesota 55114
All rights reserved.

Printed in the United States of America.

ISBN 1-55597-198-9
9 8 7 6 5 4 3 2
First Printing, 1994

Library of Congress Cataloging-in-Publication Data
Huỳnh, Jade Ngọc Quang,
  South wind changing / Jade Ngọc Quang Huỳnh.
   p. cm.
   1. Huỳnh, Jade Ngọc Quang, 1957– . 2. Vietnamese Americans—
Biography. I. Title.
E184.V53H88 1994
973'.049592'0092—dc20
[B] 93-11803

ACKNOWLEDGMENTS

I would like to thank Joe McGinniss, my agent Cynthia A. Cannell, Wayne
Hoffman-Ogier, Arturo Vivante, Meredith Steinbach, artist Hieu De, Nick
Carbo, Mark Andres, Joan and Ken Costin, Maxine Swayze, Olga and John Skow,
Margaret Rog, Ellen Foos, and many others.

The author would also like to express thanks to his ghosteditor Robert Monroe,
who assisted and gave suggestions for this book.

FOR MY FAMILY

Book I

CHAPTER 1

I was crying as I came into this world in 1957, the year of the Rooster, born into a family of seventeen children, on an island at the end of the Mekong Delta in South Vietnam. No one could have known, then, how much of my life was to be a continuation of those tears.

My parents had grown up on opposite sides of the Mekong River and had been married through the traditional Confucian arrangement. The island where I was born was tranquil and would remain unaffected by the events which were taking place around it until the TET offensive 1968, when we were thrown into the arms of a war which would claim the lives of six of my brothers and sisters.

My story begins at the beginning of the nineteenth century, during the time my great grandfather, named Khoa, came to live in the newly settled rice-growing region of Vietnam, eventually making his home in the village of An Tan in the province of Vinh Binh. Khoa was poor and illiterate and had a very difficult time adjusting in his new home. Because of his illiteracy, fellow villagers tried to take advantage of him by taking away whatever he made, laughing at him for his lack of education.

Discouraged, Khoa decided to move on and search for a better place to live. But one night he had a dream: he saw a general, clad in ancient armor, riding on a horse and surrounded by soldiers. The general spoke to him saying, "Do not leave this land. Stay here and I will protect you and help you." Afraid of disobeying the general's advice, Khoa stayed in Vinh Binh. In the months that followed, whenever people tried to harm him they would become inexplicably frightened and give up the chase. A few years later, while digging in his field, Khoa found a large pot filled with gold which someone had apparently forgotten (in my country people often bury their treasure). Grateful for his good fortune, advanced in age and having become one of the wealthiest landowners in Vinh Binh, he built a temple in thanksgiving.

Later in life, Khoa became embroiled in an argument regarding an important matter with members of his family. He insisted his point of view was correct, but eventually was proven wrong. Because he was so respected in the community, he felt ashamed that he had lost face, and in his mind, honor. Wishing to clear his name and his family's integrity, he committed suicide by drowning himself in the river—he forced himself deeper and deeper under the water by trapping himself under a heavy wooden divan.

Khoa had a son named Xuoc (my grandfather). Xuoc was the opposite in character of his father: his world consisted of gambling and womanizing. Xuoc did not try to help the people as his father had, and when Xuoc's first son, my father, was born, it was Khoa who supported the child. A bond of respect and affection developed between the boy and the old man. Khoa, being afraid that Xuoc would waste the treasure on gambling, showed only my father where he had re-buried his gold, so that my father could maintain the temple after his death.

When my father married my mother, his father Xuoc did not help them. Consequently, my father had to borrow money, at interest, from his aunt in order to start a small business. We were very poor. Our house was crudely constructed, with only a roof and no walls to give us privacy. We had so little money that my parents had only one pair of silk trousers which had to be shared between my mother and father. Whenever my father received guests, he would use the pants, while my mother, ashamed at her lack of proper attire, hid in the kitchen until the guests left. At first, we had only five chickens. One day my father, feeling pity for his hungry children, prepared to kill a chicken in order to feed us. We refused to let him kill the bird, knowing that with the chicken dead, we would not be able to have eggs to eat the following day.

I grew up in the house on the temple estate my great grandfather had built, studying Buddhism, Confucianism, Taoism and traditional earth medicine with the monks who lived and studied there. I also studied martial arts and meditation to keep me healthy, and chanting. I worked in the garden and sowed rice in the fields. Even today the smell of the new season, the freshness of the harvest, the scent of new rice when its water evaporates as it is being cooked, remains with me. I can still hear the breathing of the water buffalo in the banana grove as it lay down looking for a place to rest, chewing its cud. The peace seemed so eternal.

With time, father's business prospered, so much so that he sent all his children to school and bought houses in the city where we lived, commuting back and forth from the city to the village. Xuoc was angered by my father's "independence" from him, and during the fifteenth and thirtieth days of the month, according to the lunar calendar, he would disgrace my father in front of the whole family and relatives. Xuoc would make my father sit on the divan, situated in the place of honor, in the middle of the mansion, where shimmering black pillars surrounded us like black eyes of staring relatives, while my grandfather and grandmother would kneel on the floor beneath my father, in an attitude of submission. My grandfather held a tray containing an incense burner and a lit candle on his head saying to my father, "You are my ungrateful son. I told you to send all your children to different estates to build up the villages, to work on the rice fields and gardens, but you never listened to me." My grandfather also told my father, "It is more important to measure the rice, not the word," referring to my father's sending all his children to school. All the while my grandfather's hand would be shaking with anger as he held the tray, and all my relatives would sit listening intently, enjoying and encouraging him as he punished my father. Later, at the tomb of my great grandfather Khoa I would find my father sitting, touching the name on the stone and mumbling to himself. I would jump up from the step and sit facing him. He would rub my head. With a heavy voice he would begin to tell me about my great grandfather.

CHAPTER 2

It seems so long since I was a child. But yes, I have a memory of a time, of a place, of a day when I was twelve, when I lived with my big family in the village called An Tan, beside the Mekong River, on the outskirts of Vinh Binh, South Vietnam.

An Tan was a small village governed by an elderly group elected from a population of less than a thousand. There was a river surrounding our village and the government used the river as a borderline to separate all the regions on the map. It was a generous place for the people who lived here—most of them were farmers, and the land was flat and fertile. The area was surrounded by rice fields; everywhere was water and more water, the flood of our lives. A village shrine was the center for our activities: meetings, elections, operas, ceremonies, and the settling of conflicts among villagers took place here. The villagers grew rice every year for the main harvest and when they had free time they spent it in their gardens growing bananas, coconuts, mangos, and vegetables for their own use. My father had 20 acres of orange orchards and ten acres of rice, bought when he borrowed money (with interest) from his aunt; he built it up by himself, and prospered. My mother kept up the house as a housewife. We went to the Catholic school in the village and during the harvest my older brothers helped my father to work on the rice paddies after school, since they were stronger than I was. Our main harvest was in the spring and this was the busiest time each year. Farmers woke up early, when the rooster crowed the third time, prepared for the harvest day, and began working on the farm before the sun rose. People were everywhere—near the river, in the yard, in the garden and on the rice fields, happily chatting with one another wherever the conversation would lead.

On this spring day the buffalo had already dragged the rice stalks to the harvest floor, and the workers had stood them up in a circle on the court. My brother, Lan, a broad-backed and strong boy, brought the basket out and put some hay into it to get it ready for when my uncle needed it. My uncle led two buffaloes to the yard from the creek, and tied them together with a rope, then began to drive them in a circle on the rice stalks. As he walked them around, the buffaloes ground their hooves over the stalks, loosening the grain on the ground. Once in a while he yelled, "Basket, basket!" and Lan would jump off the nearby bench to get a basket with hay in it, so that he could catch the buffalo's dung. When the buffalo finished, my uncle whipped him to walk again. Lan took the basket and dumped it in the garden and put some new hay in it.

I was babysitting my sister, Luoi. We flew a kite on the dike, watching the farmers working on the farm, and waiting for our mother to come back home from the market. Luoi had fat cheeks, soft skin, and black eyes, and whoever saw her could not resist holding her or giving her a kiss. I loved taking care of my sister.

The south wind or *Gio Nom* blew from the South and the rice stalks rubbed against each other like a human voice whispering. Water babbled in the creek and the river as the rice plants bowed like dancers. The sun's warmth beamed down, making the water glisten in different spots. Fresh air brushed our skin—springtime was here, time for a new crop, time for us to get together for a feast, time for people to help one another winnow the rice, time for the buffaloes to get out from their hutches and get busy, time for happy songs. A time when I could see people and children everywhere and a time when people had little to worry about.

As the sun rose higher, the grain absorbed our sweat. Near the dike where we stood, flying the kite a water buffalo family was walking along eating some grass. I saw a boy sitting on the back of a big water buffalo. My sister and I came to him, asking to ride on one of the buffaloes. I sat in back of my sister and held the thread from the kite which flew in the air. Occasionally, a flock of Chim Sac birds landed on the rice stalk where they could get some ripened rice from the golden rice field, touched even now with patches of green. We yelled at them, and the chirping birds flew up in the air, landing at another spot. Luoi smiled, showing her small teeth, and we took turns holding on to the kite. Sometimes we tied the thread onto the buffalo's horns, letting the kite flap its wings by itself in the gentle south wind. We got down from the buffalo and chased grasshoppers.

The ocean-blue sky allowed no shade, as heat waves shimmered over the dry rice and grass. The tired buffaloes slish-sloshed through the mud, while the workers trudged behind them, or lingered at the dike, drinking water from a jug. My aunt stepped out from the garden into the rice field and clanged a gong, calling the workers to lunch. The smell of rice cooking rose as the smoke of village stoves brushed the coconut and areca trees, spreading into the rice paddies. From the distance, I saw a shadow move in our direction, a woman with a basket on her head. I knew it was our mother returning from the market. We rushed to her.

"Mama, mama!" we yelled.

She stepped up to us and rubbed our heads, smiling, her face red and perspiring.

"Where are your hats? I told you to wear them when you play in the sun," she scolded. "Your head is warm now. You're going to get sick, you know."

We held her hand. "Do you have some cookies, mama?"

She began to walk, while we jumped up and down, skipping backwards in front of her. She held the basket in one hand and reached inside to get a loaf of bread for us.

"Share it with your sister. Don't forget to wear your hats when you are playing in this heat," Mother said. "Mama will give you more if you remember that. Let's go home." She took off her hat, putting it on my sister.

I grabbed the bread and ran with my sister to the reed bushes where we had tied the kite. The workers in the field, on their way in for lunch, greeted my mother and asked her about the early market. I pulled the kite down and rolled up the thread. We had tied a little flute to the kite, and it made a chirping noise as it dove like a hawk. Lifting the kite, we ran after our mother and tried to avoid stepping in the mud scattered along the grass on our way home. We would enjoy our evening together, we would sleep well that night.

This was how my life was, and how, after the war mowed through it, it would never be again.

I put on my new clothes after I had New Years Eve dinner with my family at our home in the city. Then, I went with my friends downtown, waiting for the firecracker celebration at midnight. When the festivities ended I decided to go back to the village at my grandfather's house to sleep since tomorrow we had a service at the temple. It would be easy for me to greet my aunt and uncle's family to pay my respects and also get my first New Year Li Xi money. I was tired and fell asleep at once in a dreamless sleep.

Thrashing air awoke me: helicopters, low in the sky. It was dark, a few hours after midnight, I guessed. Dawn would bring the first day of the new year, the day we called Tet. I knew it was a U.S. chopper because we didn't have the southern air force in my home town. I ran to wake up my grandmother and aunt, who hardly had time to ask what it was, and Luoi, my little sister. Then my two brothers, Lan and Tam, came.

"It's fighting! The shooting is real bullets, not firecrackers!" Lan said, "Hide under the divan and listen for my signal."

Tam and Lan snatched at tables and chairs, piling them on and around the divan, as we scrambled under it. My grandmother and my aunt were shaking, speechless. Two of my brothers moved to the kitchen on the other side to bring food closer to us, in case we got stuck there.

I peeped through a hole in the boarded-up window and saw shadows moving from tree to tree. My brother Lan returned with more bags, shouting at me because I hadn't listened to him. "I told you to get under it—do you want to die?" From outside came the sound of people running and of whistling back and forth. There were more helicopters flying over the roof. It sounded as if they were about to land right on top of us. A beam of light swept over the roof, allowing me to see through a crack in the rafters. It moved from one side to another, like someone with a huge flashlight searching for something in the night. The shooting became louder and louder, and then softer and softer, spreading from one spot to another. We stayed under the divan until morning. "It's hard to breathe here. Can I go out there for a while?" I asked my brother, who sat outside on the floor next to our divan, ready to get under if something happened.

"Crawl over here and keep your mouth shut."

I crawled over to him and leaned against the thick cement wall while Luoi, exhausted, fell asleep, gently snoring. I wondered why they would fight during the holidays, when everyone celebrated our traditional New Year. I hated them for destroying my sleep. We crawled back under the divan when we heard a loud shell. My brother moved about *Nha Hau,* the guest house in my grandfather's compound, then moved to the next house. He wanted to know what the situation was outside.

Morning arrived and I thought everything was over. I tried to get back to bed to sleep but there was more noise around our house—on the porch, in the corridor, and in the temple. My grandmother, aunt, two brothers and I went to the window to look. I saw many Viet Cong in black pajamas sitting in a group discussing something. They carried guns. Then one group moved, and another group came as if they had received orders. They were being instructed by a skinny, short man with a striped scarf circled around his neck who carried a small gun. My brother signaled me with his finger to his mouth not to say anything. We went back to our divan. I heard a *Dam Gia* spy plane in the sky and the sound of a rocket shot from a helicopter. Then there was a sound like a cow mooing. (Later, I learned it was a gun that shot 3,500 bullets per minute.) We opened rice cakes to eat with the stew in a pot. My aunt and grandmother asked what we were going to do, but no one could answer the question. We knew for sure we could not get out of the house.

"I want to pee," I said.

"You can't go out. Go to the corner and do it there," my brother answered.

I looked at grandmother and saw she had already wet the fabric of her pants. We moved around the house in silence and made as little sound as possible because we did not want the

VCs to know that we were inside. The shooting continued.

In the afternoon, the fighting seemed to be getting heavier. There were more helicopters in the sky and the VCs ran to the temple court, aiming their AK-47s and shooting whenever the helicopters came in their direction. Then they ran onto the porch to hide. The helicopters shot back and circled around and around. The bullets hit the roof. We crawled under the divan. Bullets hit the wall and the tree outside. I could hear a cracking noise when the bullet hit something, as if the bullet exploded against itself. The chopper pilot was very frustrated and it seemed he shot without aiming. We were flooded with bullets. I heard VCs running to the court and shooting again with the sound of a helicopter over my head. Then I heard the helicopter circle in the air and suddenly I felt as if the air was sucking me in. Something was pressing on my chest, and it was hard for me to breathe. My back and head bounced against the wooden divan. Dirt flew up and everything fell apart—lamps, candles, incense burners, and vases shook and dropped down to the floor from the altar and table. The flower vase that my great-grandfather passed on to my grandfather fell from the top of the altar onto the floor. The earth was shaking like an earthquake. Then there was a sound—sshhhh and boomm.

I didn't know what had happened. I wanted to ask my brother but it seemed like I was deaf. I had no voice. Every one of us lay on the floor and struggled to breathe. I saw blood come out from my brother's mouth and I pulled his hand, but there was no response. Luoi trembled and cried as loud as she could, her face trembling with fear and horror as she squeezed my aunt's arm. I touched my mouth and felt something wet. There was blood on my hand. Things seemed to not exist, and the world seemed to have ended. I was in a dream yet I was not. My aunt regained her consciousness. She checked our bodies to see if we were wounded. Lan was hit very deep on his arm. She tore his shirt, poured some kerosene from the oil lamp onto the wound to prevent it from getting infected, and tied the wound to stop its bleeding. My other brother, Tam, was okay. I was hit and there were scratches everywhere on my legs with small pieces of shrapnel under my skin. Grandmother could not speak anymore; she just opened her eyes and watched. My wounded brother, Lan, looked pale; he had lost a lot of blood.

I moved out from under the divan and came to the window where I could see what had happened outside. The rocket had hit the top roof of the temple and it was burning slowly, emitting black smoke. Small pieces of cement, brick, wood, and tile were everywhere on the ground. The smell of rocket shells burning, the smell of the smoke, and the smell of blood corroded the air and flooded my nose. Some of the VCs were wounded while others helped their wounded men. The helicopter came back again to see the results and circled and shot more bullets. I didn't care to get under the divan anymore. My aunt and brother yelled at me, but I didn't hear them. I inhaled the air of burning gunpowder while smoke from the outside spread inside the house. The day became dark, too dark.

At night, on the second day of the New Year, we were still alive. I began to recover my hearing and the first thing I heard was my aunt crying. The groaning outside became louder, and I heard the accent of a northerner asking directions from the VC. Then, it became quiet again. When the night was almost over, I heard more noises from outside. Flares popped out from the sky and shone down for a while, then it turned dark again, until another flare came. The sound of a spy plane seemed to be in the sky twenty-four hours each day. Choppers flew back and forth like dragonflies hunting for food. By now, I could tell the location of a bullet, rocket, or shell, just by listening to the sound of them moving in the air. I wasn't scared anymore. I prayed to the Buddha and asked him that if he wanted me to die, to let me die instantly so that I wouldn't suffer from wounds. I prayed to him to protect my loved ones. I looked at everyone's weary face and felt impotent. I felt hungry but I couldn't eat anything. The fighting went on.

We had been in the house three days when the VC knocked on our door. We were afraid to answer. He shot at the lock to break it.

"Get all the things we can eat," a skinny VC ordered with his heavy accent, his eyes darting around the room. "We have to have supplies."

Five or six of them clambered into the room.

They all wore black cotton pajamas and striped shawls tucked around their necks. They looked like any one of us, but someone whispered that they looked like ghosts. They began to ransack the place in search of food. The small, thin leader strode over to my older brother Tam and me.

"Our comrades are wounded. You will bring them back to our base, up the river."

"My brother doesn't know how to paddle, sir."

"I don't care. If my wounded comrades die, then you die!" the VC yelled. His eyes bore into us, and his arms looked ready to jerk into action.

"Nephew, you stay. Let me go," my aunt said.

"I don't know how to take care of my brother's wound, aunt. I'll go," I said.

"Move it, don't chat!" the VC shouted.

I followed my brother and went out to the porch where the two wounded VC were lying. We helped them hobble where the canoe was anchored in the creek, and the VC instructed us where to leave his comrades. Another VC came to him for orders. I heard him say that his group could not get through under the heavy fire from the navy post in the city. The VC answered that if he could not get through, he would die there. I thought of my family in the city.

I sat in the front of the canoe and my brother sat in the back while the two wounded VC lay in the middle with their guns pointed at us. We rowed the canoe to the end of the village and left them where they wanted. On our way back to the house, a helicopter saw us paddling on the riverbank. They followed us and opened fire. My brother and I jumped into the water, pushing the canoe beneath the shadow of the trees at the side of the river. The chopper moved away and circled back again.

I put my nose along the side of the canoe to get some air as the chopper hovered above us in the air, waiting for any movement. Bullets hit the water like heavy rain. I was only twelve but I had long legs and I could stand on the mud at the bottom of the creek. The fish were nipping along the scratched wounds on my legs while leeches smelled the blood, diving up and down in the water as if they were in a hunting group. I felt the pain beginning to aggravate me but I couldn't move. I held weed bushes with one hand and with the other I held the bottom of the canoe to stop it from being blown by the wind of the chopper.

We waited for the helicopter to move and then we pushed the canoe to the shadow of another tree along the creek, but the chopper kept following us. Tam signaled me to release the canoe and he pushed it out to the current. The helicopter circled in the sky, came back and hovered over our heads. When the canoe was out of the trees and had reached the middle of the river, I saw it catch fire and explode into pieces. The water shot at me, slapped tree branches and everything around me. I felt as if I was pushed out of the water as a heavy pressure bore down on my chest. The helicopter circled one more time to check his target, then flew away. Tam pulled me near the shore and we moved from one tree shadow to another until we got home.

As we approached, a helicopter shot a rocket at our roof and the house burst into flames. When we got inside the house we saw Luoi lying on the red tile floor, as if she were asleep among the debris. She had no wounds. There was a little smile on her soft face. I didn't have enough energy left in my body to wail, but my tears fell. We moved to the temple veranda to hide ourselves. We buried Luoi in the dark, while flares and red traces shot across the air like funeral drums beating out of order from here and there. I didn't know whether they held the funeral ceremony for her or for someone else but I wanted to cry out loud and I could not produce any sound.

On the fourth day, *mung bon*, we decided to flee to the city. It might be better there, we thought, and in any case my wounded brother needed to be treated. We could not go by canoe or boat because of the choppers. After we put some food and some clothes into a small bag which my older brother Tam carried, my aunt and I helped my wounded brother, Lan. Grandmother followed us like a shadow. When we didn't see any VC outside, we went out to the village road and crept slowly. The tree branches, weedy bushes, and grass were in tatters. The leaves fell with their own wounds, some of them caught in spiders' webs. There were big and small holes on the road and small pieces of soil were tossed everywhere.

The north wind or *Gio Bac* blew from the north, giving me a chill. The shooting went on, with bullets hitting the trees, making a cracking sound which I heard within other sounds of different beats, close to me, away from me, as they passed in the wind. My wounded brother seemed tired after just a short walk. I let him lean on my shoulder, but the odor of blood made me vomit and it seemed to be everywhere in the air. My aunt helped him and let me walk alone. I was wearing my new pants and a new shirt which were bought to celebrate the New Year. When we stopped in front of a neighbor's house, I heard a child crying in a low voice, as if he had been crying for a long time. My brother and I moved into the farmhouse and followed the faint sound of the crying.

A big hay silo stood next to some bamboo bushes and I could see a pregnant woman leaning against the hay silo, wearing a white blouse with red stains all over it, holding a baby tightly in her arms. The baby was trying to search for her breasts to suck some milk, but he was too weak. A dog was standing next to the woman and he looked hungry as saliva drooled from his mouth. He growled and showed us his fangs. My brother broke a tree branch and tried to point it at the dog to scare him away. We got closer and closer and he told me,

"Get the baby." I jumped over and pulled the child away from his dead mother.

"She doesn't want me to," I said. "She still holds him tightly."

The child was in a soft cotton shirt but the fabric had become hard like cardboard from soaking up his mother's blood. His cheeks were indented and his eyes bulged. My brother helped me to open up the mother's hands, freeing the child.

I looked at her. A bullet had gone through her head and one of her eyes was dangling on her cheek. Her head was bent down towards her bosom as if she were watching her child to see if he could reach her nipple or not. Her body fell to the side.

The dog backed up and ran behind the house. The bullets from helicopters and the U.S. air base kept racing by us, hitting the trees and crackling. We went back to our group and gave the baby some water. Then, my brother carrying the baby and I carrying the bag, we moved onto the road—but the village road had been mined with grenades at the intersection, and a barricade of sharp bamboo stakes hid in the grass, along the ditches, waiting to impale my unwary feet. I saw a small thread across the road a second before I would have stepped on it. We had to make a shortcut through the rice fields along the dike. We followed the dike, but soon the helicopter chased after us again, and we jumped off the dike and under a big tree to hide from it. In the distance, we could see the U.S. air base and if they used binoculars they could see that we were unarmed. We were just a bunch of refugees, children and women, but every time we moved, the bullets went after us as if we owed them money. When bullets hit the tree we were hiding behind, they exploded again and sent small pieces of metal whizzing by us. I could feel the wind from the shrapnel as it flew past me. The bullets hit the ground and dropped through the water into the creek and crackled on the trees. We moved and listened for the sound of the bullets, jumping off the dike and crawling along it from time to time. Sometimes we lay on the rice paddies for at least twenty minutes without moving at all. We pretended to be dead so that the helicopter would stop shooting at us. The shells and rockets exploded here and there, marking the ground. I saw several empty ponds with black smoke rims and the water from the bottom soil beginning to leak in, slowly rising, like blood coming out from a wound. The ponds looked like giant bowls sitting on a table I had never seen before. The rice was ripening into a golden color, but now there was no one to harvest the crop. The soil was dry but there was no one to irrigate it. I saw dead bodies along the rice fields, I saw corpses floating on the creek. I saw decaying humans on the dike and on the road. Dead souls were everywhere. And everywhere the smell of gunpowder, blood, and burning houses thickened the air.

The child my brother was carrying died in his arms, clutching my brother's thumb as if afraid of losing a mother's breast. Four days without milk had sapped all his strength. We had to move like hide-and-seek under the pressure of the helicopters and the bullets whizzing past us on every side, but this child could not run away from his death. We left him in the middle of the rice field without having a chance to bury him. Some of the rice grains had fallen on the wet soil and the young rice sprouted in some places.

On the road I saw thousands of refugees coming from different directions, not knowing where they were going. Men carried bags, women carried children, the elderly sat on the back of bikes for the younger to push, children ran along looking for their loved ones. People called out names, trying to find each other, while the houses and buildings burned. The artillery shells, rockets, and bullets poured from every corner, every street, every hole without mercy. They had no desire to avoid us. Finally, we arrived at our house in Vinh Binh City. My family was happy to see us alive.

Across from our home an American advisor lived in a two-story house. Around midnight I heard shooting from what sounded like next door; I ran upstairs to peek through the window and found my parents already there observing. In the street below, a big copper barrel used to store gas rolled out from the Cartex gas station, as someone crept behind it. He moved, stopped, and then shot at the American advisor, who stood on his balcony. The American advisor ducked, and aimed his gun at the empty barrel. He waited for it to move again, then fired. The bullet drummed against the barrel as the shadow behind it fell down and yelled, "Comrade, help. I've been hit!" Another barrel rumbled out from it, as the wounded VC moved. The second VC pulled the wounded one back into the gas station while the American advisor fired at them and red traces flowed along the barrel. For a while it was quiet, and then the barrel moved out again. The VC aimed at the American advisor and shot. A flare popped up and brightness lit everything; I saw the VC as clearly as the American did. The shooting broke out rapidly in the dying flare light and the VC fell down behind the barrel without a sound. Something like a strike of lightning flashed along the iron railing of our balcony. We ducked down while the loud explosion went off, then hurried downstairs to hide in our cement shelter. I heard moaning from the gas station all night long, and helicopters, and more shooting. A few days later, we evacuated to my mother's parents' house on another island on the Mekong, where there was no fighting.

CHAPTER 6

I don't know how many people died during the fighting in Tet 1968, the worst New Year of our lives. New Year was the biggest holiday in Vietnam, like Christmas season in the U.S. Some parts of the city still burned, while people tried to retrieve what was left of their lives. But the loss was never recuperated and the memories couldn't fade. My family was broken in many ways. We had lost Luoi and I knew now why she died that day without a wound. Wasn't she smart? She did not like guns and bullets, she did not like rockets and bombs and she did not want to be a victim or a witness to destruction. We lost the house in the village, and we had no money, just some grain left in our cabinet. Some of us went back to the village to help our father clean up the debris after the house had burned. On the village road there were still mines and sharp stakes and once in a while people got killed when they stepped on them.

My father went back to work on his garden growing oranges, mangos, and bananas to make a living. Although my brother tried to persuade him to learn English and work for Americans, he wanted to be independent. I remember him working in the garden, his quick hands breaking a branch, or his strong back bending as he repaired a wall.

Then the helicopters came and sprayed powder over our garden and rice field, over everything in our village, constantly. It looked red to me but people said it looked orange. I didn't know what kind of powder it was, but every time they sprayed, the leaves curled up on the plants and the trees died. The powder dropped down and dissolved into the river, stream, and creek. We drank the water daily.

The war continued on and off like a chronic disease. At night the VC controlled the village and during the day the Southern Government controlled it. We were trapped in the middle as victims. My family gave me food and love, especially my mother who never went to work—only stayed home and took care of the family, but the household job seemed to last a whole day. Every night, I heard her footsteps, the flip-flopping of her sandals, walking into our room, listening to our breathing or restlessness. If my sister or brother tossed and turned she would light the candle and go into our net to search for mosquitoes, until she assured herself that we were comfortable enough to sleep. Sometimes she just sat at the side of our bed and rubbed our backs or fanned us when the night was humid.

After we were asleep, she checked us all again and again. When I was sick, she brought me food and medicine. She held us when we cried or yelled out—after a nightmare or a spanking from my father. She kept a smile on her merry face and never cried in front of us. She loved to wear grey because it was the color of our religious uniform and she was a faithful Buddhist.

If the battle outside drew near, she would hide us in a corner of the house while my father and older brothers rushed to gather provisions, ready to evacuate. Often, my mother walked over and stood near the window, peering through the city's darkness, listening to the shells drop here and there upon the city. With every shell explosion her heart went out to her children, wondering if they were safe, if the army had been attacked; then she sighed and stepped away from the window, wishing her children were still young and happy the way we were before the war. I heard my father sneezing and calling to my mother, asking for coffee, then they comforted each other, telling each other not to worry—"Who knows about life?" Their voices became softer and softer.

And so I grew up: afraid of being thrown into the military

on the one hand, or of ending up as a member of the VC on the other. I didn't like either faction. I studied very hard, because if I failed any of my fourteen courses I would be drafted. By 1972, when I was fifteen, most of the young men my size were drafted into the army to fight, since they weren't in school. They died, leaving women, elderly people, and children in my village.

The situation in our village stabilized somewhat, and I began to build something resembling a normal life, attending high school and volunteering at Bac Ai school to teach for an adult literacy program. I studied hard and was very concerned with passing the national and university entrance exams.

My best friend was Hanh, a clever and loyal boy with a quick smile, whose legs had been weakened by polio. His walk was wobbly, and his body danced like a dolphin as he moved along. We would joke and laugh until our stomachs hurt, and I smiled so much that my friends would kid me about it. "Why are you laughing all the time?" one of them asked.

"Because my brothers and sisters don't have time to cheer up my parents," I said.

There was a girl a year older than me, named Di. I began to watch her, shyly. In class, I would steal glances at her, and my mind would wander to a full moon night, or a delicate rose beginning to bloom, showing its dark red petals and exuding its fragrances. Di's nose was high, her hair long and black against her white *ao dai* uniform. Vietnamese women usually wore *ao dai* for school, church or on holidays. I dressed up handsomely in my white shirt tucked inside blue pants. I was skinny and taller than she by a few inches. She lived with her father, a widower, and her younger sister on Co Tri Street, where my grandfather lived. Summoning my courage, I invited Di to come to my grandfather's temple in the village where I grew up, to attend a ceremony which we held twice a month during the lunar year.

After the ceremony, we sat talking on a red brick step in front of the temple, surrounded by the veranda.

"It's better to have ambition, Di. Any effort is worth undertaking to get an education," I said. "Just focus on your exam and you can figure out what you want to do after the results."

"That's easy for you to say," Di bit her lip gently.

"Look at me; Do I look worried to you? If I fail one exam they'll draft me into the army. You know what that means. But look, Di." I pointed at the passage through the courtyard.

There were grapefruit trees on the side of the mossed brick passage, with flowers blossoming in white and green. A golden beam shone through the branches like a pole ready to support any trees that fell, to help them grow normally. White petals the size of cherries dropped down from the flowers, drifted in the air like snowflakes, and landed on the moss-colored brick and on the water in the pond. Bees were busy buzzing on tree branches. I pulled Di up, ran over to the passage, and chased after the falling petals. A light wind blew, shaking the boughs and lifting the petals free.

"Smell it, smell it, Di—the air," I called.

"It's so ardent and fresh," said Di.

"How many petals did you catch?" I asked.

Di opened her palm, put it close to her open face, sniffed and counted them.

"Ten. Let me see yours."

"I have only one."

"What happened to yours?" she laughed. "Anyway, we have eleven together. That's a lucky number because you are the eleventh in the family."

I looked into her eyes and could see her happiness. When I looked at them I felt as if I was drinking hot wine. The more I looked at her, the more light-headed I became. Di glanced at me with her black eyes.

"Do you know why I only caught one petal?" I asked.

"Why?"

"It's easier to catch one than to catch many and not be able to hold them all."

"But I can hold them all!" she exclaimed.

"Greedy," I teased. She pinched my shoulder hard.

"So what are you going to do with this one petal of yours?"

"Show me your dimple," I said, placing a petal on her dimple. "I'll cover it up with this."

"No, no!" She pushed me and ran on the path towards the gazebo on the side of the river.

I chased after her while the birds on the grapefruit tree at the corner next to our religious flag sang a spring melody atop the branches.

"I caught you." I held her shoulder back and we were breathing heavily. We walked at a slow pace to the river until we came to the gazebo. The water was high, halfway up the steps that connected the gazebo floor to the river. At the entrance to the large, rectangular gazebo, *Nha Mat,* two stone lions sat on each side of the gate named *Ong Lan.* The gazebo's roof was supported by six pillars, while a low, red brick railing ran around the patio. A small gate in the railing led to the steps down to the river.

"Do you want to sit on the step or the rail?" I asked Di.

She sat on the rail, breathing lightly, and rolled her satin pants up over her ankles.

"On the step, it's closer to the water."

I opened the gate for her so she could get down to sit on the step, while I sat on the rail behind her.

"Do you want to make a wish with these petals?" She turned around, showed me the petals in her hand. I took some out of her hand and dropped them back into her palm.

"They are pretty, white, and delicate aren't they?"

"Yes, because they're a virgin color and pure," she said. "Look, there is no other color on them."

She lay her hand down into the water, then opened it, letting the petals float free from her hand.

"Blow them. Push them out to the main current." She blew them and some of the petals drifted away.

In the middle of the river, some buffalo were bathing. From time to time, they would slap their faces down in the water. A family of bugs flew in the air and then landed on the buffalo's heads again. Up in the sky, a family of swallows dove back and forth. Sometimes one of them would land on a buffalo's horns, as if taking a break, its wings tired, until its flock flew back, dove down and it flew up with them again. Across the river in the distance there was a hut where the buffalo lived. Noon was almost ending now. A boy was building a fire, shoveling some of the cow dung into it to make more smoke, getting ready to call the buffaloes back for their sleep. In the distance the betel nut tree swayed from side to side in the wind.

"Ngoc, look, look!" Di called me and pointed to the surface of the water. "It's a tiny spider."

I saw the bug scampering on top of the water, leaving a gossamer trail behind, a short line, like a child drawing on an Etch-A-Sketch toy. The spider, the size of a small ant and shaped like a grasshopper, floated on the water against the waves. It bounced up and down on the tiny tides made when the water buffalo slapped his face against the river. I became lost in thought.

"How can he do that?" Di uttered, wrinkling her face. "Floating on the water!" She looked at me, puzzled.

"I don't know. I wish I had an answer." I held a stick, tracing her image in the water as if I were painting her portrait.

"I finished your painting."

She looked at me with her mouth wide open. I pointed to her reflection in the water.

"Oh, don't tease me. You are just trying to scare my spider away," Di pouted. She glanced at me and blinked her eye.

"Hold it, there is something in your eye. Let me get it out for you."

"No, I don't want you to," she said.

"Why? It might hurt you if you don't let me get it out."

She moved her smooth face over to me.

"Something is in there. See?" I said, and picked a tiny piece of dirt from her curled eyelash. "Do you know what I found in there?"

"Yourself," she said.

From that time on, I would meet Di at her house each morning and walk her to school. We talked about our families, our futures, our dreams. Sometimes, I rode by her house and looked for her or she rode by mine to search for me.

Di failed the national exam that year and returned to school again for a second chance when I was in twelfth grade. On our last day of high school, we had a farewell party for our class.

There were not many boys in my class by now, but many girls, especially this year. I went to look for Di in the Twelve C2 section. On the veranda, many students and teachers stood talking and laughing, while other students ran after each other, or sat in groups on the playground talking and asking each other what they would do during the summer. I went into the Twelve C2 class; Di wasn't there. I looked for Hanh, to wish him a nice summer and much luck on the exam. I found him standing in a corner of the classroom.

"Are you going to stay in town or go home?" I asked him, as we stood there.

"I'm going home to prepare for exam day and then come back to take the test."

"That's good. You are going to eat and sleep," I said. "I may come down there and visit you."

"Yes, come," Hanh said, smiling. "Do you know how to get to Phuoc Thien Island where my father's litchi orchard is?"

"No, tell me."

"You go to the market where they have the dock, take a passenger boat to Phuoc Thien and tell them to stop at the first stop. When you get to the village, just tell them my father's name. It takes about four hours, so when you get on the boat find a place where you can sleep. It's good for you to come because a classmate of mine is going to marry this summer in my village. We can go and have some fun."

Hanh pulled me over to the pleasant, kind-faced girl and introduced her. She invited me to go to her wedding.

"Hanh, don't forget to check with my family because they will have a party before I leave for Saigon," I said. "Make sure you are there."

"Okay," Hanh said. He walked a few paces in his odd, energetic way, then turned to face me, his eyes steady. "Are you going to leave the country?" he asked.

"I don't know yet. My brother is still working on it. But I'm not sure I want to go abroad. Maybe it's better to stay and fight like everybody else. Going abroad seems like running away from your duty."

Hanh kept looking straight at me, his eyes large.

"Why are you changing your attitude now? You told me it's much better to go out of the country, finish your studying, and then come back and do something with it. You could help change things."

"What things?" I said. I sighed. "Politics is a messy business. I have changed. Many of our friends said they wanted to do something to change the situation for our country, and now they are dead. Did anything else change? Or is it still just a bunch of idiot politicians who run the country, whether they are from the north or the south?"

"But . . . ," Hanh interrupted me.

"But . . . what?" I said.

"We don't have any voice. We don't have an impact on our government. You have a chance to get into the system and do something about it. Now you refuse. What happened to your patriotism?" Hanh glared at me.

"I show my patriotism like anybody else, that's why I've decided to fight," I said.

"No, no, Ngoc. What happened to your big dream? Do you want to be a dummy like all of our government officers? You have to go abroad. If you don't go for anybody, go for me. Ahh!" Hanh cried out. I had never seen him so upset.

I let him pace a minute, then talked as coolly as I could, in a low voice.

"Look Hanh," I said. "Let me tell you how I see it," I said. Since I understand politics, I see that all the Vietnamese politicians are opportunists, more than Nationalists or anything else. Vietnam is a nation for the Vietnamese, but both the northern and the southern governments import foreign theories and foreign weapons to try to increase their own power. As long as the government depends on the U.S., Russia, or China, we will never be free."

I talked faster, excited. "We need our own government, based on Vietnamese culture, philosophy, and values. Do you see any politician who really loves this country and cares for our people? Or do you see opportunists who want to climb into a chair and be called Mr. President, who will never step down even though they know nothing about governing our country? That kind of man will only build up his personal power, making more money for himself and appointing all his relatives to high government positions. Is that patriotism to you?"

"So what kind of government do you want to see in our country?" asked Hanh, scratching his chin.

"I want to see a Vietnamese president who has no escort, a normal citizen like any other Vietnamese who is well suited for the job. But if after a period of time it is evident that the government is not working, he would have to step down and let someone take over who has the talent to run the country and help the people. If people wanted to see the president, they could come to his house and eat what he had and stay at his house and talk to him anytime. I don't want to see any military, because we can use diplomacy to solve problems. One of the most important things is that I want all the Vietnamese to have an education and expose themselves to the world to broaden their minds. Our country has a self-sufficient economy. We don't need aid from any other nation, if we know how to apply good technology to our farmlands. We need not only a strong, liberal leader, but a model for our country."

"Maybe you could be that kind of leader, Ngoc!" Hanh exclaimed. "Go abroad, get an education, learn about technology and science, bring your knowledge back here and help us to cultivate our land and our people."

"Thank you, Hanh," I smiled. Then sighed. "It's too late though. Kissinger and Le Duc Tho met secretly in Paris for two-and-a-half years and signed a contract like a couple of real estate agents. The Paris Accord sells our country to the Soviet

Union in 1972. I don't know who these realtors represent."

"I know," Hanh tried, "but there must be a way, some solution for our country."

"I'm not a genius," I said, "I'm a human being like yourself. I have no control over our politics or our government. I have a headache now. Forget it. Let's enjoy our last day."

The bell rang again and the students began to gather on the playground for an award ceremony. We walked over to the court and lined up. The principal delivered his speech and called the teachers' council to give out the awards.

"The first-place award goes to Huỳnh Quang Ngọc of Twelve C for Academic Achievement and Citizenship for the whole year."

Hanh pushed me out of the line.

"Come on, go get it."

Everyone applauded and some of my friends shouted out. I went to the platform to receive my gift, which was wrapped in school paper. My teachers, so familiar with my face, whispered, "Good luck" to me. I went back to my place. My classmates patted me on the shoulder, congratulating me. Some in the back of the line pushed people up front and then the ones in front pushed back.

"Give me some of your gifts if you don't want them," somebody shouted from the back.

The announcer warned us to quiet down. Some of us got tired so we sat down on the ground, even though this was not allowed during a ceremony.

"Hey, cover for me," someone behind me whispered. "Don't let them see me sit down."

The ceremony continued. The second-place winner was a girl in Twelve B, third place went to a boy in Twelve A. It finally ended at noon. We went home and I heard some people sobbing along the sidewalk, because they were leaving school and friends behind.

In the middle of that month, when the moon was full, I went to a temple service to pray for my future. During the service I sat next to my mother and we bowed on the smooth red-and-white tile floor. I heard my mother mumbling, saw her looking at the altar where the bright candles and sandalwood incense burned. Her eyes closed for a moment.

"Buddha, please guide my son through life and help him overcome all its obstacles. Let him pass his exam and go on with his own life. I could give birth to him, but I cannot give birth to his soul. Only you can." She held a stick of incense between her hands and bowed. "I am not afraid of suffering, but if I see my son happy, then I am happy for him. I don't want to see the young tree, not yet fully grown, chopped down by people. Please give him health, listen to his prayers, teach him to know about his family, his relatives, teach him about himself and where he comes from . . . he is in your hands."

The gong chimed. Everyone bowed, sinking into their own prayers. When the service ended, my mother handed me a bamboo vase full of sticks by which I could ask the Buddha about my future. I shook the vase, pulled out a stick, and read the number on it. Then I went to my father and asked for the book telling which passage of the Buddha's teachings corresponded to this number. We read the passage: the Buddha compared me to the life of a famous Chinese philosopher, To Tan. I would be rich or poor depending on my career in education. He told me that in my past life I had been a good Buddhist and had a good heart, and so he had always blessed me. He also said that even though there was a long road, with the hardest part of the journey still ahead, I would succeed. I remember the prediction from the book even to this day. When my mother heard my father explaining what the Buddha had said, her happiness showed in her face, she laughed, and she talked more than on any other day.

We all went into the kitchen and sat down on the long bench to eat our lunch. Today we ate only vegetables, as we did every fifteenth and thirtieth day of the lunar month. My father picked up his chopsticks, bowed, and ate a mouthful of rice without any other food. He explained to me why we should begin every meal this way, saying that this showed respect to the people who plant and harvest the rice and use their sweat to make it grow. "Son," he said, "whether you use money to pay for the rice is not important. What's important is to remember the people who labored to cultivate the rice for you to eat today."

I heard my fourth aunt, Bieu, asking my eleventh aunt, Di's stepmother, "What is Di doing lately at home?"

"She is helping us with the business and taking care of my child."

"How old is she now?" Aunt Bieu asked.

"Nineteen."

"Pass me the pumpkin with the coconut milk, Bieu," my grandmother chimed in.

My aunt passed her the dish and continued to talk. "Don't you think it's time for her to get married? I know of a nice family near my house, very well respected."

"I don't know, she's really helping me out right now," said Di's stepmother.

"Do you want me to be a matchmaker? I can be a good one," Aunt Bieu pressed on. "I'm just afraid Di will marry too late like you."

"What do you think, Anh Ba?" Di's mother called to my father at another bench.

My father looked up from his food.

"About what?"

"About Di's marriage."

My father looked at me as if he wanted to ask me.

"It depends on her, I guess," he said finally. "But I don't think it's good to rush into it." He put down his bowl, grabbed a banana, and ate it.

"Well," Bieu blustered on, "the family has a lot of estates. They don't have any genetic diseases that I know of. They have only one son and his father is dead so he has to run the whole estate. They are looking for someone to marry their son. I think your family and their family are of the same class."

"Is he going to school?" I asked.

"He never went, but he's a good farmer."

"How do you expect him to marry Di when she's educated and he's not? She cannot farm; he cannot read. What is the benefit?" I almost shouted. I glanced at my father; he was looking at me with a smile on his face. My face felt as if it was burning up.

"Making children, son!" my aunt exclaimed.

"Oh, is that all we care about? You really want to be a matchmaker? I hope you have a big roast pig to eat if the match works out," I said. "Otherwise, everything will be blamed on you."

Everybody laughed.

"I have matched couples many times. There's no problem," Aunt Bieu responded.

My father whispered in my ear, "You are talking like an adult now, son. Do you like Di?"

I ate faster to avoid answering his question. I rose, bowed, left the table, and walked to the back of *Nha Hau,* the guest house, where I could see the stone wall around the foundation of the house, riddled with thousands of holes. I saw Di and my sister, Kha, sitting at the corner of the stone path where a hay mat was spread under shadows of a tree. As I looked at Di sitting so peacefully, her open face caressed by her long black hair, I thought of what I had just said, and I knew for the first time that I was in love with her. The fierceness with which I had opposed the prearranged marriage still swirled inside me, mixing with other feelings. I wondered what would happen to Di if she were married to a peasant. I sank into thought.

My father left the table and began to paint with his brush on some red paper to get the scroll ready for the next service in the temple. Though his father had never sent him to school, wanting him to take care of the estate instead, my father had educated himself with the help of one of the monks who came to visit the temple. He used the old Vietnamese characters, since his command of the new phonetic alphabet was only passable. He was big and strong. Besides farming and managing the estate for my grandfather, he practiced kung fu and taught it to his children and relatives. His body was beautiful with muscle tissues, vibrant like iron in a variety of shapes, his face like a sculpture. He never showed his emotion or shared his thoughts, and always went after his goal until he got it. He was the opposite, physically and mentally, of my sensitive, gentle, and fragile mother. She had never had a chance to go to high school, had never finished elementary school, never learned to read or write. My sister-in-law tried to teach her but mother always said: "Do you know how many nieces and nephews I have? They can read for me. Anyway, I'm old." Then she would laugh, her voice bubbling like water.

My sister-in-law would threaten her, saying, "If you don't know how to read, girls at school will write love letters to your sons and take your sons away from you."

My mother was a wonderful cook and always cooked for us herself, even when we could afford a maid, worrying that someone else might not cook the way she wanted and we would get sick if we didn't eat good food. She was a woman who accepted her fate, whether it was happy or sad. She would never complain, and she delighted in pleasing people. If something made her sad she would hide in a corner and cry. If one of us came to her she would wipe her tears away, pretending nothing had happened.

I took the national exam for two days. I felt very good about what I did, believing I would pass. A week after I finished my mother packed a bag for me to leave for Saigon, so that I could familiarize myself with the big city before starting as a student at the university there. She folded every shirt and pair of pants and put them neatly into a suitcase. She put some money in my wallet and handed me some money also.

"Put it in a different pocket; If you lose one, you will still have the other. Watch out for pickpockets."

She handed me a little green bottle that smelled like Ben-Gay. "Use this when you get a headache or upset stomach. Put some on your temples and your neck and massage it in. If you have a stomachache rub it there," she said, demonstrating to me. "Like this, like this, son."

"Yes, mama. I'm a big boy now; don't worry about me."

"Saigon is a big city. Watch out where you go because you might get lost. Stop by to see your brother. If you run out of money, ask your aunt for some."

My parents were expecting me to become a doctor like my older brother, but I wanted to be a literature professor or a lawyer. It seemed there would be a wonderful future ahead of me whatever I chose, but then again, who knew what tomorrow would bring? I did not want to let my parents down; I wanted to show that I loved them.

Mama opened the closet and found her box where she kept her jewelry, took out a gold chain with a Buddha on it, and put it around my neck. She also gave me a small diamond ring.

"Hold on to your necklace. Don't sell it. The Buddha will help you. If you have an emergency you can sell the ring." She repeated this to me many times, to make sure I would remember. My mother bought a matching jewelry set for all her children, which she would give to us when we went away or if we got married. I remembered seeing her, whenever one of my brothers or sisters went away; she would walk in and out of the house, pacing back and forth. She would talk with one of her friends on the porch, but her eyes would be on the road where the bus would pass by. Now it was time for me to leave. My mother stepped over to me, her gentle, wrinkled face near my chest—how much taller than her I was now! She reached for my face and held my cheeks in her hands, her brown eyes looking deep into mine. "Goodbye, son."

"Goodbye, mama."

My brother and sister took me to the bus station. I checked the schedule, bought my ticket and found a bench to sit on while I was waiting. There were a lot of people and many vendors selling food, cigarettes, sugarcane, and coconut.

"Do you want to buy some cigarettes?" a boy asked me, putting his tray down next to me.

"Hey, you are Duc's brother, is that right?" I asked him.

He looked at me, trying to place my face.

"Yes, I'm Duc's brother," he replied.

"Where is he?"

"He's in the army. Are you going to buy some cigarettes?" he asked again.

"Will he be coming back soon? Say hello for me. What is your name?"

"Tung."

"I don't smoke, but I'll buy a pack of cigarettes."

His face lit up when he heard me say yes. The driver started the engine, calling to the passengers to board. I got on the bus, waving to my brother and sister. The bus moved out of the station and headed north, towards Highway Four to Saigon. I saw my mother looking at my bus as it passed by. I could see Tung's dispirited image at the bus station. I wondered about my family and how I could help Tung and my people.

A few weeks later I took the university entrance exam. It was easier than I had thought. By now I missed my family terribly, and I decided to make a visit back home since it was still summer and I could enjoy myself while waiting for the results of the test. During this time I saw a lot of my grandfather, Xuoc. His daily routine included chanting the sutra, meditating, and offering services at the temple. He would explain to me about life cycles, reincarnation, and nirvana, our real "original home" where we would live eternally without sickness, age, suffering, or death. He and I had an odd bet: if he died before I saw him again, he would win the wager; but if he survived, then he had to pay the money to me. I always took the bet since there was no way I could lose—if I saw him, I collected, but if he were to win, he wouldn't be in much of a condition to take my money. Anyway, I knew he wasn't going to die, because he was amazingly strong for his age—seventy-nine.

In the afternoons I would come to where he sat in his big chair, holding his rosary beads, his eyes closed as he concentrated on his meditation. I would sit down on his bed without saying a word, waiting for him to finish. His head was getting bald now, with snowy white hair gathered into a tiny bun at the back.

He opened his eyes, bowed three times, and laid his rosary beads on a red cloth atop a tray.

"Hello, grandfather. How are you?"

"Very good," he said. "But your grandmother won't let me go back to my estate at the temple," he wrinkled his face. "I know I will die this month and I want to be close to my ancestors," continued grandfather.

"Are you sure, grandfather?" I asked. "How do you know you will die?"

"When I was asleep, your ancestors called, telling me to get ready for my journey."

"So exactly what date is that?"

"August twenty-fourth."

"Do you want to bet? You have lost so many times now." I grinned at him cleverly. "I don't want to force you, but only if you're willing."

"Certainly, son," he smiled. "You enjoy my money, don't you?"

"Not too bad, grandfather. I just spend it here and there," I said. "It's not as much fun for you if you just give me the money."

I thought death was an exciting game. He asked me to get some tea for him from the painted ceramic pot on the table. I gave him a hot cup and he sipped it.

"How much do you want this time?" I asked. "How about five thousand dong."

"Sounds good," he nodded, and we laughed. The house grew merry with our talk as the day wore on.

That night though, as I strolled near my grandfather's house, I felt uneasy. I called Toto, a white-and-black-spotted dog whom I liked as a companion. I sensed something would happen to me but I did not know what, and I felt restless and lonely under the full moon. Toto, asleep somewhere at the back of the house, heard my whistle, and ran to me. I patted him and we strolled to the garden where I pulled a few branches down to find some ripe fruit to pick, waking up some of the chao chao birds in the trees, who flew away. The smell of flowers cleansed the air as pollen fragrances floated from the corner of the temple to the courtyard. I wandered, peeling the skin off of an orange. Toto went ahead of me and I followed him through the gate to the bridge connecting our side of the river to our neighbors. I sat down and peered into the water, where the moon showed its reflection. I threw the orange peelings, and they splattered over the water, breaking the moon's face into tiny waves. Then the face appeared again. The current began to withdraw now, making me feel drunk watching. I wanted to lift the moon out of the water, to hold it in my palm so that I could touch it, but it fell from my fingers. Toto barked in a low voice at the end of the bridge, then ran back to me. I saw a shadow sitting beneath a plum tree. I went over. It was the neighbor girl, enjoying the night as I was.

"Are you scared of ghosts?" I asked, sitting down.

"If I were I wouldn't be here," she answered.

"Are you searching for poetry?"

"Are you?" she responded in a challenging voice.

"No. But I can't sleep and Toto asked me to take a walk with him."

"How can you blame it on a poor little thing when he cannot talk? Why don't you just say you can't sleep on a beautiful night like tonight?" She rubbed Toto's head.

"Maybe. How about you?"

"I do as any other who tries to find verses."

Suddenly, we were in silence. She leaned on the plum tree with her long hair, dressed in her black, white-spotted pajamas, ready for bed. Once in a while she pulled some strands of hair to the front of her face, looked a bit at it as if she were tasting them. Her mother came out, calling her in, and I started back to my grandfather's house to sleep. But I hesitated; something about the moon, the river, called me. Or perhaps I did not want to go into the house. I decided to sleep on the bridge with Toto for the night.

My aunt left by boat at early dawn for Di's wedding. She had arranged to marry Di off to an uneducated peasant with her matchmaker's sweet talk. I wanted to stop the wedding but I had no power. I myself was not ready to get married yet. I felt superfluous and life seemed devoid of meaning for me. Uncle Bay Bung had offered his chanting services at the temple at 5:00 a.m. Grandmother cooked breakfast, preparing food for us to eat.

"Would you get your grandfather?" she asked me.

"Yes, grandmother."

I climbed over the window from a brick wall that connected the kitchen to *Nha Hau*, the guest house. I called my grandfather, then went to his bed.

"Grandfather, breakfast is ready."

There was no reply. The net still hung down, not rolled up yet. I saw him lying there, on his back. I called again.

I stepped closer, and rolled up the net on the wooden bar above my head. He lay on his back, his head under a small red pillow. I grasped my grandfather's hand, pulling it to wake him up, but when I touched his hand I withdrew it immediately—I had touched a coldness I had never experienced before. I looked at him. His face did not seem to be in the same world as I was.

"Grandmother, uncle. Come quickly!" I yelled out loud.

My grandmother and Uncle Nam ran to see what had happened. I pointed to grandfather, who lay there as peacefully as someone drunk in his sleep.

Grandmother touched him, feeling his feet.

"Go, call your father. Your grandfather is gone."

I ran out of the room but my feet dragged like cement. "Is he really dead?" I thought. "He won't pay my bet this time, instead I have to pay him. He knew it somehow." I ran outside to the side of the creek, called my father, and then came back in the house. My father arrived along with the guests for the temple service. He was very calm but I knew he was shaking inside to suppress his emotion; he was the oldest in the family, and he had to be a model for us, maintaining his control. I felt his sadness but "men don't cry" was a part of my culture. The house became noisy, but there was no crying at all.

The news spread out to our relatives, to the village, and to Di's wedding. Uncle Nam went up to the temple, lit the candles, burned incense, and opened the Buddha sutra to chant, praying for my grandfather's funeral. I helped my father to give grandfather his last bath. Afterwards, we dressed him up: grandmother put a veil of red lace over his face, and father cut off all the buttons on his clothes. We had a belief that if the buttons were stuck on the bones of the deceased then the siblings of the deceased wouldn't prosper for two generations, and if one of the buttons dropped into the skull the siblings would have a fatal disease. My aunt opened all the drawers and took out his clothes, deciding which ones to give away and which ones to put in the coffin. In accordance with traditional belief, I put one Buddha rosary bead necklace on his abdomen to scare off any ghouls who might try to eat his intestines. We took all of the front doors and back doors down, and gathered chairs, tables, and benches where people could sit. The stoves were busy as steam puffed from one pot and then another.

I helped my father, along with ten other people, to carry the coffin. We placed it on two small benches in the middle of the guest house, *Nha Hau*. The lid, of solid wood, was heavier than the coffin itself. The candles were lit. After assigning duties that needed to be carried out, my father turned to a large dark cabinet and began to search through stacks of old books. I saw many volumes covered with dust, some of them faded, but with the paper still strong. Mice had chewed parts of the books and shredded pages lying on the shelf. He took one out, blowing the dust off.

"What are you looking for, father?" I asked.

"An old astrology notebook that I wrote," he answered.

"What for?"

"I have to locate a piece of land where it will be good to bury your grandfather."

I moved some of the books to one side. The larger ones were a meter long and half a meter wide, the width of books written with ancient Vietnamese characters, which resembled Chinese. Some of the pages were torn out.

"Here it is," my father said as he pulled a heavy volume out from the shelf.

I closed the closet, followed him to the table, and we sat down. He carefully turned page after page and stopped when he spotted it. I saw a palm drawn with many characters displayed. He counted something on his fingers, and told me, "Today is a good day to bury your grandfather." He continued to make calculations.

"It has to be exactly twelve noon when we lower the coffin down into the grave. The rain is going to fall when we place it in. This is an excellent sign for our future. If we don't make it today then we will have to wait three days for his funeral. Your grandfather died on a good day for his children." He turned to another page where I saw many different drawings in various shapes.

"Go get your uncle and some other people who can dig the grave while I go to find a place before it is too late, son."

"Yes, sir."

I fetched my uncle and three other people. We gathered shovels and followed my father to the place near the pond where the creek ran swiftly. My father walked around to look.

"Right here," he pointed.

"His head must face the east where the sun rises. If your family has a temple, whoever you bury should face in the direction of the temple," he added.

He took the shovel and drew a line on the ground before digging the first chunk of soil. We cleared the weeds, the marshes and chopped the banana bushes to widen the space. The air was fresh as the sun's beams kissed the earth's surface, the lake, the trees . . . the grass, and me. I began to sweat, and took off my shirt. The wind blasted once in a while, making the surroundings shake like a man with cold chills.

"I think it is deep enough," my father said.

We stopped and cleaned ourselves off. Three incense sticks had been burning at the side of the grave, and were now already half gone. The sounds of a wooden instrument shaped like a hollow fish and a gong from the temple mixed with my uncle's voice. He chanted for my grandfather's death, to lead his way to another world. I called all the relatives and people to come to see my grandfather for the last time. We surrounded his bed.

"I cannot see my great-grandfather," the small voice of my niece shouted at my back.

I turned around and picked her up so she could she him.

"Is great-grandfather asleep?" she asked.

"Something like that, but he will never wake up again," I answered.

"Why?"

"Because he died."

"What is that?" she asked, curious.

"People are born and people die. When you are an adult you will understand what I'm saying."

"Big, about your size, Uncle." She made a sign with her hands, and went on asking many questions, but I didn't have answers.

My father announced that it was time for him to place my grandfather in the casket. Two of my uncles hadn't come back from Saigon yet, but we couldn't wait. My grandmother gave a little piece of gold to my father to put in my grandfather's mouth so that he could have money for his next life. Some of my relatives went back to the preparations they had been making before, while others stayed and watched us.

In the kitchen, the food was ready to take up to the temple to place on the altars. People busied themselves, hurrying in and out of the house. I heard a child's voice sobbing somewhere as if she had fallen down, then her mother's voice asking her what was wrong.

We lifted grandfather up, placed him inside the casket and then packed cotton round him, and the clothes my grandmother wanted him to have. We checked everything for the last time, lowered the solid wood lid and hammered it down. I placed a set of candle holders on the top of the lid and lit the candles. Their glow reached the small altar in front of his coffin. I went out to the water barrel to wash my face, and then followed along to the temple for the service.

It was 10:30 a.m. on August 24th, the date my grandfather

said he would die. The big gong clanged while we chanted after the lead of my father's voice, who had now replaced my grandfather in that capacity. He sat between two people at the central altar, his face severe and determined, but benevolent. The atmosphere of the ceremony was high-spirited. We bowed each time the small gong was hit. I breathed the warmth of the service, my family, and our relatives. When the service ended, we prayed for our grandfather to have a wonderful trip to his new world. No one dropped a tear for him because we believe that to die is to free oneself. If we were to cry, the dead spirit would feel sorry for us, and this would make it harder for him or her to begin a new life.

At exactly twelve noon, we carried the coffin out to the grave, and lowered it down to the clay bottom. We began to shovel dirt in. A drop of water spattered the dirt lying loose on the coffin lid. The wind began to blow, and grew faster and harder, moving black clouds above our heads. Rain fell through the weak sunbeams, sprinkling and then drumming hard as we kept shoveling the soil into my grandfather's grave. When we finished, the rain stopped. The sky became clear again. My father smiled, satisfied with what he had predicted. It was one of the few downpours that month. We mixed cement powder with sand, gravel, and water, then spread it on top of the grave and began to build a tomb structure for him with bricks. His name, the day he was born and the day he died was engraved on the stone in front. I planted a special sugarcane in front of the grave with some marigold flower bushes at the side. My two uncles, the thirteenth and fourteenth of grandfather's children finally came, bowing to their father at his grave, paying their last respects.

We turned, walked away, and began to pick up our daily routine of life again. Lunch was served late that day. We ate and chatted; some of the guests came late and I had to go to the temple to give them incense and light the lamps for them so that they could bow to my grandfather.

When I returned, my father, mother, uncles, aunts, and cousins were all dressed up, ready to go to Di's wedding. My sister Kha came to me.

"Are you sure you don't want to go Di's wedding?" she asked.

"No, I don't like my aunt's decision," I said. "I want no part of it."

"You're not her father—only her father can make that decision," Kha said. "Di will be very unhappy if you do not come."

"Well, I know, but I don't understand why Di accepts being married to someone like that—an uneducated peasant!" I cried out.

"Does she have any choice, brother? She married under family pressure but that's the only way for her to pay back love and respect to her family, whether she loves him or not. The old way is marry first and love will come later."

"Forget it," I said, "I'm not going. I'm going to the city to get ready to return to Saigon for my school."

"Why don't you wait and go back with our two uncles?" she suggested.

"No, I have things to do."

"I'll see you before you go then," Kha said.

"Yeah." I looked away. "Just send her my congratulations and tell her to have a happy life."

"Okay, sir." Kha bowed with a demure gesture as if she were in front of a king, trying to make me laugh.

She left. I stared out over the fields, to where the river glided silently along. On the horizon, a few lines twittered and then sank. The birds faded and merged with the farthest smudge of trees. The sky was empty.

I set off on the road to the city. When I arrived at our house, my brother handed me a telegram: Saigon University had admitted me for the 1974-75 academic year. I stood there, my hands and head feeling heavy. It was said that a funeral brought good news, and a wedding bad; and now Di's wedding and grandfather's funeral had happened on the same day. I didn't know what to believe but perhaps it was good for me to go to the university and I wouldn't be graduating.

I went to Saigon and stayed with my aunt's family in District One on Phan Thanh Gian Avenue, where she had a bakery and restaurant. I helped her with her business, and everyone seemed happy to see me. On the weekend we went to different places so I could become familiar with the city. Saigon was beautiful, with colorful crowds of people, bright streetlights, open spaces, and elegant boulevards. I wasn't surprised to hear that people called Saigon the "Pearl of the Orient" and "The Paris of Asia." I visited the university and attended orientation.

On the first day of school, I was busy with registration, trying to become familiar with the place, and trying to make friends in my class. The class started but my head seemed not to be working very well. There were too many things that I couldn't express or reveal to anyone about. My cousin teased me that I was in love. At school, we talked more about the war moving toward us than we discussed our lessons. News and rumors spread as the U.S. proposals and the southern government's responses clashed.

I missed home and went back for a visit. My brother, who served in the air force in Can Tho, was there. He informed us about the U.S. evacuation plan and told us to be alert. He was very handsome in his grey pilot's uniform with shining gold insignia on his lapels to show his rank; I was proud of my brother. I stayed for a few days and went back to Saigon. That was my last chance to see all of my relatives.

On April 15, my birthday (according to my new birth certificate—my parents had lost the record of the exact day I was born), I planned to visit home. But that proved impossible: I heard from my aunt that Highway Four, the way home, was barricaded with mines. Everyone seemed hurried, worry showing in their faces.

I used my aunt's phone to call one of my relatives in the military police in Vinh Binh to inquire about my family. There wasn't much news. My cousin, Luyen, ran in and out from the police department to let us know what was going on. He told us not to go anywhere if we didn't have to, while he looked for someone who could secure a place for the family on a boat fleeing the country.

The news was announced on television and radio that the U.S. and South Vietnamese armies had withdrawn from the central highlands back to Saigon, the last line of defense. Phuoc Long, Quang Tri and Da Nang had all been lost to the northern enemy some time ago. A new wave of refugees headed south, into Saigon. Confusion reigned. On April 24, a curfew went into effect, sealing off the city.

People began to flock to the U.S. embassy. My cousin, a friend, and I went to wait there with the crowd, hoping they would let us in and help us evacuate. But since we didn't know anybody at the embassy, we didn't have much of a chance. American marines surrounded the compound, directing a few selected people into the embassy. It was impossible to get in. We walked to the French embassy. They were taking extra security precautions and wouldn't let us in either. We gave up and went home.

On April 21, 1975, President Thieu resigned and left for Hong Kong. A month before Tran Van Huong took over, he had transferred his huge assets to his brother, the ambassador to Hong Kong. General Ky delivered a speech at the Catholic church saying that he would stay to fight with the people, but after the speech, he disappeared fast. Duong Van Minh became president; his first important act was to order all foreigners to leave the country within twenty-four hours, while he prepared negotiations. Nobody seemed to care about our country anymore, nobody cared for our people anymore, and I tried to run away from the coming execution. What could I expect from these opportunists? Everyone lost hope. Soldiers left their units to go back to their families, hoping they could help them with something.

We were standing on Phan Thanh Gian Avenue watching people scurry back and forth, when an M-48 tank appeared at the intersection, lurching around like a mad dog, shooting into the air with all the ammunition it had left. The tank stopped and two soldiers popped out of the hatch. They jumped to the ground, tore their uniforms off and threw them down in the street, and ran. An army jeep raced around with a speaker announcing the news. Duong Van Minh had unconditionally surrendered and was asking all the southern soldiers to put down their weapons.

The northern army thundered into the presidential palace with a T-54 tank, knocking down the gate. They tore down the southern flag with three red stripes on a yellow background. Over the palace they raised their red flag with one yellow star in the middle. It was April 30, 1975, the last day of the Republic of Vietnam. The whole city turned chaotic. A Russian Molotova truck carrying northern soldiers barrelled into the city and shooting broke out here and there. Many people ran out into the street to welcome the new comrades, the new government for a new future, but no one knew what it would lead to. It was to be the darkest day for the southerners. The war was over for Americans, but a new revolution, a new regime, and a new Vietnamese class conflict had just begun.

My friend Hanh and I went to Vung Tau to search for a way to escape, but to no avail. The new government ordered all the southern soldiers, officers, security, police—anyone who was at all related to the southern government—to report to a certain place. I told my aunt that I was leaving for home because I thought it would be safer there, with my family in a small town. I went home to Vinh Binh, but I couldn't see any of my brothers because they were all stranded in different places. A public speaker on a telephone pole along the road announced the order for everyone to register with the new authorities, no matter if you were a teacher, student, or civilian. They ordered people to give up their books, magazines, tapes, newspapers. Any literature in the south was to be destroyed. If any was found in people's homes, the literature would be confiscated and the people would be executed.

In Vinh Binh, we had to go to a meeting every day to receive a new education from the Communist Party. The secret police were everywhere, checking on people. If they suspected anyone of anything they would arrest him or her.

Every week we had to go to the meeting at Ward eight and march on the hot street with thousands of sweating people chanting "Long live Ho Chi Minh, long live the Communist Party!" The black tar melted under our bare feet. We had to welcome the new government by singing their victory song as we held up the red banner with the Communist Party sign. We had to carry Ho Chi Minh's picture in front and yell out loud to condemn the betrayers who followed the U.S. and the southern government.

I remember one day very clearly. We had marched to the soccer field. We stood in front of a platform in rows, blending in with the secret police. One of the VCs stepped up to the microphone to direct the program. The new national anthem played. The master of ceremonies introduced an executioner in a cowskin-colored uniform. The executioner pulled some papers from his briefcase and read from them. With a stern and cold expression he announced the name, the age of the person, the city where he lived, and told us that this young man was working for the CIA.

"He is our traitor, he is against our party, our government, and our people! Is he guilty?" he shouted into the speaker.

"Yes, yes!" everyone shouted.

"Take him out for the people to see who he is," he ordered the guard.

The guard stepped off the platform, then pulled up a young man about my age, clean and handsome, with his hands cuffed at his back. I guessed he was one of the southern colonels' or generals' sons. I wasn't sure, but by looking at him I could guess what kind of class he was from.

"Are we going to execute him?" he yelled into the microphone again.

"Yes, yes!" the crowd shouted.

Then, the executioner moved on to another paper with another name appearing on his list and the process began again. When he reached ten people, he stopped in order for the comrades to tie the prisoners up at poles in front of us. He ordered the guards to take off their blindfolds and asked them, "Do you have anything to say for your last request?"

"We don't have any guilt. We love this country! Long live the Republic of Vietnam!" the prisoners all shouted as loud as they could. It was like an electric wave being sent through us.

The guards blindfolded them. Several yelled that they didn't want their eyes covered. The guards held their guns up, aimed at the young men, and shot them. I saw their blood sprinkle all over as their bodies shook while their heads fell to one side and they died. I felt as if I was being pushed closer to the pole.

"Long live Ho Chi Minh! Long live the Communist Party!" the executioner shouted into the microphone, applauding.

The execution had sparked the crowd. They repeated what the executioner said and clapped their hands to worship the leader without any hesitation.

Later, we marched to the cemetery to watch as they used a bulldozer to raze all the southern soldiers' graves.

"These people are against us. They are traitors and we have

no place for them!" the VC leader yelled to us. He turned to a children's group assembled there. "If any of you know some-one who is in hiding or betraying us, you have to report to the secret police at once. You are our future. You are the children of Uncle Ho, you are following in his footsteps."

The bulldozers revved, and the smell of decay thickened the air. Coffins broke as the bulldozers ripped through them, and worms crawled out. We could not move until they ordered us to leave.

On Sunday, May 15, 1975, the secret police invaded our house and threw us out. They searched under our beds, in ev-ery closet and every corner of the house where they thought they might find valuables, even in the toilet. They let each of us take one shirt and one pair of pants. My mother held her shirt and pants while pleading with them for permission to burn some incense at the altars for our ancestors for the last time. The VC consented. She lit the long sticks, and moved about the altars, placing them in the incense burners. She kneeled and bowed to pray.

As she bowed to four directions, I saw her glance to see if any of the Viet Cong were watching her. Then, quickly, she rose, stepped behind the statue, and from a small hole in the wall snatched a fabric belt filled with jewelry, which she bun-dled into the roll of clothes she was carrying as she sat down again. Later it would buy our food. My parents, older and younger sisters, and two youngest brothers went back to the village. They put my father on the people's court to execute him. But people defended him, saying that he was rich because he had worked hard and not because he had received land from my grandfather. He narrowly escaped death. All of my broth-ers were placed in labor camps. I didn't know whether my brother, the pilot, had escaped or was killed. There was no news. I pleaded with the police to let me return to my school. They agreed.

I came back to Saigon, hoping to blend in with the big crowd, staying with my aunt's family.

One day, my aunt asked me to go to the black market to buy some food. I walked down the street where they sold goods, and I didn't know that the police had raided the area. A police-man ran by chasing someone, but his quarry escaped, and he stopped, his chest heaving. He turned to me.

"Where are your papers?"

I showed him my identification. He took it and looked at it, his eyes hot, the skin of his face mottled with frustration.

"What is your occupation?" the policeman asked.

"I am a student."

He grabbed my hands and handcuffed them at my back, pointing his AK-47 at my ribs and commanding me to move. People stared at me as we began to walk. I didn't know what my crime was. The VC policeman jailed me at the ward shelter for a week and ordered me to write a confession every day, list-ing all of my background from my great-grandfather's genera-tion to the present. They moved me into a big group with many southern soldiers who had been sent to them for "re-education." In early June 1975, a few months after my eigh-teenth birthday, I was sent to a labor camp. No one knew what had happened to me. I could see my aunt's face, waiting for me to bring back the food to cook a meal that would never be.

Book II

CHAPTER I

My first taste of a labor camp was at Hiep Tam town, the site of a U.S. helicopter field abandoned after the war. It was about twenty-five acres with three barracks, three watch towers, several bunkers, and over thirty chopper garages made from sandbags, where the Americans had hid the helicopters. Several barbed wire fences circled our camp to keep us from escaping. The VC packed more than 500 prisoners into each of the barracks, which had no toilet and no place to wash. A guard told us that we would only be here from three to ten days, and then we could go home to our families. Yet I also heard them whispering to each other, and laughing: three to ten days for them, but three to ten years for us.

At first, they treated us nicely and encouraged us to tell the truth in our confession papers, so that we could go home. Nobody knew that at the end of the month our papers would become "evidence" that would allow them to sentence us to serve time in a "re-education camp." A lot of the prisoners were trapped with this gimmick, but I told them a lie and stuck with it through my time in jail.

They divided us into groups of twenty prisoners each, gave us three axes, and ordered us to convert the whole air field into a garden. We took turns using the ax to break the tar-and-cement runways piece by piece, piling the broken rock into one spot under the boiling sun. Our hands blistered but we weren't allowed to stop. We formed a line to transfer the dirt and soil from the rice field to the newly uncovered ground to make a garden. We dug two wells about twenty-four meters deep to get water, dumped the sand out of the sandbags and tied pieces of bags together to make a rope for the well. We sewed the rest of the sandbags together to make walls for our barracks. After six months, our hands had turned numb and the big heavy axes had been ground into tiny hammers.

Every night the guards held a meeting at which we were expected to criticize ourselves about how poorly we had worked that day. Each group had to pick the laziest one and a guard would punish that person by putting him in a small metal box of connex which the Americans had used to store their ammunition. We had to take turns appointing someone to receive this kind of punishment, because if we didn't pick someone out, the guard would tell us that we weren't honestly criticizing each other and more trouble would come. The metal box was oven-hot during the day and freezing at night; everyone had to taste this torture at least once during our time at the camp. You were lucky to be let out in two days, and fortunate to be alive if they put you in the box for a week.

We began to grow vegetables: lettuce, tomatoes, cucumbers, corn, beans, and peppers, but the crop wasn't good because the soil was dull and too full of clay. The guard ordered us to "increase our production," but how could we? They announced a slogan: "With our human labor we can turn rocks and pebbles into rice." The guard said that if we could reach a set level, they would release us and let us go home. Everybody was happy again when they heard the word "home," after a long, depressed period at the camp. At the meeting the guard told us: "Use your human waste as fertilizer. We do this in the north every day."

We dug a rectangle in the soil about one foot deep for our toilet and every day twelve people would squat around the rim to do our business. On the other side, a few meters away, other prisoners watched and waited to catch our excrement in a big ladle, competing against each other for a piece of shit to fertilize our vegetables, afraid that if we didn't make our vegetables grow bigger we would get in trouble. One prisoner ran over to the hole where we were squatting and put his ladle beneath one of the prisoners.

"What are you doing?" the squatting man shouted at him.

"It's okay. Just do your business. I just want to make sure it all gets into my ladle."

"Go away!" he yelled angrily. "I cannot shit if you are around. I'll kill you if you talk anymore."

The whole group, which had been squatting there stood up, pulling up their pants, ready to threaten him. He ran back to the other side to wait.

When they got the fertilizer, they mixed it with water and showered the vegetables. It seemed to be working very well since the vegetables were growing bigger. Sometimes we just covered the toilet hole with soil and dirt and built a garden over it and dug another toilet at other sites in the camp.

We didn't have any newspapers, magazines, or books to read, but there were plenty of stories in our barracks, things that actually happened to us or to people we knew. There was a former green beret captain who slept two beds away from me. He had a beautiful young wife who came to visit him, but she didn't have any money to bribe the guard to let her see her husband. The guard chief told her that if she wanted to see her husband she would have to sleep with him first. And if she refused, he would single him out for "special treatment." Afraid, she did not see how she could refuse. One day, she told her husband that she couldn't come to visit him for six months— she was having a hard time taking care of the children at home. But in fact, her stomach was growing rounder: she gave birth to a baby girl. She resumed her duty, visiting her husband and this time she brought their four-year-old boy to see his father. She wanted to hide the truth because she knew it wouldn't help her or her husband at all in this situation. She didn't know whether her husband would forgive her or not if he knew what she had done. The boy had a conversation with his father the former captain, who was presently a prisoner.

"What do you do at home?" the captain asked. "Are you a good boy?"

"Yes, I'm a good boy, father," he said proudly. "I play and watch my little sister for mother."

The captain knew that he hadn't slept with his wife at all and how could his wife have another baby? Was she a prostitute, he thought. How could she do something like this to me? The captain looked at his wife helplessly, without a word, and tears fell. His face reddened, he stood up and ran back to his barracks while his wife ran after him to beg his forgiveness.

"It isn't my fault. I didn't do anything wrong. I love you and I have to support the children. Nobody helped me. I was always faithful to you, but after Saigon fell, and with you locked up in here, what could I do? The guards can kill you anytime they want but I wanted my son to have a father."

The husband looked at her, then shut the barracks door on his wife and child. The guard came to take her into the booth for his usual payment.

That night, the captain killed himself by biting off his tongue. I didn't know if he died because he felt he had nothing to live for anymore or if the shame of losing face in front of everyone was too much for him. No one except the captain will know exactly what he went through.

CHAPTER 2

After six months at Hiep Tam, I was transferred to a new camp. It was located in a thick jungle, approximately fifty kilometers from the town of Ha Tien and not far from the Cambodian border. The Khmer Rouge had seized power in Cambodia, ousting the Lon Nol government shortly after the fall of Saigon. As Vietnam and Cambodia had been enemies since the beginning of recorded history, everyone watched this border area with apprehension.

The camp had been a VC base during the fight between the north and the south but was abandoned when the VC rushed to the city after their victory. We had twenty huts for 500 prisoners. There were sixty guards in five cabins. One was a northerner named Son or comrade Son, the chief of the squadron. The rest were Viet Cong, including the second chief of our camp, a southerner named Chu Tu. Periodically, the VC shipped prisoners out after reviewing the confession papers. Most of the time I never saw the prisoners come back to the camp again after they moved them out. No one knew whether they executed them or sent them to other labor camps in the north.

They divided us into groups and labeled us with numbers. My group was L-19, the number of our hut. Our work consisted of clearing the jungle and creating a rice field and garden. We worked from five in the morning until seven at night. After that we came back to the camp for their meeting and confession time. They wouldn't let us go to sleep until midnight, so we would be lucky to get five hours of sleep a night. The food they gave us was never quite enough. Their policy was to let us die slowly, stealing from us any strength to fight back. They forced our labor and kept us busy so we would never have any time to scheme against them. If someone provoked them, they would punish us all and shoot that person in front of us as if they were telling us, "I'll shoot anyone I want."

The guards gave each group different assignments. My

group had to chop bamboo shoots, cut them into small slices, and weave them together to make a wall for our huts. We had to nail this wall from inside so that if we pushed it to escape, the wall could not fall over and if someone pushed against it from the outside, it could trap us in. We made the ceiling of barbed wire and tree trunks. We were building our own jail.

In my first week there, the guard took us to an abandoned outpost near the city to search for mines and salvage barbed wire.

"I want it done today," the skinny guard ordered us in his sleepy voice, rubbing the AK-47 strapped across his chest.

Twenty-five of us squatted in the wild grass and weeds about one meter apart, moving our hands back and forth, trying to find the mines. The VC stood up on the hill watching us. We pulled the weeds gently. One of the prisoners began to jump up and down yelling like a child, "Look, look what I found!" Everyone flattened to the ground, so I did the same. The prisoner began to run around dangling the mine, a small rectangle, like it was a toy. I felt coldness on my back and I guessed it would explode any minute, but a VC came and told him to put it down. He poked his AK-47 at the prisoner and made him go back to work. We began to feel the ground again, like blind men searching for their way. I moved the tall grass aside and pulled the grass up along the barbed wire fence, which shook forcefully. I heard something cracking as if someone had stepped on an old branch. A mine exploded. One of the prisoners fell to the ground, as the pressure of the explosion pushed me back. All of a sudden, everything became silent.

I heard someone wailing and felt something itching on my leg. It was blood. The VC came to me.

"You're not going to die. Just a few scratches," he said. "Help this wounded person to the tree there."

I looked at my neighbor lying on the ground with blood all over his belly. He breathed very lightly, his eyes open wide. I tore his pants, put my shirt on his stomach and moved him under the shadow of the tree.

"Back to work. Let him take a break!" the guard shouted to us.

I didn't know whether I or my neighbor caused the explosion. He was dying without any help. I felt a pain soaking deeply into my soul.

I never saw any first aid kit or any medicine at all at any time in that camp. If anything happened, the wounded would simply die, either suffering slowly or dying instantly. We depended on nature, whatever we could find to help our bodies heal.

My neighbor died in an hour from loss of blood. We dug a grave for him at the outpost and shoveled him back to the dust. I felt helpless and frustrated. Suddenly I touched something in the grass and I knew it wasn't grass. It was strange-feeling. I held and looked at it very carefully. It was a wire the size of a fishing rod that connected to a fence. I saw the grenade dangling on one of the barbed wires.

"Help, it's a grenade!" I yelled.

"Don't move!" someone shouted back.

I was stunned, as if someone had pulled me down to the ground. Some prisoners ran over but one of them shouted, "Go back if you don't want to die."

They quietly moved back and let one prisoner approach me. Most of them used to be soldiers so they knew these things very well, but I knew nothing of grenades. He looked at me with his tired eyes and slowly moved close to the fence, lightly like a ghost. Everyone held his breath. I felt as if the wind might blow and sway the grenade back and forth. My heart beat faster every second that passed. The prisoner grabbed the grenade and untied the wire that I held. He pulled a little pin off the head of the grenade that connected to my wire and replaced it with a secure one.

"If you fall on the wire or move one more step you will surely follow your neighbor."

I shook my head and a chill ran up my spine.

The guard came and took the grenade. We found some more mines but had no more explosions that day. We rolled the barbed wire on a tree trunk, taking it back to the labor camp to fence our jail. We also carried back twenty 155-mm shells from storage. When we arrived at the camp, we used a handsaw to cut the shells and used the large cannon shell as a stamper to smooth the dirt road and the top of the dike. We used the copper from the shells to make pots and pans, and crafts. I thought about my neighbor all day and all night long, and I wondered why I hadn't been killed.

"What are you thinking? You look terrible." It was Hung, one of the men in my hut. "Watch out, the guard is coming toward you."

"I don't care," I replied. "We're going to die anyway."

The guard was wearing his yellow uniform, a cold expression on his face. His baggy eyes had hatred in them and he shoved his gun into my stomach, pushing me as I sat. "Come with me," he said.

I stood up, stumbled alongside him to the bushes nearby. The guard said, "I saw you talking with the man next to you. Is he your friend?"

"No," I answered, "he isn't my friend. He just wanted a cigarette."

"I don't want any excuse. Go back to your place."

I turned and had walked a couple steps when he said, "Hold it!" He came up to me, placed his rifle under my chin while reaching into my pocket to search for my cigarettes. He took one out, put it on his lip and said, "It would be fun if I lit it with my gun, wouldn't it?" He grinned at me as if it was a joke. He put my cigarettes back in my pocket, asking me, "What did you tell your friend?"

"I told him I had only one left."

He told me I could go. I went back to my place and the guard followed. He stood in front of all of us asking, "Do you have any friends in this group?" Some of us raised our hands. Then he separated those of us who had raised our hands. He asked, "Who are your friends? Point them out and stand next to them."

The guard divided us, placing each of us in different groups. Nobody knew anyone. He drew up a work schedule for us. He assigned me and another fellow to cut down bamboo trees. He gave us a knife and an ax and said, "Get started."

While we worked, I developed a code language. The signals consisted of winking the eyes or knocking on wood. The number of winks or knocks corresponded with the alphabet. We

began to communicate with our silent language. His name was
Hung, the small man I had spoken to before, the man whom
the guard had questioned me about.

I asked what had happened to him and his family. I found
that he had a mother still at home along with two sisters. His
father had died on the battlefield when Hung was young. He
was the only son in his family who had survived. He had to
care for his mother and two sisters—but how could he manage
it in this situation? He had left school when he was young because he failed the twelfth-grade exam, so he had no choice but
to join the army.

Hung seemed very intelligent. His forehead was big and his
eyebrows were shaped like swords. He had brown eyes and a
long nose, wide at the base, and thin lips. He had high cheek
bones, his hair was black as coal, and his body was frail like a
delicate bamboo tree. He walked so lightly that I imagined if a
strong wind blew it would sweep him off his feet like a tornado that sucks houses from the ground. We told each other
about our lives and we came to understand each other well.

It was dawn and still dark outside but somewhere at the end
of the horizon the sun began to rise. I looked at the bamboo
fences, wondering how long I would be here. The bamboo
poles looked like the bars of an enormous bird cage. How nice
it would be, I thought, to fly up high in the sky, to smell the
air after it rains. I wanted to jump from branch to branch. I
wanted to take a deep breath, holding it there forever. Not
long before, I had had the freedom to do everything according
to my own free will. I had never realized, before, how beautiful
that was.

"Time for work," the guard shouted.

Everybody jumped up as if emerging from a dream. We
headed towards the stream; the guard told us to build a dam
across it. None of us wanted to go into the cold water; it
seemed even colder than it actually was, because we hadn't had
enough food to eat. The guards fired shots over our heads; we
jumped into the water like frogs.

We took bamboo trees, shoved them into the soil and tied
them together with weeds, working far out into the river. We
worked the whole day there, but the dam still wasn't finished.

The sun settled down after a long day; at the end of the horizon there were many beautiful colors, a whole rainbow of shades. All the trees seemed tired, as if they had had a long day, too. The trees seemed like my closest friends, I thought, even if they never speak. I could do anything to them, but the trees would never take revenge.

"Hung," I said, "Do you want some crickets?"

"Yes."

I reached into my pocket and gave a few to him. I whispered, "Eat them when you build a fire tonight." He winked at me secretively. Then he gave me some edible leaves and said, "We have to keep ourselves in good shape."

"What the hell for?" I smiled at him.

"Shut up. The guard is coming."

The guard strutted past but he didn't notice us talking. Hung and I continued to converse on our way back to the hut.

CHAPTER 4

After a few weeks in the labor camp, I began to know my way around. I discovered that there were some people who worked in the jungle for their living not far from here—I could hear them chatting through the trees, and I knew there were many trails around this area. One day when we walked to work there were some people sitting on the trail throwing us bits of food—rice cake, cookies—when the guard wasn't watching. They whispered, "Don't worry, we have let your people know." Hung and I looked at each other in astonishment. We wondered how they knew. Who were they anyway?

About a week later, Hung's mother came to the camp with these people. They stood far away from where we were, but I could see tears glinting on her cheeks; she didn't say anything.

At noon, when we arrived at the hut, his mother stood on the trail where the people had given us food. She waved her hands at him, pretending to fix her hat, because she knew Hung would get into trouble if the guard noticed the prisoner having relatives at the camp. No one was allowed to visit at this time. Hung winked at me, and gave the signal which I understood to mean, "Be careful not to do anything that would make the guard suspicious."

During the long night, I talked to Hung as we sat at the fire cooking some sweet potato. He had found a lizard and offered to share it with me. He asked me, "Are you sure you didn't make the guards suspicious?" I shook my head. I asked him what he would do. He didn't say anything and just stared at the ground.

The night was beautiful but I felt sick. I lay down on the pile of hay which served as my mattress. It was soft and helped me fall asleep faster than usual—or perhaps it was not the softness, but exhaustion from so much hard work. I looked up at the sky; it was clear with the half-moon hanging over the hut. There were so many stars—some very bright, bigger than others; some tiny, far away. They would clear up the darkness. I was totally lost at that moment. I was both excited and frightened, lost between dreaming and reality. I saw some stars falling and remembered my grandfather telling me: "When you see a star fall it means one life has gone." How many stars were up there? How many people in this world stood for them? I wished all the people had lucky stars. Dawn came finally; I didn't have to work this day because I had permission from comrade Son to stay at my hut to rest because I was sick.

Hung's mother came again. This time she carried two bags which seemed too heavy for her. Her eyes were the deepest brown, like an autumn lake. They were the most beautiful eyes I had ever seen—the eyes of a mother! Have you ever watched the surface of the water waving toward the rushes at the side of the lake, hearing them brush against each other? Hung's mother's eyes were like a paradise with endless love to share. Whenever I looked at them, whether I was sad or happy, they always seemed to be saying, "I am here for you . . ." Her eyelashes surrounded her eyes like the rushes growing wild around a lake. I wanted to run to my friend to tell him that his mother was here, but I couldn't.

Hung's mother's nose was perfect, and there were many wrinkles on her face and on her forehead. Every wrinkle stood for an event she had been through, for all her knowledge and experience of life. She had a beautiful laugh, smiles often washing over her face.

She walked over to the guards in their booth. She began to talk to one of them and sat down for a while. I saw her take a can of food from her bag and gave it to the guard. He opened the can and began to eat.

"Were you hungry?" Hung's mother asked.

"Yeah, I never ate such good food before," replied the guard.

"Why not?" asked Hung's mother.

"Because I never went to the city. When we won the war, I wanted to go but I couldn't. I had to hold the prisoners here because it was ordered by our northerner, Bac Ky comrade. No one would permit me to go to the city."

"You are still young. One day, you'll be in a higher position. You might even be able to go to the city to work there," Hung's mother said.

"I have no chance," the guard sighed. "The northern soldiers come here telling us what to do. They hold all the positions higher than us, just like here. We had one northern fellow, Son, as our boss; we had to do what he said. We had to pretend to believe him when he claimed to have gone to school in Moscow, even though we knew he was lying."

The wind whistled like a siren, like a howling wolf, as if a tornado was approaching from the distance. I lost track of these separate voices. The tree limbs began to bend, the grass swayed, bamboo trees began to scrape together, their leaves rattling. Black clouds appeared, covering the whole sky like a net to capture fish. Lightning moved rapidly, stabs of electric shock. Thunder rumbled in the sky like bombing missions. The rain began. I listened to the raindrops falling on the roof of the hut, trying to imagine it as the rhythm of a song softly lulling me to sleep, but I didn't have any kind of happiness. I wondered whether the peaceful happiness I dreamed of as a child was just an illusion.

The water began to soak into the pile of hay I was lying on. I couldn't think any longer, I couldn't hold any feeling for even one moment. Look! There were some crickets moving out from their holes because the rain was flooding their home. They jumped all around in bewilderment in front of me as if performing a wild dance. A lizard with his slithery body moved leisurely toward the little innocent crickets. The lizard's eyes popped out from its head. It moved its head from side to side, licking its chops. It opened its mouth, clamping it shut again like someone who didn't have enough sleep. I reached for a branch but couldn't grasp it, nor could I move because of my swollen legs. I imagined having the cricket for dinner, before the lizard got him. My mouth was filled with saliva. I swallowed and turned myself over to catch the cricket but my hand was pressed firmly to the ground by a big foot, which squeezed down harder and harder. A bulky shadow loomed over me; I tried to get my hand up but it was stuck there. The pain was moving up to my head; it was more painful than my legs.

"What were you doing?" the guard asked.

"I was turning over because my back was wet," I replied.

"Don't be smart with me. I saw you. I told you that no one could have anything to eat without my order." He kicked my stomach. I shriveled up like a snail but he grabbed my shoulder and threw me out of the hut into the pouring rain. I lay there quietly; the rest depended on fate.

Soon I began to feel my stomach grumbling, my body quivering. I didn't feel sorrow or pity for myself. "This is my life," I thought. The memories of my family, of all the people that I loved came flooding back. "I have to get out of this place," I mumbled. The rain kept torturing me like a thousand needles pricking my skin. I saw my friend Hung walk by me on his way back to the hut but he just glanced at me helplessly. There was nothing he could do. Dusk came without any warning. It was dark, the darkest night of the month. Seeing light from an oil lamp fluttering inside the hut, I kept repeating to myself my determination to survive, until I fell asleep.

"Who let you in here?" the northern guard asked with his heavy accent.

"I let myself in," Hung's mother replied, putting down her plastic bag on the ground inside the guard booth. It was the next afternoon, and she had returned.

"How did you know this place?"

"I live in the city near here, why wouldn't I know? I'm old, you know, but I still get around."

"What business do you have here?"

"I want to visit my son, Hung."

"What did you bring with you? Let me check your belongings." He began to remove the things from her bag while he was talking. "You have food; who are these clothes for? Do you have any papers?"

"No, I don't. But I have this."

She gave him money wrapped up in newspaper. He put it in his pocket and told her, "You stay here and wait. I'll be back later."

He grabbed a couple things from her bag as he walked away. "This is our new tax." He smiled scornfully, then disappeared.

Hung's mother looked at the surroundings. Twenty-five huts were clustered in a circle, guarded by three security booths. Two were watchtowers with machine guns at their summits; one was perched on the ground near where she was sitting. She heard the guards in the hut close to the booth complaining: "Damn it, it wasn't my turn to take them back to the rice field. I watched them all last night. There was stirring around in the prisoners' hut so I shot, and they shut up. If they pull this next time I'll shoot them all in the head, one by one."

"I couldn't find him anywhere, lady," the guard told Hung's mother as he walked into the booth.

She turned around, facing the guard with a despairing look.

"Are you sure he's not around somewhere?" she asked.

"I went out to the rice field, and his group was supposed to be working there, but I couldn't find him. I thought maybe he had been transferred to another group this morning but I'm not sure. It's late now. I can't help you, come back another time," he said.

"Is it okay if I stay here to wait till tomorrow?"

"No, it's not safe to stay here for security reasons. Come back later."

She stood there getting her things together. She pulled something from her bag and gave it to the guard saying, "You can have this food. If you have a chance, give these clothes to my son with the jar of sugar." She smiled in a tired way. All her gums showed when she opened her mouth, like a baby asking for milk. She had lost all her teeth. Her lips wrapped around her gums while her mouth was tightly shut, forming dimples, the dimples of old age, not infancy, the dimples of time. Her dark, wrinkled, golden skin resembled a road map. She began to walk out of the booth slowly. She felt defeated because she had lost her battle to find her son; one heard this in her heavy steps.

I went to sleep and wondered about Hung's mother, who reminded me of my mother. I felt the cold and woke up in the foggy mist of early morning. There wasn't enough light yet to see clearly because the rain from yesterday still hung in the air. The still woods slept. I could hear the retreating steps of a deer walking farther and farther into the distance. Somewhere near the bamboo bushes, the wild rooster cried out. I could hear all the animals preparing for a new hunting day. It seemed as if the whole universe stood inert, yet time rolled quickly by. I didn't know what to think of my experiences. Everything happened abruptly, like a storm sinking a little sailboat unexpectedly on the ocean—I was indifferent for the first time since the beginning of the war; I was lost. I saw my future not as light but as a looming darkness.

The sun peeked through the branches of the trees resting on the land. Some of the branches hanging over the green grass, as if asking for kisses as the wind moved them back and forth in rhythm with the morning breezes. The young, green grass was endlessly growing, like baby's hair. The mist and fog combined to make drops of water that fell from leaf to stem and then to leaf again, until finally falling to the grass. The shining sun beamed its yellow light through the leaves while the water dripped and dripped. The sun reflected through the water, sparkling as if it was a whole diamond forest. The water trickled down onto the golden, dead leaves on the ground. I could hear the drops of water as they struck the leaves, musical gems that sounded like beautiful notes as they soaked the earth.

The area around the labor camp began to change: we were turning the jungle into gardens. We grew sugarcane, bananas, corn, lettuce, tomatoes, hot peppers, and yucca root. We had the right to grow them but not the right to eat them. Like when the guards said we could defecate, but not urinate, on pain of castration. We tended the garden and watched the produce grow, our mouths watering. I felt like I was half dead and half alive.

We harvested the corn, salads, and cabbages, sorted the good and bad, and brought them to the highway for the VC to take away to sell. We didn't know where or to whom. We had to steal anything we could eat; we even picked edible leaves we found on the road or wherever we worked. We caught crickets or lizards and ate them raw because we could not let the guards see this. If the guards saw you, you would find yourself at the "guillotine center," the place where the VC held our meeting each evening. The guard tied the thumb of your left hand to your right toe and the right thumb to your left toe and let you stay at the guillotine center for a few hours, donating blood to mosquitoes. If the guard wanted to kill you he would leave you there all night. You died in horror, your face sunken, pale as a banana leaf from loss of blood, your mouth wide open. I could tell you about beatings, but they seemed almost routine: we were beaten whenever the guard felt like it.

I didn't know what to think anymore. I became numb and indifferent. I lived day by day and consoled myself with the thought that perhaps I was being punished for being cruel to others in past lives. I missed my family terribly and I wondered what had happened to them. What was my mother doing right now? I bet she was crying and I hoped she hadn't become blind because she was getting old. She had eleven children and eight of them were in jail. What did she think? How could she bear that kind of life? How about father? I bet he was worrying as always and getting skinnier. I knew he wouldn't cry. What could I say to my sisters and brothers? I prayed to my

Buddha to help them and myself. I heard the temple gong bang with its harmonious and warm sound, soothing me.

"Hey, I'm starving. Do you want to cook some yucca root?" Hung whispered. We were squatting in our hut.

"We don't have any," I answered.

"We have plenty in our garden." He smiled sarcastically.

"You mean we're going to steal again?"

"No, it's ours. We grew them. The guard didn't grow them."

"But they have a right to beat us up if we eat our crop," I said.

"Don't be a scaredy-cat. Let's go."

We woke a few other prisoners we trusted, and told them to build a fire for boiling water. Hung and I sidled out into the night, then crawled under the barbed wire fencing and into the garden. It was midnight. I recognized some of the stars in the sky. The weather was cool and it wasn't too dark.

We crept along the dike to the yucca root garden where we would dig some. I felt a cold chill when I stepped on the dewy grass. Hung found a spot and began digging a hole beneath the yucca tree, cutting the roots with his pocket knife. He put them in a bag and covered the hole up to make it look as if nothing had happened. He gave me the bag and moved to another spot to get some more. We could not get all the root in one spot because the tree would die and the VC would know. We took a little here and there from the furrow. And then I heard footsteps. I snatched a piece of soil and skipped it towards Hung, then jumped behind a bush nearby. I didn't know if Hung had received my signal. Several flashlights appeared, moving closer to our spot. I heard the sharp sound of metal cocking. I held my breath and tried to stop my beating heart, which seemed so loud the guard would notice.

"Come out with your hands up," one of the guards shouted and pointed his flashlight.

I stayed put, since I didn't feel any gun pointing at my back. They always bluffed—that was their trick. Everything became quiet and the guard moved along the furrow. He called out to his comrade walking along the garden, then disappeared into the dark. I lay in the bush not too far from the furrow, waiting a while before I made my move. I felt something thud on my back and thought it was Hung's signal for me to go back. I held the yucca bag and crept along the dike until I arrived at the hut. I gave the bag to my neighbors to cook the roots. They peeled off the skin and put them in the boiling water.

"What took you so long? Where is Hung?" one of them whispered.

"Hung couldn't get out because of the guard." I answered with broken breaths.

Four prisoners stood at each side of the hut to watch for the guards. We sat down in a circle around the fire. We were afraid someone would see the sparks from the fire even though it had been placed in a hole in the ground. We opened our mouths, sucked in the cooking smell, and exhaled with our noses, like we were some sort of filter machine.

"Smells good. Is it done?" one of the inmates asked in a low voice.

"Almost. Keep watching," I said.

I wondered what was happening to Hung.

"What can you do with the yucca skin?" someone asked.

"I'll bury them," I said.

I dug a hole in the ground and buried the skin to keep the guard from finding the evidence. It was almost morning now. I heard some shooting in the distance. We shared the yucca root and buried the fire. Hung still wasn't back.

When day broke, the camp was strangely quiet with no activity at all, though it was broad daylight. Strangely, there were few VC to be seen as if they were all meeting somewhere. Worried about Hung, I decided to go to the bathroom, our "communication center." I waited in line for a toilet, in the overpowering smell. I tried to identify a familiar face, to communicate with someone. I sat in the toilet finally and my connection sat next to me. I asked him about Hung. He said he didn't know. I asked him why we hadn't gone to work that day and why the guards weren't saying anything. He said there was some fighting near the border but he didn't know for sure who was fighting. I asked him if anyone in the camp was missing. He answered no. I asked him to check on Hung and let me know. We left the toilet.

Our group didn't report that Hung was missing because that would be dangerous for him if he had escaped. He would need all the time he could get. Besides, we could take advantage of the situation. The guards ordered us to dig trenches and holes around our camp and inside our huts. They told us that the Cambodians had attacked the border and that if any fighting reached our camp we would need to take cover in the trenches and holes. They said that they were protecting us from the Cambodians. I thought, if the Cambodians attack again, I will escape in the chaos. The morning went by; the situation was still tense. We had a meeting at the guillotine center and Chu Tu, one of the guards, pulled me to the side.

"Don't hide in the trenches," he paused, his face weary. "The trenches and holes are targets for grenades."

It figures, I thought, and the VC said they were protecting us. I thanked Chu Tu but still suspected him. Chu Tu was a southerner who had joined the north to fight the French in 1945, and had stayed there until the fall of Saigon when he returned to the south. He was the assistant chief for our camp, but it seemed that all the power was in comrade Son's hands. Chu Tu seemed to carry a big resentment against the north; I had used this to get to know him, hoping to turn him against comrade Son, hoping the more numerous VC guards might rebel against the northerners. I went to the "communication center" to pass Chu Tu's warning on to my fellow prisoners, and ask them if there was a way we could take advantage of the situation.

I learned from them what had happened to Hung. He had escaped, but was captured by guards from another camp nearby. They held him and tortured him before sending him back to our camp.

That evening, the guards came to our hut and escorted twenty-four of us to the "guillotine center." They ordered us to stand in a circle, beat each other, and yell, "You have to report to a comrade if someone escapes." We kept hitting each other until we couldn't move our hands. Our skin bruised and swelled. They pulled our arms back and tied our toes to our thumbs and left us in the sun to burn. They didn't give us any food or water for a whole day. I felt terribly hungry and cold, but there was nothing to eat; I swallowed my saliva, in pain. The more pain I felt the more I hated the VC. I couldn't stand the color of their uniforms; it looked like the color of a cow and I named them "yellow cow" meaning uneducated and stupid . . . every negative thing I could think of. I became determined to escape. I could not stand this pain any longer.

My body grew colder, even though it was hot and humid in the afternoon. My stomach growled. The hungrier I felt the colder I got. I wished they would just shoot us.

Hung was sent back to our camp, half dead with torture marks. His whole body was skin, bones, and bruises. It seemed like they would never heal. His eyes were sunken beneath messed-up hair which he didn't care to comb. Hair was growing everywhere on his face. He looked like an old man when he walked, his back hunched. I could imagine all his bones broken to pieces. He seemed like a dead ghost wandering about the camp. His clothes had holes everywhere. He appeared to have no energy, no feelings, no life any longer. We gave him medicine and asked him to take it, but he didn't say much. We looked at him, knowing he wouldn't survive.

He told us how they tormented him in the other camp. They filled up a barrel with water, put him in it, and closed the lid. They hit it with a stick for a minute and then took him out. He said he didn't know anything but blood, which came from his eyes, nose, ears, and mouth. Besides that, he had to cut trees down and carry them back to the camp. Hearing his story, I felt like I couldn't breathe because something clogged my throat as if someone had put a bag over my head and tied it to suffocate me. We tried to help each other as we could. I didn't know when it would end.

The guard mixed us with different inmates in a different hut. I was in a new hut with different prisoners, not sure of the make-up in this new group. Luckily Hung was here too. I watched them slowly, and reacted. They gave me some water and roast sweet potato as a sign of welcome.

The next day we went to work on the rice paddy. I had an easy job irrigating water into fields while two prisoners put ropes around their necks and pulled the plow behind with one inmate holding it to make furrows. Some picked weeds and grass and dug a little trench for the water to run. This was a new area that the VC had assigned to us. I observed it very carefully, searching for ways of escape.

A few weeks later, Hung's mother arrived at the camp. She bribed comrade Son and asked him to release Hung. The guard led her to him. Hung sat down on the ground and stared into space. He didn't run over to his mother to embrace her; he didn't say a word. He wanted to, but he just sat there. His mother ran over to him as if she hadn't seen her son for years. Gently, she held his face, kissing him.

"Son, do you recognize your mama? Aren't you happy to see me?" she whispered, choked by tears. He didn't say anything, but nodded his head. Gradually, he raised his arm to his mother's shoulder, tried to hold it there, then revealed his gloomy smile. His mother held his hand, squeezing it, looked to the front and then the back, as if she was afraid he would run away from her.

"Look at this, son. Your hand looks the same as when you were young, but now with more wrinkles and roughness," said Hung's mother. "Do you miss your sister, son?"

He nodded his head again. "Yes, mama."

"They want to come and see you, but I won't let them. I want you to come home, son. The house is so empty without you. I feel so lonely since your father died." Tears fell from her eyes, and she turned her head to the side quickly as if she feared Hung would see her crying.

"Yes, I will, mama."

"I found a beautiful girl for you. I want you to marry her," she said. "Do you want to know her name? Tuyet. How do you like that name, son?"

"It's beautiful, mama," he murmured.

She rubbed his back, tried to lift him up, but he was too heavy for her.

"You cannot stay here long, lady. You have to report to comrade Son. Hurry!" the guard shouted at her, and walked out of the hut. But it seemed she didn't hear him speaking to her. I didn't want to see them get in trouble. I came over to them, explained the situation and promised to take care of Hung for her. I helped her up. Hung brushed his hand at me feebly, signalling me to take her away. I felt like I would collapse on the ground, but I rallied enough energy to walk with Hung's mother.

"I have to go now. Goodbye, son. Come home early."

She stepped away from me, held her son's face again and kissed him. I picked up her hat and the shawl to cover her shoulders. We walked out.

"Yes, I'll remember, mama . . . ," he mumbled, staring at the doorway where she had walked out.

When we came out of the hut, Hung's mother ran back in as if she had forgotten something. She came to Hung, pulled out some money and a few bars of gold, giving them to him.

"Give this to comrade Son and he will let you go. Don't forget, don't forget."

She ran out of the hut.

CHAPTER 8

It was sometime in August of 1976, I don't remember the exact day, but there was a half-moon far away in the night sky; a dim light shone through the restless woods. I heard the frogs croaking louder and softer, starting and stopping continuously. Along with this croaking sound crickets were making shrill, chirping noises like they were composing "wild-nature" music. It made me feel like I was at a concert, but this particular one had only one audience—me. I was lost in thought. Then I heard heavy, brisk footsteps running along the bamboo fences, and the clicking of grenades jostling on the belts of the guards. Then the sharp metal sound of the AK-47s being cocked, ready to shoot. I shivered and looked out from the hut. Many shadows were moving in different directions.

"Shoot him, shoot him now, comrade."

"He went this way. Let's go," someone shouted back. There were two guards approaching my hut. One of them came inside the hut, grasped Hung's thin neck and threw him on the ground.

"Come on, move it," the guard shouted, while he used his gun to scramble his belongings.

Hung staggered out of the hut as the guard shoved the gun in his back. I didn't know what was going on, but I had an awful feeling. I wanted to stop Hung from going, but I didn't know what to do. I saw Hung's shadow appear under the unsettled moon, then disappear past the booth. I was frightened. I heard some gun shots vaguely in the distance, violently disturbing the night, and I felt like I had just been shot.

Everyone in the hut was awake, but we stayed quiet. I wondered what had happened to Hung, what would happen to us now. Would anyone know about this after the war was over, or was this the beginning of a new war—the war in which brothers kill brothers? Torture was happening everywhere in the labor camps around the country, but people did not seem to know or care, especially the people who negotiated this kind of "peace" for Vietnam. Happy to celebrate their victory after

Saigon fell, the north took over all the southern cities and people called this a "happy reunification." The happier they were the more bitterness I felt. I looked at the heads of my fellow prisoners in the dark and I wondered if anyone else felt like this. Or did they try not to think about it? I didn't hear anything except my own thoughts echoing inside my head: "Am I going to weep? No, I'm going to fight, whatever the circumstances, till the last drop of blood." I bit my lip harder, clenched my fists, stared at the moon going down at the side of the forest. Within myself there were only two things left—impotent hatred and the thirst for revenge.

At last, the wild rooster cried out somewhere in the bamboo bushes for his family. He was our dawn every morning. We got up restlessly to begin a new day. What happened last night stayed with me. "Am I going to die? And how? I have to find a way out!" I mumbled to myself. It was then that I remembered something my grandfather had said: "You are a good fighter and a good fighter has to be a leader himself; a good leader is a leader who doesn't need to show up at the battlefield." Was it true, grandfather? I am at battle right now. I must start planning. First: we need to unite, we prisoners. Then what? Rebel, kill them, or escape? If we revolt, some inmates will oppose it. Then what will happen? If we want to kill the guards, how will we go about it? The guards have weapons; we don't. How about escape? I could escape myself. I don't need any force from outside or inside. No one is going to get hurt. I only need a knife and a match.

And if they shoot me? Then I die faster than if I were tortured, or starved, or worked to death. I will be happy this way. The thought kept drifting through my mind, like a slow-motion picture. I grabbed my latanier leaf hat, placing it on my head. We formed a single line, walked out of the hut, picking up our tools as usual.

"Hey, you! Come here," the guard shouted.

"Are you talking to me?" I asked.

"Yeah, you. Are you deaf?"

I went to him hesitantly and he threw me a shovel.

"Are you in the L-19 group?"

"Yeah."

"Rice field today."

I walked away from him, following the group to the rice field. I noticed there were four guards in the group. One walked in front, two in the middle, and one at the end of the line. We reached the rice field outside of the woods about three kilometers from the clearing where our huts were.

"Build the dike around the rice field in order to retain the water for the rice to grow," the guard said, while he demonstrated with his hands.

The soil was neither dry nor muddy. We stepped down, began to dig.

"Do you understand clearly?" the guard asked.

"Yes, comrade."

He walked toward the woods and sat down beneath a tree, his eyes set on us. We formed a human conveyor belt, digging soil and passing it man to man down to the dike.

"Can you dig less?" I asked the man next to me.

"What's the matter with you? Too much?" he said with a sarcastic look.

"Yes, I can't carry it."

"That's your problem," the man said.

I was angry and yanked the shovel away from him when he was digging in the soil; he lost his balance and splashed into the water. He jumped up, trying to grab me, but I had already stepped away from him. He was furious, having missed his chance at revenge.

"Come on, break it up," a man in the group said.

"If he would dig less I would stop," I said.

"Yeah, do him a favor. He's a new guy, Chung," the group yelled at him. Then the guard appeared.

"What's going on here?" the guard asked.

"Nothing," I said.

"You again?" the guard called to me. "Come here."

I walked up to him. He hit my jaw with his elbow, swung his body around, and jabbed his rifle into my ribs. I tasted salt in my mouth as I fell to the ground. I wiped my face, and there was blood. I looked at Chung, who was glancing at the group with a look that said, "I'm not your enemy, the guard is our enemy." But everybody just turned away.

Go back to work. If you make any more trouble, you will be at the guillotine," the guard shouted.

I walked back to my work station, already feeling the tight rope around my thumbs and toes. The pain went through my veins, spreading throughout my body. I felt cold and quivery. I began to gather the soil, to pass it on endlessly.

Time went by slowly, from one hour to the next. Noon arrived finally; I knew this because the sun was beating down on my head. I didn't know what time we could eat. My stomach was growling, my heart was beating harder, faster every second. My legs were trembling. I had no more energy left. I conveyed a piece of soil to one of the men on the line, but it felt it weighed a ton. My hands moved slower and slower; I felt weaker and weaker.

"Time to eat," the guard yelled.

We all scrubbed our hands and cleaned our faces with the dirty water where we dug. I felt refreshed, even though the water wasn't clean. I learned a good lesson: anything that is dirty has its own purity.

We all lined up, walking along the grassy trail back to the camp.

"Comrade. I found him," comrade Son happily called to the other guard that was walking with us.

"Who?" the tired guard asked.

"The man last night," Son replied.

"Where?" He turned around, and walked with Son toward the forest. We all looked at each other, following the guards like we were robots. There were many trees along the trail, with ferns and green moss on the muddy ground and dew on the grass where the shade was deep. Weeds crawled around, consorting with all the wild crawling plants. The forest was dense. We walked by a couple of ditches. It seemed to me there had been a struggle here some time ago. In the ditch, there were many dead leaves with mud scattered about. Small broken branches and stems from a young tree covered the trail. I saw handprints in the mud and on the tree. It looked like someone had been holding on to the tree, then had fallen down. I noticed the mud spots splattered on the ground. In the distance they grew more uneven. I saw the footprints: it appeared that someone had been limping here. Beneath the tree was a man lying on the grass with his head bent.

Everybody rushed to him. I saw a plastic bag carefully folded beneath the leaves. I picked it up, stuffed it in my pocket. I approached the dead man. One of his eyes was dangling on his cheek. His other eye stared at the pale blue sky and grey clouds. He was looking at the tall tree, whose shadow covered him like a blanket, as if he was searching for something up there.

There was a small indentation on one side of his forehead, with a big bruise. I knelt, and touched his head there: it was as soft as jello, moving in and out under his messy black hair. It looked like someone had used a hammer to strike his head. He had a broken nose; one side of his cheek was stretched up towards his eye and it made his mouth look a little like a half smile. His skin had turned green and his body was as cold as ice. He looked young—thirty-six. His arms were stretched apart while his legs were crossed together. He looked like he was going to be put on a cross . . . or had just been taken from one. He was very frail under his dirty white shirt and black trousers. I saw a little red hole on his stomach where the shirt had been torn apart. Around the hole the skin had turned brown. The brown color had streaked down to his thighs. The guard bent down and frisked the dead body but found nothing except the wedding ring on the corpse's finger. The guard took his knife from the holster, cut the finger off and pocketed the ring.

"I knew him. He was in the L-21 hut group near mine," Teo said.

"Are you sure?" the guard asked.

"Yes, I'm sure because I was working with his group in the sweet potato garden last week."

"Take him back to the hut," the guard ordered.

Two of us grabbed his legs, two his arms; we heaved him up and walked onto the trail with the guard at our backs, his gun aimed at us. We walked about five hundred meters but the odor of the body was overwhelming. I was gagging. I released his legs, falling to the ground.

"What's wrong with you? You never seen a dead body before?" the guard scolded, his face stern. While I was vomiting, the men constructed a stretcher consisting of branches, which they then tied to the body.

"Move it, I don't have all day!" the guard shouted. We elevated the dead body and began walking. It seemed like the trail was getting longer and longer. Finally, we arrived at the security booth.

"Put him down here," the sweating guard said as he walked into the booth.

"What is it, comrade?" the guard in the booth asked.

"We found the piece to the puzzle," our boss said, and burst out laughing. "What do you think? Did you get your share yet?"

They winked at each other, with self-satisfied grins. One of them turned to us.

"Go in to eat. Come right back for your next assignment."

We walked slowly to the usual place to get our food, but everything had been put away except for a small pot. Each of us took a coconut bowl and poured the watery rice from the pot into our bowls. There was more water than rice. I could count each grain in my bowl—plus one cockroach, displaying his belly and looking at me with his innocent eyes. It reminded me of the dead body we had just brought back. I wasn't sure of my feelings at this moment, but I still brought the bowl up to my mouth and swallowed the rice. I felt something tickling in my throat. I started to choke.

Hung never came back and his body was never found. No one knew for sure whether he was dead or alive. We listed him in our collective Missing In Action memory. That evening, I went to our "communication center" to learn what I could. I found that the scene last night had been a setup. Some of the guards were jealous of those who had received bribes from Hung and the man from the L-21 hut; they threatened to call for an investigation. To get rid of the evidence, the bribe-takers had terminated their victims—Hung, and the man I found.

The afternoon slipped by slowly as I finished my lunch. I was still hungry but there was nothing left to eat. I tried to keep my mind off my hunger but my stomach kept torturing me. I got up but had to sit down again because I was dizzy. I cupped my hand over my eyes, held it there for a moment, then opened it slowly. I saw a black cloud appear in the sky; the sun was barely shining, as if it didn't have any more strength. The wind was whispering gently through the trees, then suddenly died down.

"Are you okay?" one of my friends, Thanh, asked.

"I'm all right, just a little dizzy."

He grasped my hand and helped me up. We walked back to the security booth. I was thinking that my situation was getting worse. The guard walked out of the booth and came to us.

"Follow me."

We walked behind him to the meeting place in front of the shack. All of the prisoners were there, sitting in rows of fifteen. Comrade Son stood under the awning of the hut. He started his speech as if he was a general:

"From now on, no one can go out for any reason, even if you have to go to the bathroom. There was an incident last night. I think you all know what I'm talking about. He asked our permission to go out, but he ran away. So we shot him. This is a very good lesson for all of you. I am a good person because I follow the Communist rules of how to treat prisoners. I follow Uncle Ho's ways. If you don't study hard and become a good citizen, you won't have a chance to appear in front of the people's court and ask them to forgive you of your crime. You betrayed them and your country. You followed the southern puppet government, the U.S. regime. This is the time for you to do something to pay us back, to prove your sincerity to our people. If you don't, you may stay here forever. Make your decision. I want you to write down your family history, your background and whether you feel guilty or innocent. I want the truth. If you lie we know what to do." He had a low, grating voice. Someone gave him a glass of water. He drank it, continued. "People are the owners, the government is the worker for the people, and the Communist Party manages peoples' businesses. Long live Ho Chi Minh," he yelled.

"Long live Ho Chi Minh," we repeated after him, like a broken record.

He paused for a moment while the guard walked over to the front row to tell them to stand up.

"Come here!" he pointed to a new captive who wore glasses.

The guard shoved the new man in the back with his gun to make him walk up to Son.

"You look handsome with your glasses. You are an intellectual from the south, huh? You know too much. You are the one who had a revolution against us, against our people, against our country for over twenty years and our people had to bleed all that time. You are a traitor, you are an idealist. Am I right, our citizens?" he rasped in his heavy accent full of scorn. Then he grinned.

"Yes, comrade, yes, comrade. He's our traitor!" we all shouted as if we were furious. Many guns were held at our backs ready to fire. I felt so bitter since every bad thing I said about others made my mouth dirty. Did I have any choice? The prisoner wearing glasses said softly:

"No, comrade, I'm not an intellectual person. I'm a mechanic in the army and I never held a gun to anyone. Look, look at my hands. They're all dirty with calluses. I'm not a traitor. Please forgive me!" He raised his voice louder and louder, repeatedly, but the crowd's voices were overpowering his.

"Don't lie to the party," Comrade Son shouted. "I have all your files here. You were working for the secret police. You have to confess to us now!"

The crowd quieted. The prisoner kneeled down and crawled over to him and begged for forgiveness. "I'm not a traitor, please forgive me!" he patted his hands on Son's legs and bowed down; Son pushed him away. He crawled back again, but this time the guard who stood next to Son raised his gun and knocked him down. The blood began to dribble from his mouth.

"Who will volunteer to punish our traitor?" comrade Son asked.

One of the men in the antenna group, the prisoners who spied for the guards, stood up and walked over to him like a dog obeying his master. Son threw him a rope. He held it, pulled the prisoner's arms to his back and firmly tied the left thumb to the right toe and the left toe to the right thumb. He jerked the man toward the flag pole, dragging him in the dirt like an animal. I didn't know if I was an animal or a human being at this moment. The antenna group man walked over, picked up the glasses and gave them to Son while the captive was moaning, trying to get up on his feet. He couldn't see anything without his glasses, his face was close to the ground. He pushed with his head, trying to sit up, but he didn't succeed. Son walked over to him and pulled him up. The inmate stood silently, his mouth bleeding. Son held his glasses in front of his face.

"Are you trying to act blind? We are the people; we are the justice. We know you so well, traitor. Why don't you come and get them?" Son waved the glasses in front of his face and the captive stood still. "You ignore me." Son dropped the glasses into the dirt, lifted his foot, then brought it down grinding glass into the dust. He laughed. The leader of the antenna group walked over to the captive, spit in his face, and kicked his stomach. The man fell down. The guard yanked him up. The next inmate stepped forward to continue the execution. We all lined up in a line, spit on him, and called him traitor. We held our confession papers, giving them to the guard as we walked up.

The guard called on individuals to stand up and make a remark. Abruptly a huge shadow covered the whole area. Rain drip-dropped on my hat. It rained harder every moment. The guard raised his voice louder and louder to lecture about his Communist theory. He tried to speak over the rain so we could hear him. The louder he spoke the stronger the rain fell. I got wet, but I was happy because I didn't have to listen to him rattle on. Water flooded the ground, running down the side of the hut. We were wet like soaked rats. I looked around the group. Each row of people looked like gravestones in a cemetery. We sat still, thinking to ourselves. Some cold, some hard, and some joyous faces. I didn't know exactly what they were thinking, but felt I could see into their minds. I knew they wished they were home with their families, with their wives and children. How will we get out of this trap? I thought. They just promise, but nothing is done. Look! The rain dropped down in a puddle at my side, making bubbles. The bubbles disappeared. Again, the rain dropped. More bubbles, then gone, so quickly.

"Come on! Let's go back to the hut," Thanh called to me. I stood up and walked with him.

"What do you think?" I asked.

"Politics, all lies. They make promises but don't keep them," he said.

"What do you plan to do?" I asked.

"Lower your voice," he whispered. We looked around, but nobody was in sight.

"Do you have anything to eat?" I said.

"Yeah, some burned rice," said Thanh.

"Where do you hide it?"

"Close to where I sleep so I can eat at night," he said. "I'll give you some when I go to sleep, but don't let anybody know."

"Sure." He went to his spot; I went to mine.

There was mud all around the hut and we walked barefoot. Footprints were everywhere, some big, some small, in different shapes. Inside, the hut looked like a pigpen. I placed the bamboo frame on the floor, and put some hay over it. I had a nice bed—I felt so happy, like a child who sees his mother coming home from the market. It reminded me of when I was young. I would pretend to build a house with a bed in my father's backyard. I remembered my brothers, sisters, and friends playing together. What had happened to my family? I wanted badly to see them. I wanted to put my head on my mother's chest, feel her warmth and tenderness. I longed for my father's embrace. I wanted to hold my sister's hands, share her happiness and sorrow. When I was in trouble, I ran to my brother. Now, I wanted to sit down with my friend beneath the shadow of a tree, near a creek with a waterfall. I wanted to sit down on the green grass and look at the flowers bloom and smell the freshness of early spring.

My friend and I told each other our stories. Where were my loved ones? Here are my kisses, my embrace, my love, and my prayers. I want to send them all to you, I was thinking. I wanted to bury my head in my pillow—the pillow I used to sleep with, the pillow I used to fight with. Oh, my happiness, my happiness.

"You can borrow my linen bag." Thanh patted me on the shoulder, winked, and handed me the bag. I knew there was some food in the bag, and I looked at him, showing my gratefulness. He turned around and walked away. I lay down on my bed, reached into the bag to get the dried burned rice. I put it in my mouth, chewed it slowly. It was soft and mushy with a bittersweet taste. I swallowed it like a sweet drop of water which people in the desert thirst for. I let my happiness soak through all my body tissues, spread out to my veins, to my blood which ran to my heart. I could feel it beating faster and steadily. It felt as if my heart was going to jump out of my chest, and so I pressed my hand over it on my shirt pocket.

I felt something hard. I took it out—it was the plastic bag that I had picked up next to the corpse. I opened the bag, and pulled out a photograph of the dead man's family, some documents, and a letter to his wife.

I read:

Em,

What will I say to you now? I don't know if this letter will reach you or not. It would be easy for me to say I'm sorry, but this was unbearable. I couldn't hold onto my life any more, any longer. I had to run. If they shoot me, I will die faster than by being tortured here. I know I hold the love for you and our children, but what can I do . . . ? Will you understand me? I wish I could have found another world where there was peace, happiness which I could share with you and our children . . . I wanted to take my family there but how could I? I don't want to compare the life of being tortured and the love that is out there for me. I don't care to look into these two things because I know it would be impossible for me to escape. Here are my kisses to you, hugs for my little daughter and son. I hope you raise them to be real human beings. Our son to be like me, our daughter

to be like you. Send my love to my family and your family. If this let-
ter comes to you, it will be very fortunate for me. If it doesn't come to
you it was my acceptance of fate. Whether I come to you through my
spirit or body; dead or alive.

Farewell—dear,
Anh

The pencil writing was scattered across the page and towards the bottom it looked like his hand had been shaking. I
looked at his family picture and I saw him standing next to his
wife. He was holding his son. His wife was pregnant though
she looked very young. I didn't know how old this photograph
was, but I could see it was from his youth—the time of tri-
umphs and fighting for victory. What had happened to this
generation, all the young, brave men that stood up for our
country, for honor and duty? I looked at myself, felt that I was
born at the wrong time. Where was my patriotism? I knew I
had it in my blood, but it wouldn't come out. I had to wait to
take my chances. I felt I wanted to prove something to myself
at this moment—do something for this family. I would hide
the nylon bag which I had just opened. I promised myself I
would take it back to his family if I could get out of this place.
I prayed that his spirit would help me escape safely so that I
could bring his message to his family. Where was his soul wandering? Did he have a place to rest? Did he know how to find
his way home? Or was he just one of the wandering souls who
have no place to go, no family to love, like a wasted person
roaming the city? Or did he just die and that's the end?

Outside, the night stood still, waiting for the new day. The
moon was dim, shining through the hut, through the bamboo
wall. All kinds of animals were on the prowl, ready for a hunting night, but leaves had folded on the trees for the sleeping
night. I could hear animals calling each other to prepare for
their journey. They were whispering through the trees, in the
thickets. The air was getting cooler. It seemed as if the whole
universe was ready for a new beginning of life. How long have
I been here? I couldn't remember. I touched the bamboo wall
to count the marks on it: more than 350 days. It seemed like
my whole life. I couldn't sleep, thinking of the memories now
long past.

Suddenly, there was a strange noise outside the hut. My eyes followed the rustling, looked beyond the barbed wire fence at the back of the security booth. I saw a dark shadow crawling towards the dead body which we carried in on our way back to the camp in the afternoon and left near the fence, not having had time to bury it yet. The shadow stopped at the corpse for a moment, then the figure moved back, vanishing beyond the fence. I couldn't figure out what was going on. Were there any guards in the booth? Were they watching us? There wasn't any action. Could it be that the remnants of the South Vietnamese army had invaded the place and the guards had run off? But why was it so quiet then? If they had invaded the area I would have heard shooting. Maybe they attacked using a special force. I had heard of incidents like this lately. I was more hopeful.

I raised my head, looked at the booth and beyond the barbed wire fence. Everything was still quiet. The moon hid its face behind the trees. I could hear the birds flapping their wings and flying away. In the distance, the rooster crowed. Above, the North Star shone, mixing together with the dawn which was finally arriving. The sky became brighter and brighter. I had not slept.

The old folks have a saying: If you're awake all night, you know how long the night is. I understood that now. I got up and walked out of the hut to prepare for another working day. I went to the shack to pick up the tools.

"I'm in L-19 group. Where shall I work today?" I asked.

"You cook, but before you begin, call your friend Thanh and get a shovel," Chu Tu ordered. "Come back after."

I went back to my hut to find Thanh but halfway there I saw him coming towards me.

"Thanh, we work together today."

"What is our job?"

"Chu Tu told me to have you get a shovel and see him before we cook."

"So we cook today. That's good," Thanh looked at me, smiling while we walked.

"What are you smiling about?" I asked.

"Nothing, really."

We stopped at the shack to get shovels and went to the well to look for Chu Tu. I saw him squatting like a frog at the side of the well.

"What do you want us to do, Chu Tu?"

"Make me some tea first," he said while he was washing his face. We walked to the place where we cooked.

"And don't forget to fill the barrels up with water," Chu Tu yelled at us.

I chopped some wood, then built a fire while Thanh got a kettle, filled it with water and put it over the fire.

"What will we cook for lunch?"

"White rice for our comrades. Leftover rice mixed together with sweet potato and old corn for us as usual."

"Do we have any sweet potatoes?"

"No, but we have a small bag of old corn left," Thanh said while he was checking the ingredients. I saw steam coming from the spout on the kettle. It began to boil.

"I'm going to Chu Tu's hut to get his cup. I'll be back." I ran out of the place. I came to Chu Tu as he was talking to some of the other comrades. I got his cup and he told me to make some for these other comrades too. I went back to make the tea and carried it to them.

"Would you like sugar in your tea, Chu Tu?" Thanh asked.

"Yes, here is my jar of sugar."

Thanh took it and opened it. He got a spoon to scoop the sugar out of the jar, put some in the cups and stirred them.

"These cups too, Thanh." I gave them to him.

He put more sugar in the cups a second time, but he didn't stir them. I looked at him curiously, opening my eyes wider. I tried to ask him but he looked at me, winking his eye. I remained silent. We handed the tea to them and walked out of the hut. We came to the well, dropped the bucket into the water, then hoisted it up. Thanh poured the bucket of water into the barrel until it was full.

"Why did you do that before with the sugar?"

He didn't say a word but gave me a smile. You are learning, I thought.

"You and Thanh come here," Chu Tu called us.

We ran over to him.

"What do you want us to do?"

"Clean the cups and get your shovels," said Chu Tu. "Come to the security booth after you're done."

We brought the cups to the well to wash them. Thanh put a little water in the cup, drank it. I looked into the cups, and saw there was some sugar left on the bottom. Now I knew his purpose. I hadn't tasted sugar in a long time. I used my finger to scoop the sugar, placed it on my tongue, and slowly let it melt. I didn't want to swallow it. I just wanted to let it soak in my mouth, I wanted to see what the taste was, as if I had never tasted it before in my life. I smiled to myself.

"Are you dreaming?" Thanh called me. "Let's go."

I felt invigorated. I didn't know where all this energy was coming from. I felt like I was a new person. I got up.

"Yes, let's go."

We walked to the security booth to see Chu Tu. He walked out of the booth to the gate. He waited at the gate till we arrived.

"Go dig a hole to bury the body you brought back yesterday," he said, and pointed to the side of the gate.

We began to chop the weeds and surrounding grass away. Afterwards, we dug.

"When you're finished, come and get me," Chu Tu said.

He walked back to the booth to talk to the other guard.

"Thank you for the sugar, Thanh," I said.

"What are you thanking me for? Are we friends or what?"

"Yeah, we are friends."

CHAPTER 10

As we were digging, my mind wandered back over the past months. I was thinking about Thanh. He was a nice fellow and a good companion. He wore a hat wherever he went, in rain or sun. I was nineteen and he was eleven years older, wasn't married, and had a younger sister my age. He used to speak of her often. He said he'd take me to meet her if we ever got out of here. He always smiled after he said that.

Thanh's mother had died during the war when he was small. His father had remarried and his sister stayed with them. He knew his sister was suffering under her stepmother and that she never opened up to anyone. That was a part of him also. Thanh had a bigger frame than me. His muscles were very firm. Whenever he walked, his steps were as heavy as an elephant's—strong, confident—nothing could stop him. His face was oval-shaped, with a high nose, a black moustache, and a wide mouth with small teeth compared to his body, which made him look rather comical. He had thin lips with a long chin, and his unyielding eyebrows slanted together like an upside-down roof. I imagined rain dropping down on his big forehead and running along his eyebrows to the top of his nose, then gently running down like a steady stream along his cheeks. His long eyelashes curled up over his black eyes.

Thanh had been a lieutenant in a green beret group, but then had transferred to a special force called *Biet Cach;* they had fought to take back An Loc, Binh Long, and other cities in the central highland near the Cambodian border during the Tet Offensive of '68. His entire group had been killed: only he survived. Now he had ended up here. He had first impressed me when a guard had come to search our belongings for weapons, on a tip from someone in the antenna group. Thanh wanted to kill the antenna member, but we couldn't identify who had done it. I knew these people were scheming to ruin us. They wouldn't deserve to live if we found them.

"Look at this hole," Thanh called to me, from the pit.

"What hole?"

"This one." Thanh used the shovel to make the hole bigger.

I bent down to look into the hole. It was dry and smooth, with some rat footprints around the hole.

"Hey, do you think we'll have rat meat today?" I asked.

"I don't think so. The hole is old. I don't think there are any rats living here." I stood up beside the grave.

"I heard something," Thanh said.

"What is it?"

"Don't stand there!" he yelled at me. I jumped into the crypt alongside Thanh.

"Why?"

"Come here and listen to this."

I put my ear close to the hole. I heard a hissing noise, but I didn't see anything in there because it was dark.

"It's a snake. Don't you know? If you stand up there, there might be another hole where a snake can come out to bite you. Go and get a branch."

I jumped out of the pit to get a stick, then came back.

"You stand on the pile of soil, and yell if you see a snake come out."

Thanh continued digging towards the hole. The closer he got, the louder the hissing sound became.

"It's a snake, it's a snake!" I yelled, pointing at the movement.

The thick, slithery body crawled out of the hole where I had stood before. Thanh leaped up from the pit, ran after the snake, grabbed his shovel, and chopped at the snake with it. The snake came halfway out, cocked its head, shot out its pink tongue and pecked at the shovel. Thanh lifted the shovel up, ready to strike again. This time I saw the snake's head move from side to side. His piercing eyes stared out from his large head, flaring from his thin neck. On the top of his neck were spots of different colors. It looked like a strange tattoo. I couldn't recognize it. There was one big patch in the middle with some small marks surrounding it. I used my branch stick and whipped at the snake's head but he dodged it. When the snake moved towards him, Thanh struck it with his shovel. The snake fell down on the ground. We hit it a couple more times to make sure we had killed it. The snake surrendered, its last battle finished.

When Thanh picked up the snake, its body was still moving as if it were alive. The snake's dark blue skin was slippery, scaley, and cold. It had rings around its body. We couldn't tell what kind of snake it was since we had smashed its head. It was about eight feet long and six inches thick. We knew it was a dangerous snake on account of its spots.

"We're going to have a good meal," I said.

"Do you want to prepare it?" Thanh asked.

"You clean it, I'll cook." I said.

"You have to ask Chu Tu first."

We were so busy with the snake that we forgot to dig the grave. Chu Tu came unexpectedly.

"What happened? Did you finish the grave?" he shouted.

"Look what we have, Chu Tu. Can we eat this?"

"Snake, huh, good meat. Give me some after you cook it. Dig the grave then. Hurry."

We began to dig further into the ground, but water started to rise in the pit. Thanh dug, I scooped out water, throwing it aside. Suddenly I realized what I was doing. "I'm digging someone's grave." I felt cold from the water down below. This is your new bed, your last home, isn't it? I'm digging this grave for somebody today; who will dig for me tomorrow? Is the Buddhist concept right? They believe that our bodies are built up with the combinations of fire, air, dust, and water. Is fire our body temperature, is air our breath? Is dust our body tissue? Is water our blood? Were we a part of nature? If so, we will come back to it. Ashes to ashes, dust to dust . . . What is our purpose for existence? Is life a crime? But what is our crime? Do we ask to be born to this world? We are born, age, sicken, and die. And does this all mean anything, does it lead to something? Will we end up at the same resting place? Does death make all of us equals?

"Did you see a dead body near the booth when we walked by this morning?" Thanh asked me.

"I didn't notice it."

"Do you want to be buried or burned when you die?" he asked.

"I want to be burned because I believe my soul can leave my body more freely," I said.

"Do you believe in another world?"

"Yes, but I'm not sure."

"Does it really matter if you're buried or burned?" Thanh asked.

"No, but people like to have a ceremony."

"Do you think it's silly when you see people cry at their relative's funeral?" he asked. "When their relatives are alive they don't show any affection toward them."

"Silly, yeah," I answered. "To me, I do everything for my loved ones. I give all my love to them. When it comes to the end, I walk them to the grave, drop a few flowers on it. I don't have to weep to make myself feel better. I don't hate or feel sorry for myself."

"Let's go back to the booth." We climbed out of the pit and walked back.

"We finished, Chu Tu," said Thanh.

Chu Tu walked out from the booth to the dead body that we had left near the gate the day before.

"Go bury him. When you're done, come back to make lunch."

I looked at the dead body. He looked the same as yesterday. His face was dark purple, and he had no clothes on. Flies were lighting on his mouth, buzzing in his ears, the odor from his body attracting them more than ever. I remembered that yesterday, when we brought him back, he still had his clothes on. But he had none now.

When you were born you were bare. Then, your parents clothed you to show their affection. You didn't know whether you wanted that or not, but it became a habit. You had to use a cover all your life, but now someone has taken off your clothes. You lie here exposed again, just like the first time you came into this world. You must face yourself as you are now; and I will have to see myself just as clearly, someday. What else do we have in common, from the beginning to the end? What did you give to life, what did you take with you? Did you leave anything behind? Yes, your material world, your love, your sorrow, your happiness . . . and what happened to your suffering? You don't have to worry now, you don't have to think about it anymore . . . You are through with life, you're all done and gone.

Let us be ourselves, let us speak, let us breathe, and let us live . . . You are the bird out of the cage, free to fly as high as the sky. If you look down below you can see us chasing after your shadow.

"Do you want to hold his hands or his legs?" Thanh asked me.

"Is it easier if we both hold his hands to drag him?"

"Let's see if we can lift him." Both of us raised him off the ground.

"Why don't we use the stretcher we made?" I suggested.

"Yeah, let's do it."

We put him on the stretcher to carry him to the grave. His odor began to aggravate me. I started coughing.

"Would you walk a little faster? I feel like I'm going to vomit."

We were halfway there now. I felt as if all my energy was gone. We put the stretcher down.

"You can't handle it anymore?" asked Thanh.

"It's okay."

He knew it was too much for me, so he pulled it himself. I just walked behind him to the crypt.

"How will we bury him, faceup or face down?"

"It doesn't matter," I coughed. I looked at his poor body. "But I remember my father told me that if you bury someone face down, then when their star falls, their body will turn over to face the sky. And then someone will be born into the family with a special talent."

"Are you sure?"

"No, but the old people say that," I said. "The crown of his head has to face the sunrise."

"How do you know so much about this?" Thanh said.

"My grandparents told me a lot of stories."

"So what should we do?"

"Just push him into the grave to find out his fate."

"Okay, let's do it."

We counted to three, pushed him down; he landed on his stomach.

We started covering the body with the soil. His body sank into the dirt, disappearing. We kept putting soil over it till there was a little hill over the grave. We patted it down.

"Is he a Catholic or Buddhist?"

"I don't know," said Thanh.

"In all religions, they teach people to be good, pray for them whether they're dead or alive. I think we should make a cross or a sign so his relatives can identify him if they come."

I looked up at the sky. It was clear; the hot sun seemed to want to burn everything under its radiance. It felt more humid, making us perspire. I took shorter breaths, like a chicken panting beneath a tree on a hot summer afternoon. I just wanted to jump into the river, float atop the water, and let it take me away somewhere . . .

"Are you dreaming again?" Thanh asked me.

"Life is a dream, isn't it?"

"Yes, it's a dream." His voice was getting softer and softer. I held the cross in front of the grave while Thanh hammered it into the ground with the shovel. We're finally done, I thought. It was exhausting getting up to go back to the hut. I held the tail of the snake, pulling it along the path, as Thanh carried the shovel on his shoulder.

We stopped by the well to have some water. I felt coolness inside my chest as the water moved down to my stomach while Thanh gulped water. We walked back to make lunch.

"Oh, we forgot to get some sweet potato."

"Why don't you go to the garden to get them? I will chop the wood for the fire to cook the rice for the comrades." I grabbed a basket and hoe and went to the garden. I raked the soil from the dike where the sweet potatoes were growing. I cut the stems off the potatoes, filled the basket, and carried them back to the well. In a big pot I put corn kernels, rice, and sliced potatoes, mixing everything together and washing it all. I filled the water up to the rim, called Thanh to help me, and together we took it back to set it on the three-stone stove to cook.

"Can you watch this pot of rice for me?" asked Thanh. "I want to find Chu Tu."

He walked to the hut and came back with Chu Tu. We made a bamboo table to put the food on. Chu Tu came and sat on it while we were cooking. The pot began to boil. I took some wood away so it would have medium heat to prevent the bottom from burning. But when I took it out, Thanh put it back. I remembered what he had done with the sugar, and the burned rice which he had given me another night. He winked at me with a smile on his face.

"Thanh, why don't you clean the snake?" Chu Tu told him.

Thanh picked up the snake and burned it over the fire. He turned the snake around and around till the scales popped off. I could smell the skin burning. He brought it back to me. I opened up the stomach, cleaned out the insides. I saved the liver and some other parts I could use. I boiled the snake with salt, taking the spine and rib bones out to get the meat. I chopped the meat very thin, mixing it with the other parts and some onion from the garden for flavor. I added some salt, stuffing everything into the skin. I tied the ends up to keep the juices in. Afterwards, I barbecued this big sausage. The burning smell of the rice came out stronger. Both of us put the fire out. The smell of the snake barbecue sauce with the rice made me drool. I didn't realize it. I could hear Thanh swallow. The juices kept dripping down onto the fire, making a sizzling sound. The stronger the smell of the cooking, the more we swallowed. I checked the sausage to see if it was done. I sliced it piece by piece.

"Let me taste it," Chu Tu said.

I gave him a piece and he ate it as if he'd never eaten before. I took a bite and I could not believe that a snake could taste so wonderful, rich, and flavorful. After we finished eating, we washed all the pots and bowls at the well. We scrubbed the pots with a coconut skin to get the leftovers out. Thanh tore a piece of banana leaf, putting the burned rice on it. Next he folded it and put it on top of the lid of the barrel of drinking water.

"Are you going to hide it?"

"No, let them see it."

"Why?"

"Trust me, I know what I'm doing."

Chu Tu and a guard came to the well to drink some water at the barrel while we were washing. Chu Tu saw the banana wrap. He opened it to see what was inside, and he put it back.

"Are you ready?" Chu Tu asked.

"Yes, we're almost done," I replied.

We brought everything back, put it all on the bamboo table where we had cooked. We went with Chu Tu.

"Go get two baskets and some bags," Chu Tu said.

Thanh went back to the tool shack to get the supplies. He ran after us as we walked out of the gate.

"Go and get four more people," Chu Tu told me. I walked back to the group where we ate, asking some of them to come with me. Thanh winked at me when I walked by him. I didn't know what he meant at first. Then I remembered the banana wrap which we hadn't concealed yet. I nodded my head to let him know I understood him.

I stopped by the well to drink some water but my real purpose was to get the banana wrap. I held the coconut shell inside the barrel to get the water and I drank it. I looked around to see if anyone was coming in my direction; no one was in sight. I looked on the top of the other barrel, but the banana wrap was gone. What had happened? Had someone taken it or had the guard thrown it away? I remembered when Thanh winked at me about the banana wrap. I knew he wanted me to hide it, or maybe I misunderstood him. I would ask him later.

"Come on, I don't have all day," Chu Tu yelled.

I ran to the prisoner's group, called four people to follow me, and came to Chu Tu.

We began to walk out of the gate to follow the trail toward the highway.

"If any one of you makes me suspicious, I'll shoot!" Chu Tu told us as we were walking.

I saw the trees' shadows hanging over the trail. Gradually, the afternoon came. The humidity made me feel breathless and slothful in the hot summer sun. It reminded me of my youth, of places where my friends and I had hung out. I never realized how wonderful those moments I shared with my friends were until now. I didn't want to do anything except lie down on the grass, look up at the pink and blue sky, and watch the birds flying. I was chasing a dream that seemed so immense I couldn't hold on to it.

"Chu Tu, do you go home on the holidays? I see you work all the time," Thanh asked him.

"No, I want to go home to retire, but I still feel an obligation to my country. I think the war has ended, but it is harder to struggle with this new revolution than to fight on the battlefield."

"Do you have a family?" I asked.

"Yes, I have a wife and three children. I got married to a northern woman when I lived in Hanoi. I regrouped to follow Ho Chi Minh to fight the French in 1945, but then the war was still going on."

"What war was that, Chu Tu?" I asked.

"You see, after the war ended, we were supposed to run the government in the south as Uncle Ho had planned, but now all the northern comrades control the whole country. We have no voice, no power, and that's why I'm still here."

As I listened to the conversation, an idea developed in my mind: Why don't I draw the northern and southern guards into deeper conflict? I knew the southerners hated the northerners but I didn't realize that the VC liberation front hated the north too. They both were members of the Communist Party. I hated the yellow uniform; we called them yellow cowards. Let them fight to kill each other; I could be in the middle, and watch them fight like chickens. I could place bets and be the winner no matter what.

"It's good to be home, Chu Tu," I said.

"Yes," he said. "I'm going home soon."

"Why not? If I were you, I'd do the same."

Silence came suddenly. Everybody seemed to be concentrating on something. I let my mind wander. It seemed like it was the first time I was escaping from this deadly place, but it was only in my mind. I took a deep breath in the afternoon air, feeling the gentle wind sweep over my face. It was like a little wave on the ocean brushing the sand. I looked at the path, which was curving like a slithery snake. My eyes landed on a cross-section of the path.

"Stop here for a break," Chu Tu called while he put his hand on his gun belt, sitting down at the side of the path. He took slow breaths, too tired to supervise us, holding on to his gun more tightly. We sat down at the side facing him.

"Give me some water," Chu Tu said.

"Here." Thanh held out the pitcher and gave it to him.

He chugged the water down.

"Do you feel better, Chu Tu?" I asked.

"Yeah, but I'm old. I don't know where all my energy has gone with this little walk. I don't feel the same as when I was young and went to the north to fight the French. I wish I had the same energy, and passion that I had in my younger days."

"You'll be fine."

We sat there for a while to wait for Chu Tu. Thanh was leaning against the tree, plucking grass. All the other men were pacing up and down impatiently. Chu Tu's eyes were partly closed like he was half asleep. One hand was behind his head, the other was holding his gun. I looked at his K-54. It looked well polished. I turned around to look at Thanh and the four other captives. I wondered if Chu Tu had a good aim. He stood up.

"Let's go."

We walked faster on the trail now as the afternoon began to fall. Finally we reached the highway. We stood there about ten minutes; nothing happened except one car passed by.

"They told me they would be here early, but where are they?" Chu Tu said with much anger in his voice.

"Who, Chu Tu?"

"The convoy."

"What for, Chu Tu?"

"To get our supplies." While we were talking, we saw the army truck coming closer.

"Maybe that's the one."

"When it stops, I'll believe it."

I felt dizzy as I sat at the shoulder of the highway. The heat was rising up off the highway like water rippling. It was very hard for anybody to breathe. The blacktop looked ready to melt. It burned our feet whenever we walked on it. The army truck passed by, making a suction noise like a vacuum ready to suck me in. The air brushed by me powerfully, then vanished into empty space. The highway stretched away as far as I could see, empty, the temperature rising.

"What time is it, Thanh?" asked Chu Tu.

"I don't know, Chu Tu. I don't have a watch."

"Oh, I forgot; I do have it." He looked at his watch, mumbling to himself. "Thirty minutes already. Where are they?" Chu Tu said angrily.

We stood up and sat down. We waited and waited. Time passed by, the sun showed its bright red face slowly falling down beyond the woods. Up in the sky, many beautiful colors were blending together, from blue to pink with red. I noticed there were no houses or people. It was the middle of nowhere. Trees of different sizes lined both sides of the highway. The grass was growing wild. A gigantic hill stood in the distance. There was a flat valley and a vast field running alongside the hill. The sweat rolled down Chu Tu's face. He used his hand to wipe it, scratching his head intolerantly. He looked as if he had taken a hot shower. He walked back and forth, adjusting his gun belt, taking off his hat and putting it on again.

"Damn, where are they?"

The sun went down; dusk came upon us like a dark shadow. I heard a hum in the distance. Clearer and clearer it came. The lights came toward us like eyes staring into the darkness, but it was too little a light to cover up the immense space. The lights brightened; the engine grew louder. The truck stopped at the side of the highway.

"Come on, let's get them." Chu Tu walked over to the truck with us behind him. He walked over to the driver's side.

"What took you so long, comrade?" whined Chu Tu.

"We got drunk at the restaurant in town, comrade," the driver shouted with his sliding, laughing voice. He opened the door, jumped out, and walked to the back pulling the cargo cover aside.

"There are your supplies, comrade."

"How many bags does your list say we get?"

"Five bags of kernels, two bags of rice, and you leave one bag of rice here for me. We're in short supply," He grinned at Chu Tu.

"What shortage are you talking about? We have to feed the prisoners in the jungle, you know."

"To keep the black market going—that's the shortage, comrade. How do we live in the city if we don't have an underground market?" The driver grinned, his face loose and greasy.

Chu Tu was looking at his list, mumbling to himself: "Five kernel bags, two bags of rice. What is this comrade talking about?" Chu Tu wanted to make sure he got it right. He was wondering about it, looking naive.

"Climb up there to take it down," Chu Tu yelled to us.

Thanh jumped up to help the other two strapping men drag the bags off the truck while Chu Tu stood aside at the rear to watch us. He reached into his pocket to get his tobacco bag. He opened the bag, taking the tobacco, placing it in a small piece of newspaper which he cut. He rolled himself a cigarette. He put it on his lip, searching for a match, but he couldn't find one.

"Do you have a light, comrade?"

"Sure. Why do you smoke this? Try this American cigarette." The truck driver took a Marlboro pack out, gave one to Chu Tu, took one for himself. He leaned over to light Chu Tu's cigarette; Chu Tu sucked the cigarette in deeply, letting the smoke come out slowly.

"Is it good, comrade?"

"Yeah, where did you get it?"

"Black market; if you want to get anything, it's there."

"Is it expensive?"

"With my income plus your income in one month we wouldn't make enough for one pack. But with one bag of rice, my short supply as I call it, I can make it."

"You like to drive the truck?" said Chu Tu.

"It's not too bad, comrade. I make a living. How about you, do you like the jungle? Do you treat your prisoners right as Uncle Ho wants you to?"

"It's my duty," Chu Tu said sarcastically.

"Here are a couple more cigarettes for you. Don't be angry

if I'm late, comrade. I'll see you next time. Do you need anything from the city?"

"Would you mail these letters?"

"Sure." He took the letters from Chu Tu, walked to his truck, pulled the cover down, climbed in the cab, and started the engine. The headlights shined into the darkness, moving slowly, fading into the night. The air was cooler after the long hot day, helping me breathe more easily. The earth seemed to be revitalized again. The trees, grass, flowers, and weeds with all kinds of organisms began to live again like they were fighting for life.

"Thanh, did you give the bags to the driver?" Chu Tu asked.

"I did. Six empty bags, wasn't it?"

"Yeah."

We divided into pairs, each pair tying two bags on a pole, then hoisting the pole onto our shoulders. We shuffled back on the path into the jungle. Chu Tu walked in front of us with his flashlight waving up and down. He turned around, aiming the flashlight at us along the trail. We went back down the trail with our heavy load. We walked on the path for a while.

"Ouch!" Chu Tu shouted when he fell down. We almost tripped over him. We put our load down, helped him up.

"What happened?"

"A little ditch. Damn it! When I went along Ho Chi Minh's trail in Laos it was tough, but nothing happened. Now I walk in these woods and look what happens to me!"

"Why don't you go to work in the city, Chu Tu?" I asked gently. "You deserve it since you won the war."

"You're right, but the stupid northerners are still my boss. I can't do a damn thing."

"Fight for it, Chu Tu!"

"Yeah." He said fiercely, grinding his teeth.

"Let me see your foot. Would you point the flashlight at your foot? Why don't you sit down." Chu Tu sat down on the side of the trail and showed his foot. I lifted his foot up, examining it. I pressed it in different places.

"Does it hurt here?"

"No."

I moved my fingers to his ankle, pressing it firmly.

"Oooooooohh!" Chu Tu said.

"It hurts, huh?"

"Yeah."

I began to massage his foot so the blood would circulate easily.

"Feel better now?"

He didn't say anything but nodded his head.

"You're okay, Chu Tu. There isn't anything broken."

"Can you walk now?" Thanh asked while he lifted him. Chu Tu stood up, limped a few steps.

"It's all right. Let's get a move on."

He suggested this, but his hand was still on his gun. I noticed it even when he sat down. The flashlight was pointed at the ground. We began to move gradually, like a little hunting group that had lost its way at night.

I thought: Why not just kill Chu Tu and escape? I had a chance when he was sitting down holding his leg. I knew Thanh was on my side, but I wasn't sure about the four other men. What would happen if I did it, and the other men were in the antenna group? They would get me for sure. They would take me to their hut for their killing. I understood the antenna group very well. They would do anything, whether they benefited from it or not. They were the kind of people who liked to gossip. They were blind without anger, without love, without trust. They were blind to life.

No, it was not worth it. I had a larger purpose: If I could draw this VC and the northern guard into a deeper conflict, then all the prisoners would benefit. If I killed Chu Tu, I would be free but what would they do to all the other captives? They would torture them in ways I didn't want to imagine, trying to make them pay for what someone else had done. I didn't want to exchange myself for all the other prisoners. The time wasn't ripe yet. I trudged on.

I remembered reading something in a book at school saying that if you can devote yourself to the majority with a good reason, do it. But if you see yourself devoting your life to the merely individual without a good reason, don't do it. I had been thinking without realizing the heavy weight I was carrying.

"Bay, open the gate!" Chu Tu exclaimed. Nobody responded. He flashed his light, ran it along the gate and called again. The young guard, Bay, ran to the gate, clutching his AK-47. He rubbed his eyes as if he had just woken up.

"Oh, Chu Tu."

"Open the damn gate."

Bay opened the bamboo and barbed-wire gate. We walked inside.

"Put all the supplies in the storage area and go to sleep."

Chu Tu called one of the four prisoners to go and make some tea for him. He went back to his hut. Bay closed the gate behind us. The night was cool, carrying a fresh breeze which was less humid. But I was still perspiring. I took a deep breath, walked back to my hut, lay down on the spot, and fell asleep.

Some days later, Hung's mother showed up at the gate, her shawl dusty and her face weary from the long walk. Comrade Son ordered the guard at the booth to tell Hung's mother that her son had died because of a sickness; they showed her the new grave next to the gate which wasn't Hung's but that of the man I had buried. I saw Hung's mother standing in front of it, trying to find evidence that would make her believe he was dead, but there wasn't any name on the grave, only a cross which I had drawn on the soil. She jumped on the crypt and scratched at the dirt as if she wanted to know what was underneath. She called out her son's name. "Where are you, my son? Your mama is here. If you are dead please give me a sign." There was nothing for her to see. The green grass was stubbly and had just begun to grow, but now it lay in her hands.

Tiredly she stood up, reached for a branch, pulled it down and broke it. She put it in front of the grave like flowers, not knowing whether the grave was her son's. Gathering up her bag, she walked a few steps, then turned around and looked back, as if she wanted to ask a question of whoever was in the grave. I wanted to run over to her, but I couldn't while the guard was there; the guard stepped over and told her to go away. She shuffled off, her eyes on the ground.

Whenever I saw comrade Son I thought of Hung and I wanted to kill him. I crept out of the hut that night to burn a whole field of sugarcane in revenge. The entire camp was punished, and comrade Son was determined to find who the vandal was. I smiled to myself, and began to formulate a new plan.

Every evening we had a meeting in which comrade Son lectured us about Ho Chi Minh and the Communist Party. Comrade Son was a northerner, the feared and fawned upon chief of the labor camp, a very clever and cruel person. He talked a constant stream of Communist propaganda, none of which made any sense to me; he was full of shit. I hated him; if I had a chance I would kill him.

Son and those like him were opportunists rather than Communists or Nationalists, or whatever they labeled themselves. In truth, no one really cared about the Vietnamese people. No one cared for my country, least of all their glorious leader; if they did, the Vietnamese war would never have happened. Why did Ho Chi Minh say he fought for our independence at the same time that he depended on the aid of the Soviet Union and China? The south fought against the Communists for independence and freedom and they depended on U.S. aid. Tell me how you can fight for independence when you rely so heavily on someone else? How was it independence when they fed you and told you what to do? Maybe it would have been better for them not to fight at all. As it was, comrade Son repeated foreign doctrine like a broken record, and we just became bored with this brainwashing.

And so, that night, I met with some of my trusted friends, and we came up with a scheme. During the next meeting, we would shout, "Snake!" and then run away, effectively breaking up the meeting. Besides, we didn't want to donate our blood for mosquitoes every evening. The guards were our first enemy, the mosquitoes were our second, and the antenna group was our third. If you spoke about "the third," we knew it was about the antenna group, if we talked about "the second," it was the mosquitoes and if we talked about "the first," it was the guards. In the evening, we burned a torch and built a fire as usual to prepare for the meeting. We lined up in rows, sitting down in the packed dirt yard which we called the guillotine table or the center of civilization, surrounded by our huts. I chuckled at the thought that perhaps they were really all in the same class. We saluted comrade Son, then Ho Chi Minh and the glorious Communist Party, and applauded. Son carped about a few trivial matters and announced what he was going to do for the next few days and we wrote our confessions and self-criticism. After they collected them comrade Son rambled on about things he had learned by heart, while the guards stood around with their AK-47s watching our every move. The jungle was asleep. The night was dark and humid.

It had been about thirty minutes since comrade Son had begun to speak. He started to sweat. He wiped his forehead with his black pajama sleeve, pausing for a moment and swallowing his saliva.

"Snake! snake!" a shout ripped through the air. The prisoner who had been designated, jumped up from his spot in the corner.

Everyone stood up.

"Where, where is it?" we yelled.

The guards jerked their guns from their shoulders, and trained them on us.

"It went this way!" someone cried out.

We began to move in different directions.

"Sit down, now!" comrade Son yelled as loud as he could. "Don't bullshit me!"

He was hot and angry but the crowd was still moving, agitated. The guards backed away from us, afraid of a riot, afraid of revenge. They cocked their guns.

Comrade Son tensed like a tiger, his expression fierce, ready to strike. He shouted again but no one listened; he pulled out his K-54 Soviet-made rifle and pulled one of the inmates near him by the man's collar and shot into the air. Still we didn't listen; he pointed his gun at the middle of the prisoner's head and pulled the trigger. Blood splashed out everywhere. Son shot a few more bullets to make sure we heard his shooting. The prisoner died without a word. We froze and stood in silence while comrade Son dragged the dead prisoner across the ground in front of us until the man's shirt fell off.

"Is this the snake you are talking about?" comrade Son said. "Where is there another?"

He walked around us, poking his gun at our heads. There was no response, just a mosquito buzzing in the dark. I didn't believe that I would be a good soldier because I couldn't hold a gun and shoot someone like that. I looked at the gun and the black metal, and felt a chill. The night seemed permanent.

We settled back into our routine, depressed. Time wore on, and our bodies and minds continued to wear out. I began work in the woods where the banana trees grew. One morning, I cut all the drooping banana leaves to get to the stems, which we used as a rope to tie shoots of bamboo together. We then took the bamboo to the river and stuck them in the mud, building two lines across the river which we covered with grass and mud. We walked over it to make it firm. We kept mixing grass into the mud until it was as dense and sturdy as the ground. The current flowed into our newly made dam and the water slowly rose.

"Look, look," one of the prisoners yelled, pointing at the current.

We looked in the direction he had pointed and saw a banana raft drifting towards us. We pulled it to the side of the river while the guard ran over. On the raft lay the naked bodies of two girls, decapitated and with bruises all over their bodies. In their vaginas were two sticks. On a pole flapped the Khmer Rouge flag with the sign of Angkor Wat, above a blood-spattered note saying "We are coming soon to kill all you Vietnamese dogs."

"Bury them," the guard ordered us, not showing any emotion.

We worked on, exchanging excited, anxious glances, while the guards whispered to each other in quick, low tones. There had been rumors that the VC leaders themselves might want a war with Cambodia; after all, they had one of the world's largest armies to feed and a dying economy. Conquest might be the only way. When it was almost dark, we marched back to our shack. I was all wet, covered with mud. I felt so exhausted that I didn't even want to take a shower. I fell asleep immediately.

I was awakened by footsteps close to my hut, guard's footsteps. Everything was dark—always a mysterious darkness. Thanh and I wanted to find out, to venture. To risk our own lives without any expectation. The footsteps began to move inside the hut.

"Up, up!" the guard screamed, rattling a stick along the bamboo fence, shattering the stillness like a hammer hitting our heads over and over again. Everyone ran in different directions; people's voices babbled everywhere. I snatched my bag, threw all my belongings into it and ran out of the hut.

"Quiet, walk in a straight line!" the guard hollered.

The calmness of the jungle turned into chaos. I didn't know what had happened. In different places I still heard the whispers, voices babbling. Then all activity stopped, quiet, spread out against the dark. The whole universe seemed to be standing still. The wind stopped blowing. The air was isolated in one spot on the earth. I saw a line moving slowly into the woods. It was vague, like the ghost of a whole army running away. I didn't know where we were going, but my legs kept walking. I could imagine that I walked into the darkness, into a room which held an immense echo, a vast airiness, a deep depth. It was as if we were heading into an underground cavern leading to a nowhere world. I could see myself falling off a cliff at the end of the line.

"You, come with me," the guard whispered in my ear, pulling me out of the line.

I walked beside him to another group of people. They were whispering. I also heard shooting. It was getting closer. A bullet whizzed over our heads, then more, hitting the trees with a violent crack. My spine stiffened.

"You and Thanh help this comrade."

I saw Thanh holding onto a stretcher made out of branches. Chu Tu was lying on it, holding his leg, moaning.

"Are you okay, Chu Tu?"

"My leg." He groaned again.

"Move, move, hurry," ordered the guard.

Thanh and I quietly looked at each other, bending down at the same time and picking up the stretcher. We moved back into the line, carrying Chu Tu. We walked and walked, as if our journey would never end. It was so calm we could hear our own breathing, faster and faster, moment by moment. The shooting rushed at our backs, chasing us. Finally the night began to clear at the end of the horizon. The clouds were moving from place to place, yielding to the sunrise like a blanket removed from a light. Chu Tu had been groaning most of the way, but had fallen asleep for a while. Now, he lifted his head up saying, "Water, water." We stopped and gently set down the stretcher.

"Comrade, do you have some water? Chu Tu wants it."

The comrade turned and walked back. He reached for his canteen on his belt, giving it to me.

"Give him a little."

I opened it while Thanh lifted Chu Tu's head up. I put it on his mouth. He took a sip, then another.

"Do you feel better?"

"A little."

I put my hand on the mouth of the canteen, got a little water on my hand to put on his forehead. His head felt hot, feverish.

"What happened to you, Chu Tu?"

"Damn, those Cambodians! I went to the outpost at the border to check the army group. I didn't know they had already invaded it, that's why I got shot in the leg. Luckily, I got back here."

His face was all sweaty and pale since he had lost blood. He bit his lip occasionally as if he was in much pain. I glanced at his leg; the pant was torn apart. A lot of blood had soaked his first aid bandage.

"Let's go; we can't stay too long."

I gave the canteen back to the guard. We hoisted the stretcher and continued on the path behind him. As we walked, I thought, "Why do I have to save this man instead of letting him die? He made me, Thanh, and all the captives suffer. Why don't I trip over something, drop the stretcher, let Chu Tu die? No, it's silly. It's cowardly to fight with someone when they can't fight back. My father had a saying, "Never kill a person who has fallen from a horse." I wanted to feel proud of myself, follow the good tradition of my family. Chu Tu was in my hands now. If I killed Chu Tu, maybe the other comrade would kill me. The killing would go on and on, never ending. "Be loving, merciful, forgive, and forget," I consoled myself. I felt my legs getting heavier. I could hear my footsteps on the ground. Sweat was running down my face.

We finally came to the highway and set up camp. I looked up at the sky in the direction of our huts and the guards' cabins, and saw big clouds of black smoke swirling up. It seemed fighting was going on there, but I didn't know who it would be for sure; Cambodians or the southern army. The comrades ordered us to find water and when we couldn't find a stream nearby, we had to dig a well.

"Do it faster," one of the comrades said. "Find something to cook."

We dug three meters deep but we hadn't found any water yet. Thanh stood inside the hole, using the shovel, pushing it down with his foot. Another prisoner picked up the soil, passed it to me, and I threw it to the side.

"Thanh, do you know what's going on over there?" someone pointed at the smoke.

"Don't point at it; the guard will see you."

"I don't know what happened, but I heard the guards talking last night. The Cambodians attacked the border."

"Is there any water yet?" someone on the line asked.

"Not yet. If we dig one more meter and we don't find any water, we'll have to go to another place," answered Thanh. And another voice, "Hey, why don't we run away while they're busy fighting?"

"Yeah, yeah!" I said.

The group started jabbering. We were all excited.

"I don't know," Thanh said calmly.

Somebody was hushing everyone in the group. The guard came.

"Is there any water?"

"My feet feel wet. We're getting there."

"Hurry up." The guard walked away to let us dig. Thanh dug a couple more times and the water started coming out of a small hole. He passed the shovel up and we bent down to help him up out of the hole. We walked over to where Chu Tu was lying down. He was still asleep. The northern guard came, told Thanh and me to follow him, to his spot. We saw a bag of corn lying there.

"Make something with this," he pointed at the bag.

"We have to wait for the water to clear up, comrade."

"While you wait, go get some wood and start stacking it."

We walked away and he yelled, "Come back here!"

We came back. "Remember," he said, "if one of you runs away, I shoot all of you."

We began to gather wood. When we came back to the well, there was some water. We used a can, hooked it to the banana rope, and put it into the well to get the water. We cooked corn for the comrades and the prisoners. Everyone had a small cup of corn for a whole day. We were starving more than before because we couldn't take our supplies with us. I didn't know how long we would last. If we had still been living in our old camp we could at least have gotten our food from the garden.

"Comrade, can we go around to trap animals?" asked Thanh.

"Yeah. Make sure you don't go any further than three kilometers. We can't protect you."

"Yes, comrade."

"May we borrow a knife?"

"I don't have one. Go ask comrade Son."

I went back to the spot near the well to get a bag. Thanh went to get a knife. We walked into the woods to cut some weeds to use as a rope. Then we chopped some bamboo branches to make traps. When we had all the materials, we went around to find animal footprints and trails. We found some rat tracks. We examined the trail.

"What do you think?" I asked Thanh. He sat down and scratched the soil.

"It's still wet. The footprints seem like they're new. I think a rat uses this path."

"Let's build a trap."

I dug the soil while Thanh used bamboo branches to make a rack. We used chopped bamboo limbs, tied them together into the shape of a rectangle about one-third meter in length and twenty centimeters in width. We placed the soil over the rack like a little grave. We blocked the path on one side. Next, we put the little grave on the side of the blocked area. We used bamboo limbs to fence around the trap, left a small path in front of it so the rat could go in to eat the food underneath.

We used two small branches that looked like a slingshot. We stuck them in the dirt in front of the trap, put a pole over it, pulled the rope up over the bar, and placed a stick leaning over it. Finally, we connected it to the bamboo stick under the trap. We put some kernels behind the bamboo stick to attract the rat. When the rat touched the bamboo branch, the trap would close, capturing it.

"Are you all set?"

"Yes, we will catch some rats."

"You're making me hungry when you say that."

"I'm hungry too."

We swallowed our saliva.

"Come on, let's go build another one."

We prowled about, looking for another trail and animal footprints. We built several more traps.

"Thanh, over here."

Thanh came over.

"What?"

"Look at this." I pointed at the trail where there were footprints of what might be a dog or pig, but I wasn't sure.

"That's interesting. I'm not sure what it is, but we may get something big."

All the thorny bamboo trees were scattered on the path. It was hard for anyone to maneuver around. There were more footprints under the bushes. It seemed that's where all the animal traffic was. We cleared a little path to reach the closest bamboo bush. We grabbed one and bent it to the surface near the footprints. We hacked the limbs down, used a rope to tie around the top of the tree, clamping to the ground. Then we made a loop from the rope to put on the path where the animals would run over it. We used a pole to keep the tree down. I put a limb in the loop that was attached to the pole so if the animal ran over it the bamboo tree would swing up, clasping the head or leg of the animal.

"I'm tired. Let's sit down for a while."

We both sat on the trail, leaned against the trees, and observed everything around us. The sun shone strongly through the trees like a laser beam. The sun looked so beautiful, like clear crystal strips in different shapes mixing with the heavy green of the leaf. I let this nature penetrate me; at the same time I took oxygen into my lungs, breathing steadily. I could feel all my body tissues begin to circulate as if they combined with nature, like rain soaking into the earth, into the atmosphere. I realized my subconscious was expanding enormously—I couldn't hold on to it any longer. I felt very light in the air. I could smell the air into which the water evaporated in tiny atoms.

"Are you asleep?"

"Sort of," I yawned, tiredly standing up.

"Let's go back to the campsite and check the trap later."

"How long from now?"

"Three or four hours, maybe."

"Shhh . . . !" Thanh stepped to the side of the tree, pointing to the other side. I looked over to where he was pointing. I saw the guard holding his gun, ready to shoot. Thanh squatted and waved to me to sit. We sat down quietly, watching the guard closely as if we were hawks. The guard moved from one position to the other like he was searching for something—us maybe, or someone else. I didn't know. He looked around, standing there silently for a brief second. He walked away in the opposite direction. We sat there about ten minutes. Then, we tip-toed back. We could see the campsite now, but it looked like no one was there.

"Where are they hiding?"

"Don't talk so loud. They are everywhere. We just saw one man, remember?"

We walked into the campsite, pretending we didn't know what had happened.

"I think we're going to get some rat today, you think so?"

"Yeah," Thanh said.

While we were talking, Thanh banged on the bamboo branches which he held under his arm. We saw about six guards sitting together talking. The guard, Son, turned to us.

"Did you get anything yet?"

"Not yet, comrade."

"How many traps did you make?"

"Ten."

"Whatever you catch today, I want two for myself since I lent you my knife."

Thanh gave the knife back to him with a smile. "It's very profitable, right, comrade?"

"That's why I only get two out of the whole catch," said comrade Son, his slick eyes grinning. A dull light glimmered off his hair, which he wore greased back with Vaseline or coconut oil.

"I know, comrade," Thanh said. "We're going to check them this evening."

"We'll let you know," I said.

"You better. "

Son laughed, turned to his group and continued to play chess. I saw them draw a chessboard in the dirt. They used rolled up bits of paper for chess figures. We walked back to the spot near the well. Someone was using a pot to boil water and had already set it on the fire. There was a prisoner sitting there feeding the fire while Chu Tu sat in his spot watching. I walked back to my spot. Thanh sat next to Chu Tu, talking to him. Next, he stood up, turning to me.

"I'll get you when we go to check the traps."

"Okay."

Thanh walked away, and I went over and sat beside Chu Tu.

"Do you feel better, Chu Tu?"

"No, it's getting worse." He had a sour grin. He tossed and turned, looking at his leg helplessly.

"Do you still have a fever?"

"Yeah. I feel like my wound is festering."

"Did you change the bandage and clean the wound?"

"I don't have any first aid left."

"That's terrible! Is someone coming to take you to the hospital in the city or what?"

"I don't know yet. We already sent a message to headquarters to let them know the situation."

"Let me help you. I'll boil some water to clean your wound. Would you like that?"

"Will it hurt?"

"I'll be gentle. Otherwise, it will have to be amputated."

I went to boil some water to clean the wound. He looked at his wound, and he seemed to be wondering about the Cambodians, hating them. After the water boiled I took it off the fire. I tried to find a clean rag but there weren't any.

"Do you have any clean rags?" I asked him.

"Look in my bag here." He handed his bag to me. I searched in the bag but there were only dirty clothes which had a bad odor.

"Wait."

I took my clean handkerchief and wet it with hot water to clean his wound. I poured some warm water over the bandage. I let it soak a little. Slowly I opened the bandage. The smell of the blood was too much for me; I was going to vomit. I held my breath, exhaled slowly, repeating this a few times to prevent myself from vomiting. Most of the torn-off muscle was all black and soft. Inside the wound, the blood was clotted, with some white pus coming out. The wound wasn't really big, but it was deep. I thought it would be a serious problem if it wasn't treated right.

"How far from here to the city, Chu Tu?"

"About twenty kilometers southeast."

I thought I could find my location, and distract his attention from his pain, by asking, "What's the closest city?"

"Ha Tien."

"I think now's a good time to go to the city."

"I'm not sure," he said with a grin.

"Come on, Chu Tu, relax; take a vacation."

"Yeah, sure. Damn northerners," he mumbled to himself, but I could hear it.

"What did you say, Chu Tu?"

"Nothing, nothing."

With the clean handkerchief I wiped the lesion a few times, cleaning all the dried blood around it. I washed the bandage very well, wrapping it around his leg. He yelped loudly. "Tie it easily."

"It's all done. Take a rest, Chu Tu." I said. "You'll feel better." He settled back, rolled himself a cigarette to smoke. He looked relieved and happier than before.

I was tired as the afternoon wore on. I put my head against the bag as a pillow, and lay down on the ground. I heard shooting again, but it was more faint, smaller, and farther away. I thought they had moved to another spot. I wished they would come nearer so that I could escape while the guards and the Cambodians were fighting, especially since I now knew my location. I had the information I needed for my escape and yet I lingered. Was this the right time or not? I could take advantage of this situation, but I didn't. Maybe I was scared of the threat from before and of what would happen to all the other prisoners if I escaped successfully. How could I be happy then? How could I feel peace within myself? My soul and conscience would be the one to torture me. I would never be at rest.

The air was hot and humid. I was barely asleep because the heat aggravated me and sweat poured from my skin, making me feel sticky. I opened my eyes and looked up at the trees. They were all standing in one spot without moving their limbs or leaves since there was no wind. The sun buried its face in the clouds, showing its last brilliant smile before dying down beside the forest. I didn't know what time it was but I guessed it was around four or five o'clock. It almost seemed as if I was on a camping trip in the summer, as if this were a lazy, enjoyable day.

"Are you going to check the trap or not?"

Thanh kicked my leg. I got up.

"Yeah."

"I want to go!" hollered Tam, one of our fellow prisoners, a young, energetic boy. He was anxious, like a child asking for permission to play.

"You better ask the comrade," I said.

He turned around and asked Chu Tu.

"Can I?"

"Okay, but you have to come back early," ordered Chu Tu.

We went back the way we came through the woods. We checked the first trap but found nothing. We checked the second: a rat was trapped inside it, flattened in his own grave.

Thanh lifted the trap, grabbed the tail of the rat, and dangled it in front of Tam and me.

"Look what we have!" said Thanh delightedly.

"Yeah, yeah we're going to have a good meal today."

We yelled happily, looking at the rat. It was flat as a pancake. I could imagine the pavement truck rolling over and squashing me like a dead rat.

"May I have some too?" asked Tam.

"Sure."

"May I check the next trap?" Tam insisted.

"Okay, go ahead."

Tam walked in front of us on the path.

"Keep going till you see the big bamboo thickets, then turn right at the corner," Thanh said.

We followed him closely, moving through the forest while the sky was getting dark.

"Is this the right way?"

"Yeah, keep walking," I said.

"I feel like I'm going to get something big tonight!" exclaimed Tam.

"Why not?" We were giggling.

Thanh held the flashlight and gave it to Tam.

"Use it; it's dark now."

Tam turned on the flashlight and walked faster ahead. We couldn't keep up with him.

The night was cool; the air was fresh with a nice breeze. I felt comfortable with this weather. A memory flashed back briefly but I couldn't recall what it was or why it came to me . . . I had a weird feeling that my conscience knew, but it wasn't manifesting itself in my five senses. What was it? What was going on? I didn't know.

"Don't go so fast; we can't see anything back here!" Thanh called to Tam.

Tam slowed down and flashed the light at us.

"Not on my face—on the ground!"

We caught up with him, but he was still moving quickly ahead when we heard him yell.

"Ahhhhhh . . . !!" He fell down, dropping the flashlight.

"What happened?"

"Something bit me on my leg!"

"Squeeze your leg tightly and don't let the blood move up!" Thanh cried out.

We ran up to him. I looked for the light while Thanh squatted down to hold Tam's leg. I picked up the light, pointed it at his leg. Tam's slim body was hunched over in pain. Thanh pulled up his pant leg, tore it, then tied it snugly above Tam's knee. Two holes. He held Tam's leg under his arm with his back facing Tam while he took a knife to cut the snake bite, opening it bigger. He used his mouth to suck the blood, spitting it out repeatedly. Tam was grinding his teeth together in pain, moaning deeply. He was sweating and his hands were squeezing the dirt, the grass, anything he could grasp. I sat down, aiming the flashlight in Thanh's direction so he could see more clearly. It only lasted a second, but the time felt endless.

"Hold on Tam, hold on," said Thanh.

"I feel like I want to sleep."

"Don't go to sleep, don't!" I screamed and shook him.

"My heart feels heavy."

"No, no—stay awake!" I yelled again to break the burden, to break that tense moment, to break through the darkness, the blind jungle, and to scare all the living things away.

"Tam, look at my eyes!"

He turned his head slowly to look at me. I aimed the flashlight at him indirectly, but I could see clearly. Carefully, I peered into his eyes. I saw a two-headed snake swim across the pupils in his eyeball. Oh, no—there is no way we can save him, I thought. There was no kind of medicine that could cure this poison. I knew it was hopeless. What could I do? How could I tell him? It was a king snake, the most poisonous of all. I remembered my father telling me: whenever something bites you, swing your arm to the back of yourself, grab anything— like grass or leaves. Put it in your mouth, chew, swallow the juices and with the remaining, apply it to the wound immediately. It will stop the flow of poison through your blood for a moment, which gives you time to find a snake doctor who knows about folk medicines for all kinds of snakes. Was it too late to help? Was it? How could I tell him?

"Stay right there, don't move!" I said.

I looked for some leaves that could help him temporarily, but I couldn't find any.

"Let's go back to the campsite."

Thanh carried Tam over his shoulder. I walked behind him. With one hand I aimed the light in his path, in the other I held the tail of the rat. Gradually, we moved. We finally arrived at the campsite. We laid him down on the ground where his stuff was.

"Tam, are you all right?"

He didn't say a word but breathed lightly. Comrade Son walked over.

"What happened?"

"A snake bit him."

"Son, are there any hens around here?" Chu Tu called to Son.

"No, I don't think so. Why?"

"If you can find a hen, you could apply hen's saliva to the snake bite. Perhaps it would help."

"Are you sure?"

"Yes, we did it many times before," Chu Tu answered.

"Let me find someone who can help."

He was ready to walk away but he turned his head around saying, "Did you get any rat?" Son walked away, disappearing into the dark. The fire was dying down. There wasn't enough light or enough smoke to chase the mosquitoes away. I stood up, gathered the wood together and threw it in the fire. The wood fell apart, the fire was crackling, sparks jumping all around. The fire began to burn. My skin felt like chicken skin, even though the flames were getting bigger and hotter. I went to see how Tam was doing. Thanh was talking to him.

"I miss my mama . . ." Tam said under his breath.

"I understand how you feel, but I've never tasted this kind of experience before because my mama died when I was only in her arms," Thanh said.

"Oh, your mama died . . . You weren't that lucky," Tam said, sorry for his friend. "You didn't have much love, did you?"

"Yeah, I guess," whispered Thanh.

"What is it like to have a mama? I wonder what this kind of love is like?" Thanh added.

"Have you ever tasted a banana before? Have you ever felt the warmth of a sunny morning? Have you ever drunk the mountain stream when you were thirsty? It was like that, that kind of sweetness, that kind of warmth, that kind of freshness. It is love; it is mama," Tam said with all his energy. He put his head on his bag and cuddled upon it.

"Mama, mama . . ." mumbled Thanh.

I sat down next to them and silently shared their emotions. I didn't know what to say but I felt as if the whole world had fallen on my shoulders.

"I have a mama, too, but I wonder where she is?"

"What happened to her?" Thanh asked me anxiously.

"I don't know. I haven't seen her for years, not since I came to Saigon to study."

"I hope she is well."

Thanh was moving a stick back and forth on the ground. You could see a little dust fly up in the air through the flames.

"My chest is heavy," Tam called.

I held his head so that he could sit up.

"Here, drink some water." I held the container up to his mouth. He took a couple of sips, but started choking. I patted his back, letting him sit there until he caught his breath. I fetched some cold water from the well, and, using my handkerchief, sponged the sweat from Tam's forehead.

"Do you feel a little better now?"

"I don't see clearly," Tam said.

"Open your eyes; don't go to sleep."

I felt as if I didn't see anything either, not because of blindness, not because of the dark, but because of the moisture in my eyes. Thanh stood up, sat down, holding Tam's hand, squeezing it. I looked into his eyes. They were blinking. He turned his head away like a shy child would. I felt defeated, but we had to keep Tam awake. Thanh got up, kicked the stick away. Then he bent down, picked up a piece of soil, and threw it angrily in the bushes.

"I want some more water."

I gave him some water and he gulped it down.

"Tam, where did you live before?" I asked.

"Bien Hoa."

"Is your family still there?"

"No, Baba, Mama, my two brothers and one sister moved to Saigon after they invaded our home."

"Are they about my age?"

"Yeah, my brothers are. My sister is fourteen. You should hear her play the piano. She's wonderful," said Tam.

"I love piano. I can feel its crescendo in the air, and then suddenly vanish." I asked, "Do I sound like a pianist?"

"Yeah, I'll take you to see my sister. You and Lieu can play for me."

"I want to go, but I don't know how to play. I like to watch and listen."

"I feel cold on my spine!" Tam grumbled.

"Drink some warm water. Maybe it will help."

I got some clothes from my bag, covered him. Thanh walked over to the fire to put more wood on it. Next, he went to the well to get a pot, filled it with water, set it over the fire to boil. Chu Tu was asleep, but he woke up because his wound started to aggravate him.

"Thanh, make me a cup of tea," called Chu Tu. Thanh walked over to Chu Tu to see what he wanted. I looked at Tam lying there barely breathing. His hands were folded over his chest as if he was dreaming, far, far away. He brought his legs up and then they collapsed. He stared into the fire in a child-like way, but his eyes were too weak to stay open. It seemed like he was ready to fall asleep, a long sleep which we have only once in our lifetime. I pinched one of his legs; the one that was bitten.

"Does it hurt, Tam?" I asked.

"No, I don't feel a thing," he yawned, answering impatiently.

The night was black, maybe the blackest one I had ever known. The fire continued to sparkle, its brightness began to fade. It seemed as if it was yielding, allowing the dawn and the new day to come. Up in the sky, the North Star shone dimly. It was shining through the black clouds. The wind blew slowly, pushing the black clouds away. A small group of stars, were exchanging places, some fell down. I forgot that I was so tired. I wondered where all that energy came from, what strength kept me awake all night.

"I want to go home," Tam said.

"Yeah, I'll take you home . . . ," I mumbled.

"I can't see anymore. My heart and my eyelids are heavier. It's time for me to sleep," Tam said in a weak voice.

I called Thanh over. We both held Tam's hands. Tam gripped my hand briefly; his body rose up and then lowered in a second. He inhaled deeply, sucking in the air like a fish going up to the surface of the water to get a breath. And then he died.

"Yeah, I'll take you home . . . I'll take you home . . . Tam," I muttered.

His face looked relieved, as if he had just done something wonderful, the faintest curve of a smile on his lips. His head turned to one side as if he didn't want to see me. I straightened his arms and legs. I covered his face.

"I'm going to make something to eat," Thanh said, standing up and picking up the rat. He put it over the fire to burn the hair off. He brought the rat to the well and cleaned it. I saw Chu Tu move his head. I walked over to him.

"Do you want something, Chu Tu?"

He asked for some tea as he wiped his eyes. I looked in his bag to get the tea, but there wasn't any left.

"You don't have any more tea."

"Just get me some hot water. Oh, how is Tam?"

He turned his head towards Tam, but Tam's soul wasn't there anymore, only a lump lay there now.

"How long ago did he die?"

"A little while," I said.

"He was a fine young man. It was too early for him."

"Yeah, it was too early . . . Poor, poor young man."

I went to boil some water. My mind began to wander to an open field, into my forgotten past. I remembered one long night when we all sat around my grandfather's bed, in corners, everywhere in the room. All my relatives were there, my whole family from young to old. Every girl and boy shared the moment when my grandfather died. I didn't know what death was. I held my niece in my arms as she asked me, "Uncle, is grandfather playing a game?"

"Yes, he's playing a game, dear."

"What is it, uncle? I want to play."

"No, not now, dear. If you play you have to stop breathing, stop eating, stop drinking, stop thinking . . . stop living for a long, long time."

She fell against my arms, closed her eyes, pretending to look like my grandfather for a minute and then she jumped up. "I want to play, uncle, but I want to eat too. I can't stop eating." She was bouncing up and down, kicking my stomach. Now I knew what dying was: yielding a space for the younger one to grow. This death was the same, but the difference was that my grandfather had loved ones with him. Tam didn't have them when he needed them the most. And, one suffered and one didn't. Is there any difference between strangers' faces and familiar faces? Tam died without his loved ones. How could I let his family know? What could they do for him?

"Is the water ready?" asked Chu Tu.

"Yeah, I think so."

I poured the water into his cup and gave it to him.

"How do you feel?" I asked. "Do you want me to clean your wound now?"

"It still hurts, but I'm okay. Go ahead—clean it."

It seemed like the wound was getting better since I had cleaned it the day before, even though there was no medicine. Maybe I had good healing hands. Or was it a miracle? I wasn't sure. Thanh patted my shoulder.

"Here, eat some of this." He gave me a piece of the roasted rat.

It smelled wonderful, but I didn't feel hungry.

"I don't want any."

I gave it back to him and he told me to eat it because if I didn't I would get sick. I took a bite, chewed, and swallowed it without any feeling. He walked over to Chu Tu to give him some. Afterwards, he came over and sat down.

"Do you know how I cooked the rat? I used a bamboo branch that was about one meter long which I cut down the middle, leaving a remaining ten centimeters. Next, I put the rat in the clip to hold it in place, roasting it over the fire. Is it good? Do you like it?"

He continued to talk while I looked sullenly into the woods. Yes, because of this rat, we have to eat. We have to survive so we need food. Was it worth it for Tam to die simply because he had to eat and he was starving? It's only a mouthful! Is it worth it to fight for life, I wondered. But why do we have to stay here instead of staying with our family, our friends, enjoying good food, and sharing happiness? What makes us stay here? Who brought these circumstances to us? Are the Communists the cause of this? Is it the Americans, the northerners, or the opportunists? Is it individualism or is it just the idealism people want to practice on us? How do I know? Who cares? We're such a small voice with no power. What can we do in this big world? Whatever, Tam shared with me this little piece of rat. I prayed.

CHAPTER 14

"Come on, let's dig a grave for him." Thanh stood up to go find a shovel. We dug a grave next to where Tam was lying. Comrade Son came over.

"Where is my profit?" he asked us.

"We didn't check the trap this morning, comrade," Thanh replied.

"When you finish this you better give me my profit."

Then he walked away, ignoring our response.

The morning was muggy and very uncomfortable for working. I was tired, breathing heavily. I wasn't sure why. Maybe I had been awake the whole night and didn't realize it, or maybe it was the sudden death of my friend, or perhaps I had given up the fight for my own life. I dug the soil and it felt so heavy that I was unable to lift it. I could see the soil was rich with dead leaves that fertilized the soil. This helped all the other plants around. I wondered about my life, if I deserved to live, if I could enrich the lives of others. What could I do for people? What could I do for others? For myself? The sun rose as high as the trees above me. I felt the heat press down harder over the whole universe, but the shade gently covered us as if we were indoors. I felt homesick.

"Do you want to take a break?" asked Thanh. "You look worn out."

"Yeah."

Thanh jumped up over the grave and helped me up. We sat down in the dirt. Thanh got his tobacco bag and paper and rolled himself a cigarette. He found a match in his pocket, but it wouldn't light.

"I'll go to the fire to light my cigarette. Do you want me to get some water for you?"

"Yeah."

He walked away and left me sitting there. I looked at the grave and at Tam lying next to it. I wondered if Tam wanted to be burned or buried. He had no choice now.

"Here's some water."

I took the bowl of water from Thanh and drank it. I felt the coldness of the water run inside my chest, down to my stomach. It gave me a little chill wherever it went. I felt refreshed and I had more energy.

"Are you ready to dig some more before the sun gets hotter?" said Thanh.

"Okay, let's do it."

We jumped into the pit and Thanh dug the soil while I picked it up and threw it aside.

"You're a Buddhist. What do you believe?"

"I believe in something; I don't believe in nothing," I replied.

"Come on, explain more so I can understand it."

"The first thing you have to do is to believe in yourself; you have to treat yourself with respect and you have to save yourself for a worthy purpose, for a good way of life. When you have that kind of a mind, you can treat your family the same way you treat yourself. When you know how to treat your family, then you know how to take care of your country and all human beings."

"It sounds complicated. Just tell me if you believe in reincarnation," said Thanh.

"Yeah, why not? Look what has happened in your past and you'll know what your future will be. When you plant the apple seed, you'll have an apple whether there's a worm in it or not. You cannot have another fruit except the apple because the apple tree cannot produce an orange or any other fruit. The curse you make is the result you get."

"But I don't understand why my life ended up this way even though I didn't do anything bad except kill my enemy to protect our freedom." Thanh wrinkled his face, thinking hard. "It was the war and we had to kill. If I didn't kill my enemy, the enemy would have killed me. Did I have any alternative? War is tragic, war is irony, war is messy business, but who caused this war? You, me, or someone else, or did it just happen?" Thanh continued.

"What's your definition of hell and heaven?" I asked.

"Hell is war and heaven is peace," answered Thanh.

"You understand it now because of what you just said. We

live in this world, on this earth. There is a heaven and there is a hell both inside and outside of us, and now we live in hell, but we share, we care, we help, and understand each other. That means inside you or me we live in heaven, but outside you or me we live in hell. It's an emptiness and in that open space there are living souls traveling in that distance. There is something we have and something we don't. We can decide ourselves which place we want to live."

"But, why do good people like Tam die early, rather than the cruel people?" asked Thanh.

"Do you think this is the real world? If you say yes, then it's your real world, but if you say no then it's not your real world. They finish the things they have to do, for the Buddhists believe this is the world of illusion, the world of transition for the next step, the training school for the next journey, the world of birth, age, sickness, suffering, dying. The cruel people live longer so they can carry all their suffering; they must pay for what they have done during their lives."

"Do you think Tam died so he would have all the freedom he wanted?" asked Thanh.

"Yeah, I guess."

"Why don't we all die, so we can have all the freedom we want?" Thanh asked.

"If that were true, then we wouldn't have the existing world. We haven't yet accomplished what we have to and we haven't done the things that we need to do. Your existence and my existence have a purpose, but I don't know when it ends because I'm a human like you and I have to deal with the things you have to deal with. The Buddhist believes that when you're born to this world, everything is arranged. Even the things you eat and the things you wear."

"You mean Tam died today and we have to dig his grave for him because it was already arranged?" Thanh asked, his eyes open wide.

"That's right. If he didn't ask to come along and walk in front of us, it would have been you or I who died instead of him," I said.

"Maybe, I'm not sure," said Thanh.

Thanh and I were both quiet. We were chasing our thoughts,

silently, in our own ways. It was difficult to discuss religion, but I thought all religions had their own good philosophy. It taught people to be humane. It didn't matter how we learned —through the material or spiritual—but that we reach an understanding fairness and forgiveness. These were good laws.

Why does our society have to carry on with religion, I wondered? Is it because this society doesn't exist anymore? Is it because the people don't have anything to hold on to or anything to turn to? Society has laws, so our lives have to have religion. Religion is good; religion is not wrong, religion is our hope, religion is one root, but people separate it, practice it in different ways, whatever way suits them. There is only one religion, "a real human" religion, a religion that is caring, sharing, understanding, trusting, dignified with our extending hands which hold onto each other and build up a real world, a real civilization. We have to have hope, we have to try to do our best in order to be spiritual. I felt such sorrow and much pity for the people who tortured us, abused us, because they have narrow minds. They haven't come to an understanding: they have eyes but they are unable to see things; they have minds but they cannot think; they live in this world but they don't believe in another world; they are like frogs who live at the bottom of the water: how do they know a world exists above the water outside of the lake?

"What are you thinking? Suddenly you are quiet," Thanh said.

"I don't know, but there was a thought which passed over my head."

"What was it?"

"Let it go, like Tam. We are sad because we are going to miss him. We have to let him go; we have to let him have his freedom. He is all through with life; we should feel happy for him rather than sad. He is gone, but he's also still here, in our memory, in our eternity whenever we talk about him or think of him," I explained.

"Yeah, it seems that way."

"Are you ready to put him down in the dirt, to give him back to nature?"

"Yeah . . . ," Thanh said.

We pulled the cover off Tam's face, and it was a light purple color, wrinkly, and his cheeks were indented. His whole body was wrinkly as if the poison had shrunk all of his muscles. His eyeballs had sunk a little into his skull, and he kept a smile on his face as if he was happy to die, to enjoy the surroundings, to breathe the fresh air. He looked at the fire with his unrestricted eyes. His body was very thin, only skin and bones. We put him in the grave and covered him with soil. Then, the picture of his smiling face remained with us. I didn't know whether he smiled for himself, or for me or Thanh, or someone else. But I knew he was content with nature, happy that we didn't put him in a coffin, in a cage to be tormented, to be buried alive.

Good-bye, Tam, I thought. You finished your role in life, you have left the stage now. You have to face yourself. You have to be what you are. You have to keep your identity without anyone disturbing you. You are on your own; you don't need any help from anyone now. You are released from this false world. You know who you are now, but I wonder if you know why you were born. Do you still remember your name? Are you lucky that you lived long enough to have a name, luckier than those who died before they were given a name? At least your name stays with us and we got to know you. I heard heavy footsteps and a scraping sound coming closer to us.

"Poor young man . . ."

I turned around to see Chu Tu hobbling towards us, leaning on the tree limb which he had made into a makeshift crutch. Thanh was patting the soil down with his foot. He used the shovel to press it down over the tomb.

"How do you feel, Chu Tu?" I asked.

"I'm okay, but I think I'll get a ride back to Ha Tien this afternoon for my leg. I want you to come with me. You better go check the traps before you get in trouble with Son."

Midday was very humid; the air was sticky. I thought that nothing would survive under this heat. All the trees were drooping down as if someone was guilty, hiding his face from the judge—like the whole forest seemed to be running out of energy, running out of water, running out of air, running out of food. Thanh and I slowly walked into the jungle and checked all of the traps. We found three rats and one rabbit.

We brought them back to the campsite and went to find comrade Son. We saw him playing cards with his buddies.

"Here is your profit, comrade," I said to him.

"I can't eat it raw. Go and cook it," he hooted.

I brought the rat back to the fire and roasted it. Thanh went and got some kernels and made some lunch.

"I think we're going to starve, because we don't have many kernels left. Maybe we can cook one more time," said Thanh.

"Are you serious?"

"Yeah."

"We better do something for ourselves," I whispered.

"We still have some traps in the woods."

"How long will they last?"

"Perhaps we can make some more." While Thanh was speaking, he looked around and then he put a few handfuls of kernels in his pocket and gave me some. The day moved on gradually. The wind blew strongly and carried black clouds from somewhere on the horizon. Suddenly they drifted away above our heads. The tree limbs rattled. Branches broke apart and fell to the ground.

The campsite erupted into noise. People ran all over the place, preparing for the coming rainfall as the sky held the water that would break through and soak the earth. The gusty winds subsided and a burst of rain poured down; the wind blew again and twisted at the corner of the woods and swept over the highway. I ran over to the bamboo bushes and chopped some leaves off. I asked Thanh to carry some branches over to the fire. We built a shelter over the fire to prevent the rain from putting it out. We used some banana leaves as a cover, putting grass over the leaves to hold them down. The rain still dropped down on the fire and we kept throwing wood in the fire to cook the kernels and the rats.

"Thanh, will you make a dike around the fire to hold back the water?" I called to the other side.

"Okay, I heard you. I'm looking for a shovel!"

He ran back with a shovel in his hand and quickly constructed a dike while I watched the kernels boil and turned the rats around and around. We were all wet, as if we ourselves were rats, swimming for our lives in the water with hunting dogs chasing after us. The rain stopped.

"What's the use!" Thanh said.

Thanh threw the shovel down, turned around and smiled at me.

"We had a good shower, you know. We haven't had one for months."

Comrade Son walked over to us, dry inside his poncho.

"Is my food done?"

"Here, you can check it, comrade."

I handed him the rat and he tore a piece off and chewed it.

"It's done. Put it on my plate with some corn."

"Yes, comrade."

He took his plate and walked away. Everybody came to eat their food. I gave everyone a little bowl of kernels. Thanh, Chu Tu and I all shared a rabbit. I was so hungry that I could have eaten the whole rabbit myself but I only had a small piece along with some kernels. I could taste the smoke in the kernels and in the rabbit sections because the fire hadn't burned well. But that didn't stop me from savoring it.

The afternoon came and I felt cooler after it had rained. I could see the water evaporating from the ground in little clouds of mist. The smoke from the fire scattered all about, billowing, then subsiding. Mosquitoes were scared away by the smoke. Frogs, crickets, and all the insects began to make their music. Birds gathered into flocks, then flew away, disappearing into the forest, in rhythm with their own season. The ground turned into mud, showing our footprints all over the place, making it look like a detective had been chasing a criminal.

"Come on, let's go," Chu Tu called me.

"Would you wait a minute? I want to ask Thanh to take care of my stuff."

"Go ahead, hurry up."

I ran over to Thanh and asked him to watch my belongings because I had to go to the city with Chu Tu. It seemed somewhat ridiculous, since I didn't have anything valuable except some pajamas which we used for working clothes. They were in a linen bag. That and nothing else composed the whole of my assets. We lived close to the dirt.

"Do you have my family's address?" murmured Thanh.

"Yeah, if I have a chance I'll write them a note to let them know. I'll ask them to let all the families know where we are."

"Be careful. Don't get into trouble."

He looked at me, worry and gratitude in his eyes. I ran to Chu Tu and picked up his bag; we walked out of the campsite and toward the highway. He had a hard time walking on his wounded leg, but finally we made it to the highway. Chu Tu sat down on the shoulder of the road while I stood there watching for the bus to come, waiting to flag it down. The heat was powerful again before sunset. I felt irritable so I walked back and forth impatiently. I began to sweat, feeling sticky. Chu Tu stood up and sat down again and glanced toward the end of the highway with the expectation of going home soon. It seemed like his leg bothered him. He straightened it out. The sun disappeared in the forest and left an explosion of color reflecting over the broad sky. The day became dimmer and dimmer.

"Is there something coming?" asked Chu Tu.

"I don't see anything."

"I see a little black spot moving towards us. You sure you don't see it?"

"Yes I'm sure, Chu Tu."

"It seems like there's no bus running today. We have already waited two hours."

He gazed at his watch with disappointment.

"Yeah, it's really hard to catch the bus these days. When I was in school, the transportation was very convenient and you could go anywhere at any time as long as you had money in your pocket," I said.

"Don't say that to anybody unless you want trouble. It's okay with me because I understand the situation. I wonder what I'm fighting for! With this new upheaval, you had better close your mouth because it's best for you to learn and survive."

I thought of what he said: Is he really helping me, or does he want to fool me? I'm not sure. I wonder if he's really frustrated with the Communist Party and the northerners now? Or is he up to something?

"You know, after over thirty years of struggling, what do I have now? I'm still here in the jungle," Chu Tu said.

"Do you feel sorry for your life?" I said.

"No, I don't feel sorry for my life. I know I made a mistake. I don't blame it on the mistake because everyone has their own way to show patriotism for his country and this was mine."

"If you say that, what is my guilt? I'm a student. Why did they capture me and throw me in this place?"

"Because you are educated. When you're educated you have knowledge that will stop us from controlling you, and you're one of the people who could start a revolution against us, against our government, against the Communist Party and those like myself. When I went up north to fight the French, I hadn't finished fifth grade yet, but I could still read and write. But we're not supposed to think; when we carry out orders, we ask no questions. We do it like we're machines," Chu Tu answered.

"Do you think certain individuals in the government control the people and run the country, rather than Communist policy? I mean, it seems to me they take advantage of the situation; they label themselves with the Communist symbol to persuade others. For example, you do what you want in this place, and the northern guard does what he wants. You're a boss in your area and he's a boss in his. I'm in your hands now; you can do anything to me and if I run to the northern guard, I would belong to him and you couldn't do anything to me. Am I right?"

"It seems that way," said Chu Tu.

"Look, I see something coming!"

Chu Tu hobbled up and looked in the direction I was looking. The spot came nearer and nearer. I was waving my hand up and down. I saw an army jeep approach us with one driver and three passengers wearing the northern army uniform.

"Damn, northerners again," he mumbled.

The car passed by without even a wave.

"I don't think we'll get a ride today," I said. "Do you want to go back to get some sleep and come back tomorrow? It's getting dark now."

"Wait half an hour longer, and then we'll leave."

The evening fell gently and it was quiet. There wasn't anybody on the road. Chu Tu and I sat there hoping something would come, as if we were waiting for relatives to arrive. But nothing showed up. We stood up and walked back to the campsite. The trees were asleep and the dew was still on the grass and the stars kept sparkling. I had to support Chu Tu and lead the way because he couldn't put his wounded leg down in the mud.

We arrived at our spot safely. I let Chu Tu lie down on his spot and I went back to mine. I fell asleep without expecting to.

I woke up surrounded by noise. All the guards were running back and forth in the night and I could hear their weapons hitting each other. The sound of the bullets and grenades clanging together gave me a cold chill, made my teeth hurt. I sat up against a tree and looked toward the highway. Several cars were stopping, the occupants jumping out of the vehicles and running to the sides of the road. They turned all their lights off and began to move in the dark.

"Wake up, wake up!"

The guards forced all of us to get up and to form a group. I heard the northern accent everywhere.

"When did they attack the border?" a northerner asked the guard.

"Did you get our message a few days ago, comrade?"

"Yes, we did, but it wasn't clear," the northerner answered.

"About three days ago comrade Tu went to the outpost to check on the VC, but the Cambodians had invaded it some time before and we weren't aware of it. We didn't hear any shooting, and that's why he was wounded in the leg. We didn't have any transportation, so he has been stuck here. Can you take him to the hospital now?" the guard said.

"We'll take care of him later! Now, we have to attack our enemies and take our outpost back before the situation gets really serious. I want your prisoners to carry the supplies for the battle," the northerner ordered.

"Where are your supplies?"

"In our trucks. Get your prisoners and come with us."

The guard came to our group and brought us to the convoy on the highway.

"These are our ammunition and supplies. I want two prisoners to carry each box and move silently to the hut area where you stayed before."

We unloaded the boxes and began to move toward the trail. It was dark, but far away in the sky many stars shined down on us. We were moving like a convoy of troops in the night, going into the woods. I saw many shadows running from one spot to another at the side of the path, like ghosts. I wondered what was in the boxes. Grenades? Mortar shells? First aid or food? I didn't care because I knew this time they were going to push us into the fire, into the battle, and we didn't have anything to defend ourselves. I asked myself: Are we going to be victims; are we going to die? What will we do? What are our sins? Are we guilty for loving our country, for loving our people? Or is it our innocence that lets this happen? I didn't know.

Above us bats flew, hunting for food. Birds flew away when they heard our noise. I heard people stepping on branches, making a crackling sound, making it seem like someone was following us, like our shadows on a moonlit night. The air was wet, the space was vast, and we kept walking and walking. All the trees seemed awake. I felt like the grass was going to grab my feet and tie them up so that I couldn't move. I was poised to fall to the ground, but there wasn't any shooting yet. I wondered if we would walk into a trap, into a place where they would bury us alive. I could feel eyes peering at us. I was cold even though the air wasn't cold. Time seemed to stop; the night was endless.

"Go this way. Take the short cut!" someone whispered.

We turned into the narrow path and had to walk single file.

"Move faster and be quiet."

I tripped over something, fell on the ground, and dropped the box.

"Do you want to blow yourself up?" someone said.

I stood and held the box firmly and started walking again. A message came down the line: "Something happened at the front. Send some comrades up here and shoot any prisoner who runs away or appears suspicious." The message continued to move down the line until it reached the northern soldiers at the end. A couple of northerners moved up the line.

"Move aside, let me pass!"

They pushed us while they whispered. I couldn't believe the message that was passed: We were telling them with our own mouths to shoot us. I remembered the self-criticism we had to write at the daily meetings, how they put words in our mouths, how they beat us at the same time they said they forgave us. I thought of how they robbed people at the same time they chanted above how they helped people clean up the Empire's mess. And how they banned all our books saying it was bad education while they took these same books home to read. I remembered how they insulted our music saying it betrayed our patriotism: they said if we loved our music we wouldn't be able to fight, but they took it home and listened to it themselves. How could they kill people without any reason? What could I do for myself, for my friends, for my people?

As I walked through the dark jungle, a new determination took shape inside me. I can't just drift here, ready to fall into the trap without any desire or hope, I said to myself. I have to do something. I have to pull through; I have to survive under any circumstances, in any situation. Fight! Yes, fight, not only in my body but in my spirit. I have to make history. Not only for myself but for others. If I lose, it's only a game. I want to play, I want to play it now! I felt as if I had just invented something new, discovered the way to win. All of my energy suddenly came back, and my awareness intensified. I walked briskly. I saw things clearly now, even though it was dark.

"Slow down. Is the ghost chasing you?" muttered my partner.

"You'll be safe if you stay with me."

The night stood still and the troops kept moving. We came close to the hut area, my former living quarters. Although I couldn't see the hut, the leftover smell of a fire was still in the air. Trees were scattered about on the ground. The darkness of the night was lifting a bit. I inhaled deeply as if I were relieved of something, but only the smell of ashes filled my nostrils.

Boom, boom, boom, boom, boooommm . . . !

I dropped the box and dove to the ground. I heard a series of shots, but didn't know what direction they were coming from. The sound was very brittle, as if a tree had fallen, its limbs breaking. Someone shrieked, hurt. Another shot and another. The fighting began. Bullets landed and exploded in the tree tops. A ssshhh . . . sound going in different places. I crawled back to the trail we had just come from. Bullets hit the box I had left. It sounded like someone was using an ax to chop down a tree.

"Where is the box? If you lose that box you will die!"

The guard sat against the tree and pointed the gun at my head. I crept over to the box and pulled it back to where the guard was sitting. I didn't think this was a good idea, but I also didn't want to get shot. I left the box there and moved to the opposite side. The shooting was heavy from that direction.

"Back me up, back up for me, comrade," someone shouted.

A line of shots passed over my head, and then another. My hands slipped and I fell to the dirt. I lay there and held the ground tightly as if it was going to slip out of my hands. I turned around and looked for something to shield me from getting shot. Footsteps were running all over and jumping over the boxes and down again and running on. It seemed like a riot in the night, a confusing motions battling with the darkness.

"Run, run, run!" someone yelled.

I was caught in the middle of the battle. I couldn't move ahead or backwards or sideways. I stayed in one spot.

"Stay where you are, prisoners. If you run back we'll shoot!" a guard yelled from the back. He was louder than the shooting. I recognized the northerner's voice, heavy and fast. The shooting began to die down and faded in the distance. The sun rose with its big cheery face. I touched my face and body and realized I was still alive. The guard and the northern army man were walking around to check all the supplies and to see who was wounded and killed. One of them walked over to me and used his gun to poke my back. I rolled over and faced him.

"You're okay. Come on, clean up the mess."

I stood up, looking around me. The whole area, including the place where our hut used to be, was entirely devastated. Burnt black spots covered the ground. The grass was flattened. Trees had fallen down or were leaning against one another. All the leaves had wilted because of the heat of the fire. Some trees were scorched, while in the garden the fences had collapsed and the sweet potatoes, cucumbers, and lettuce were scattered all around on the dirt. Everything was destroyed, ruined. I gazed around me again and everything seemed fixed in my memory. I couldn't erase it.

"Come here, move these boxes to the side and take the dead bodies away," the guard called me.

I came to him and helped the other prisoners pull the boxes aside. We moved two dead Cambodians who were very young, and one of our men. We buried them together in one hole. I heard shooting toward the border. An injured northern army man sat while someone wrapped a bandage around his arm and chest. Blood was all over the ground from the dead bodies and the injured man. The northern army men kept moving toward the outpost at the border. Some stayed there and ordered us to set up a temporary base. We opened the boxes. They held food, first aid, tool supplies, all the necessary things to support the army. We had to dig a trench and build a fire on the ground for cooking. Northerners stood guard in the thickets. The air was getting sticky. The sun's rays were stronger every second. The morning weakened, and midday moved in. With sweat pouring out of us we cooked lunch for the northern army troops. Afterward, they discharged us and the guards escorted us back to the campsite; we carried the injured man with us. When we reached the highway, I saw another group of prisoners walking back to the camp we had just left. On the highway more commotion signaled that the northern army was on the road.

"Chu Tu is looking for you," Thanh told me.

"What for?"

"I don't know."

"We just put a wounded man on the truck to go to the hospital," I said. "Maybe Chu Tu can get a ride with them. Would you look for him?"

Thanh walked around the campsite and looked for Chu Tu while I went to comrade Son.

"Comrade, Chu Tu told me to go to the highway to tell the army truck to wait for him to go to the hospital."

"Okay, go."

I went to the highway. I saw Chu Tu sitting on the army truck and I came to him, while all the northerners stood around chatting.

"Are you looking for me, Chu Tu?"

"Yes, where were you?"

"I helped the northern army group to carry the supplies last night. I was caught in the middle of all the fighting until now."

"I thought another group went with them, not your group. If I had known, I would have kept you with me. Whatever, just get on the truck."

I jumped onto the truck and sat at the side near the injured man. He looked like he was sleeping on the stretcher. There was dried blood on his face. His hair was tangled and matted. He seemed young. I wondered if his wound was serious because I saw a blood-soaked bandage on his chest. He breathed slowly. I didn't know why the vehicle wasn't moving yet. It seemed like no one was in a hurry except the people who were traumatized. I glanced at Chu Tu with an inquiring look. Chu Tu looking at the wounded man solemnly, wrinkled his forehead as if he were speculating, unaware of anything around him. He glared at the northerners, who were rambling on with their bunch. He looked at the injured man and then impatiently at his leg.

"Comrade, let's go!"

"Just a minute, comrade," someone called back.

"The man is dying!"

"Okay, okay."

The northerner came over to the truck and started the motor. He backed up and turned around, screeching the tires on the blacktop, and we sped away. The truck ran smoothly for a while as we left the campsite. I glanced back and there wasn't anything in sight, only dust blowing up in the air.

CHAPTER 17

Chu Tu and I sat in the back quietly, bouncing up and down when we rode over bumpy spots. I looked to the side where vast fields were cut into portions. Young rice with green leaves was ready to bloom. Some parts were wet, some dry. Next to the rice field was a garden. The scenery changed continually as we moved up and down the hill. I felt free because I could breathe this air and smell the greenness.

"Water, water," the hurt man whimpered.

I bent down to look under the bench for a water jug, but found none. I glanced over to Chu Tu to see if he had some water with him. He didn't have any either.

"Comrade, do you have some water?" Chu Tu asked the driver.

"In the tool box under your seat."

I bent over and opened the tool box to get the jug out. I lifted the wounded man's head and gave him some water. He guzzled it down like he didn't want to stop.

"Don't let him drink too much. He'll lose more blood."

I took the jug back and put it in the tool box. Chu Tu took his tobacco bag and paper out from his pocket, rolled himself a cigarette, lit it up, and took a puff, the tip of the cigarette reddening. He exhaled slowly and the smoke came out of his nose. He took a couple more puffs.

"Are you going home after the hospital or are you coming back to our place?" I asked.

"I think I'll go home for a while, but I have to bring you back first. Maybe you'll ride back with this comrade. Don't ever think you're going to escape, unless you want the other prisoners to die."

"Yes, Chu Tu, I understand."

"Good . . ." His weary face relaxed somewhat.

"What are you going to do at home? Will your wife make something good for you? It's good to eat, you know."

I winked my eye and smirked at him. He grinned at me.

"Do you think you'll take your children to visit their grand-parents?" I added.

"I haven't thought about it yet. Retirement is all I think of. I've wanted it for a long time now. I'm really tired of fighting day after day. It's a long war."

"What are you going to do during retirement?"

"I want to go back to my parents in Tra Vinh and ask them for a piece of land to build a house, raise some chickens, pigs, cows, ducks, and settle down."

"Your life is simple; I like that."

"Do you know how long I've waited for this small dream? Over thirty years, you know that?" He looked down, reflecting.

"Why didn't you build a house and raise a family in the first place?"

"Because of the war, because I love my motherland, because of my youth. You cannot have peace when you see people suffering, your country destroyed by foreign forces."

He kept talking, but the tire made a cchhhh . . . noise and the truck jiggled. The driver pulled over to the shoulder of the road and stopped. I held the wounded man's stretcher to keep it from falling to one side as the truck tilted. The northerner leaped off and looked at the front tire. He kicked it.

"Damn it, I just changed it two weeks ago. Now it's happened again. Where am I going to get another one to replace it? These roads have to be fixed!" He smacked the hood with his hand, then walked to the back of the truck and opened a little compartment. The tire inside was flat. He slammed the cupboard shut.

"I don't think we can move anymore, comrade. I don't have another tire."

The injured man opened his eyes at the racket.

"Water, I need water."

I gave him some water. Then I sprang down onto the road to see if I could help. I saw that there were two sets of back tires on each side.

"Comrade, is it possible to take one tire off the back to replace the front one?"

"I don't know; let's try it."

He gazed at me with surprise. My feet were burning because the blacktop was scorching them. I stood on tiptoe and raised one foot up when it was hot and then raised the other. The heat was strong and it blurred my vision when I peered down the highway. I helped him jack up the back tire and put it on the front. He got in his seat and turned on the ignition. The truck backfired four or five times, without running, tired in the heat. The driver got off the truck and opened the hood to try to fix the problem. I climbed back under the shady canvas, but it was still hot. I saw Chu Tu applying some water to the injured man's forehead.

"Let me help you," I said. "Is your leg all right?"

"It's painful again because I moved around a lot today. Is the car fixed yet?"

"We fixed the tire, but now it won't start."

"Maybe it's too hot."

"Probably."

I heard the truck start up again, then stop. He started it a few times, but the truck stood still.

"What are we going to do if the vehicle doesn't run, Chu Tu?"

"If we can get a bus that comes by we'll be lucky."

"Do you think you can get it to run, comrade?" Chu Tu asked the driver.

"I don't know. I'm working on it."

We sat there sweating, laboring to breathe. The hot air brushed my lungs each time I inhaled. It was as if we were stranded in the middle of the desert with nowhere to go and nothing to do. I grabbed a hat from under the seat and fanned the wounded man, but it didn't seem to help, and the truck still wouldn't run. I wished the bus would come. I looked down the highway and saw something coming.

"Is there something coming, Chu Tu?"

"Yeah, there is." His voice seemed like it was quenched with water after a long thirst.

"Can you fan him while I signal it to stop?"

I gave the hat to him, jumped off the truck, and flagged down the bus. The driver leaped down.

"Where are you going? Do you have any baggage?"

"Ha Tien. I don't have any baggage, just two wounded men on the truck. They have to go to the hospital immediately. Do you have enough space for them?"

"Let's see." While he spoke, he hopped on the bus.

"Ladies, ladies, would you move over a little to make room for the injured people? They're hurt very badly." They all squeezed together, leaving a bench open for us.

"Can you help me get them on the bus?" I asked the bus driver's helper. He got off the bus and ran over to the truck with me and helped Chu Tu get on the bus first.

"Comrade, I'll take these injured men to the hospital. If you get the truck started, you can catch us before we get to the hospital or else just meet us there. Or follow your orders and go back to the camp," Chu Tu said.

"Okay."

We carried the man to the bus and laid him on the bench. Chu Tu sat at the end of the seat and put the man's legs over his lap. There wasn't any room left for me or the driver's helper, so I climbed up to the top of the bus where the baggage was and sat there next to a basket full of chickens and ducks hopping about, several bags of corn, and some other odds and ends. The helper stood on the step at the rear of the bus, holding the railing.

"It's all set, let's go," he yelled, slapping the side of the bus. We moved slowly.

"How far from here to Ha Tien?" I bent down and asked the bus driver's helper.

"It's about twenty kilometers."

I felt a little better because the car was moving and the wind was blowing on my face. I smelled chickens' and ducks' excrement and all the feathers fell on me when they flapped their wings. The chicken pecked at the duck; some of them sat while some of them stood and panted. The bus rolled on, then stopped to let off some passengers. I climbed down and sat on one of the empty seats.

"It's so hot," someone said.

"Yes, especially on the top where I sat," I replied.

One of the ladies glanced at me from head to toe.

"You're not from around here, are you?"

"No ma'am, I'm a prisoner in a labor camp. I'm helping these injured men to get to the hospital."

She reached in the bag at her feet and gave me a banana pie made with sweet rice and two sticks of sugarcane.

"Eat it son, eat it. You're an old soldier?"

"Sort of, ma'am."

"You remind me of my son. He died one year ago. Maybe he's happier than you. I don't know, son, I don't know."

She pulled her shawl around her neck, wiped her eyes and nose. Her eyes were red. She turned, looked out the window and said, "It's hot and dusty, son."

"Yes, ma'am . . ."

I peered at her, sharing the moment, my voice stuck somewhere in my throat. I wanted to jump in her arms and call her mama . . . I wanted to replace her son for only this moment— the moment of one's childhood, the moment of one's mother, but I sat still and held her hand.

"It's okay." I wanted to call her mama, but my voice was cracking.

"Thiem Bay, did anything happen to your village last night?" another lady asked her.

"No, but I heard someone warning that the Cambodians were coming." Her voice wasn't steady.

"I heard shooting around but I wasn't sure who was having a brawl. They asked the young people to guard the school and the village."

"I don't know what happens these days. It's not the old days anymore."

They began to talk noisily despite the clamor the bus was making, loud and low. It was chugging along like a steamboat churning through the afternoon's humidity. People were sweating and exhausted. The bus driver's helper screamed to the driver to stop the bus. It pulled over to the side.

"Ladies, ladies, we're getting close to the police station. Stand up, let me hide your bags of rice under the bench in the compartment so that you can make some money today."

They all stood up and hid their rice for the black market. The bus moved back onto the highway and ran about five kilometers before it reached the police station.

"We have to get off for the police to check our papers and the goods," the bus driver's helper shouted to us. We got off; the group was mostly women, with four elderly men and myself. Two policemen walked over to the bus. One checked the papers and one got on the bus and examined everyone's belongings. The bus driver's helper showed the guard all the stuff.

"What's in that bag?" he asked as he messed about the contents.

"Some sugarcane and cabbage, comrade," answered the driver's helper.

"What's inside that box beneath there?"

"Tool box, comrade."

After he finished, he climbed to the top and continued his snooping. He poked a hole in the bags of corn with his stick. Some of the corn dropped out.

"What's in there? How about that bag?"

"Corn, comrade."

"Who do these chickens and ducks belong to?" he yelled and looked down at us. One of the ladies ran over.

"It's mine. I have the papers here." She stood there waving the papers back and forth. He got down and skimmed the papers. I didn't know whether he could read it or not.

"Where are your papers?" he asked me.

"I don't have any. I'm with the wounded comrade, Chu Tu. I'm helping him to the hospital."

"Come with me."

I followed him to the bus.

"Comrade, is this man your prisoner?" he asked Chu Tu.

"Yes, comrade."

"What happened to you, comrade?"

"The Cambodians."

"When did it happen?"

"Last night."

He got off the bus and returned all the papers to everyone. We hopped back on the bus and departed again. Before the bus came to its destination, it stopped at the hospital to let us off. Chu Tu paid the fare because I didn't have any money. Before I got off the bus the lady held and patted my hand.

"If there is anything I can do, son . . . I'm selling things at the market in town. Here, have another pie. I know you're hungry. Take care, son."

She slipped the pie in my hand as if she was afraid someone would see it. I got off the bus and the bus driver closed the door, waving his goodbye to me. I stood there and looked as the bus faded away, trailing a cloud of smoke. I wanted to wave my hand, but instead I looked on helplessly. The orderlies had already moved the injured man to the hospital. Chu Tu limped halfway to the entrance with me behind him. The first thing I noticed was the odor of chloroform and the whiteness of everything in the hospital, from the uniforms to the walls to the beds. I caught up with Chu Tu and helped him walk over to the registration desk. As we walked down the hall, we saw many people sitting and restlessly waiting for their relatives: some of them were lying down and napping; some kids chased each other, jumping over the little cement wall and running into the garden to play; some adults were washing their linens, standing under the canvas cover to be shielded from the afternoon sun. The sun began to set for the day.

"Move, move!" the nurse shouted as she pulled the stretcher. People stepped aside but popped their heads out to see what was going on. There was a body lying on the stretcher with blood all over; the man was barely breathing. A blood bag was hooked up to him. The nurse with the stretcher disappeared behind the corner. We went to the counter to register Chu Tu.

"May I borrow a pen and a blank piece of paper?" Chu Tu asked the nurse.

"What for?"

"I want to let my wife know I'm here so she can come visit me."

"You don't need to do that; we'll take care of it for you."

The nurse smiled but I could see it was just a joke to her. She gave him a piece of paper with a pencil she took from the desk.

"Make sure you give me the pencil back. It cost a lot of money, comrade."

"Sure, cadre," he answered to the female VC.

The nurse left the office. Chu Tu filled out a form and

quickly wrote a letter to his wife. I sat there and looked outside the window. The afternoon was slowly drifting away. The wind blew gently on the coconut leaves of the palm trees outside; the leaves waved back and forth like someone waving his hand at me. Some of the old leaves had drooped down at the side of the tree trunk, holding on to their last minutes of life, while other leaves were blossoming now. I saw the side of another building; people were moving back and forth, and on the concrete wall were many bullet holes. Around the hole, a smudge of black powder remained, surrounded by other tiny holes. I wondered how long ago the war had happened in this city. It seemed as if people were trying to mend this big wound, but nothing was fixed. The damage still remained. At the corner of the building the wall was falling apart. The roof was just hanging there.

"Are you all done, comrade?" the female VC cadre asked.

"Yes."

Chu Tu handed the form to her and she looked at it quickly.

"Where is my pencil? I can't afford to buy many these days. We have to help our Party."

"Can you do something about my leg?"

"Hold on, comrade. I'll get someone. Wait here."

She walked away down the hall and disappeared behind the door. We sat there quietly and I chased my thoughts while Chu Tu chased his. I didn't realize how long we were waiting. My eyes were getting tired and I felt weak. I wanted to ask Chu Tu if I could walk around but I felt too tired to ask. Chu Tu looked like he was suffering very much and unable to wait any longer.

"Huhhh! Thirty years I've been fighting, a faithful member of the Communist Party and now what do I have? Only anguish. I wonder why we don't wait like this when we fight in the jungle?" Chu Tu mumbled to himself.

"In any society there is always some corruption; there is always something wrong. I really don't know, Chu Tu," I tried to comfort him.

He held his leg and squeezed it tightly with a sour expression on his face.

"Let me go and find them."

"Don't go out of the hospital since I cannot do anything if you get into trouble."

"Yes, Chu Tu."

I stood up and followed the hall to the door where the cadre had gone. I looked into the room, but didn't see any nurses, only sick people. Some were lying on the bed and others were lying on the ground. I walked to the next room, where a kind of babble drew me in. I saw a girl about fourteen or fifteen holding her stomach and yelling. Next to her was a lady who was trying to help her, but she didn't know what to do. She held a little handkerchief and wiped the sweat from the girl's face. The girl was tossing back and forth on the ground.

"Mama, I'm dying, and I don't know what's happening inside my stomach! I feel like someone has cut my intestines apart. Help me, mama, help me . . . I can't stand it." Her voice was wet and soft.

I looked at the girl. She had an oval face with round black eyes full of despair. She had light skin and all the hair on her arm stood up like she was cold. She looked young and pure like a child who doesn't know anything about life. Her mother held her shoulders and grabbed her and was trembling nervously as if she were cradling a baby to stop her from crying. The tears fell from her face and she was speechless. I ran out and walked down the hall fast, running from my fears. I glanced in every room, until finally I heard laughter and chatter inside a room at the end of the hall. I opened the door and peeked inside. I saw all the nurses and doctors standing around having their own little party as if there wasn't anything happening around them.

"What do you want?" someone hollered at me.

"Please, please help! There is a girl who is dying."

"Who, where?"

"Near the registration desk. Please, come with me," the cadre stumbled out from the room with her heavy steps and came with me.

"You disturbed my enjoyment. Did you know that? I sacrificed myself for the war for over fifteen years, underground in the tunnel, to save all our injured comrades. Now that the war's over, I need to enjoy my life."

"I'm sorry, ma'am, but please help someone who is dying."

"Why didn't anyone help me when they bombed the Ho Chi Minh trail?" she demanded, in her tight voice. "The underground hospital almost collapsed," the cadre continued, as if she blamed it on me. Her heavy gestures were the opposite of her light voice.

"I don't know, ma'am."

"I never went to school and I joined the guerrilla force when I was twelve and with my fifteen years of service I became a doctor. Do you think that's a good title for me?"

"Yes, ma'am."

I walked beside her and I tried to walk faster but the hall seemed endless. I could hear the girl screaming. Some of the people ran after us to see what was going on. We came to the room and her mother ran out like she couldn't bear the burden anymore.

"Get the stretcher over there," the nurse pointed.

I pulled the stretcher over to the room. I helped her put the girl on it. We strapped her hands and legs.

"Go back to the room where you found me before and tell them I want someone," she said, while she hauled the stretcher to another hall, yelling at patients to make way as the hall became crowded with people curious to see who was on the stretcher. I ran back to tell them, but no one was there except a short, middle-aged woman cleaning the kitchen.

"Ma'am, do you see any nurses or doctors around?"

"They just ate and left. Who are you looking for? Saigon doctor, northerner, or a cadre doctor?"

"I don't know, ma'am; I just want to find somebody who can help the patients out there who are in pain."

"You don't know anything about this hospital, son." She raised her heavy black eyebrows. "Who are you, anyway?"

"I'm a prisoner. I helped the wounded comrades to the hospital," I said. "Actually, they took me with them."

"I thought you looked like a prisoner. I heard them say that they never release any captive except by death." She looked around because she was afraid someone would hear her. "When will they release you, do you know?"

"I don't know, ma'am, I have to go back to the desk now

before I get in trouble."

She didn't speak anymore and continued picking up the mess on the table. I walked back to where I had left Chu Tu. He wasn't there. I paced for a little while but he didn't show up. I thought he might be in the surgery room. There was nothing in this room except a desk, a chair, and the bench I was sitting on. The whole wall was white; a few windows were open and the wind was blowing in. Some flies were making a buzzing sound as they traveled back and forth and finally flew out the window. The red brick floor allowed me to feel the weather changing when I walked on it with bare feet. I felt cold, but I didn't know whether it was because I was still hungry, even though I had eaten the two pies that the lady gave me on the bus, or because it was getting dark outside.

It was evening and the morgue building stood still like a big shadow, hiding, lurking in the darkness, ready to swallow its next victim. I wondered why this building attracted me so strongly. The palm and coconut trees were clattering against the building, making mysterious music softly, powerfully. There wasn't a real ceiling, but I could see the brick roof. The wall was peeling in some spots. Some of the kids from the hall ran into me, chasing each other in their own game. I stood up and walked out of the room to let them play, then walked back to the kitchen to talk to the cook I'd met a few hours ago when I was looking for a nurse or doctor in the kitchen, and maybe find something to eat. Inside the kitchen the oil lamp was fluttering, like fireflies scattered in the gentle night. I heard utensils clanging together, and it seemed like she was putting things away for the day to head back home and be with her children. I stood at the door and looked inside.

"Who's that?"

"Me."

"Who is me?" Her voice was heavy and when she held the lamp and walked over, you could hear the slish-sloshy sound of her sandals on the wet floor. She held the lamp up and gazed at my face carefully.

"Oh, you . . . ?" Her eyes and the whole oval of her face seemed to widen as she recognized me.

She told me to hush and pulled me in, closing the door behind us. I followed her and she pushed me into a dark corner of a closet. I sat there quietly. She moved away past the stove and I heard a door open.

"We have a meeting now, you'd better hurry," someone called out from the door.

"Yes, comrade. I'm almost done." With her shimmering eyes she seemed to work very well in the dark, the bun at the back of her head bobbing with her quick motions.

I heard the door shut. She left the oil lamp at the stove and shuffled over. She handed something to me but I couldn't see what it was. I took it, smelled it and ate it.

I tasted the sweetness like the cooked banana rice cake. I hadn't realized I was that hungry. It was so dark that I couldn't even see my hands; I used my senses to eat, like a blind person, dropping the food slowly into my mouth, licking my fingers to get every morsel.

She had left the kitchen some time ago but I didn't notice. I heard people running along the hall and some of the women calling their children to come back to their beds and sleep. Now my eyes could see dimly in the dark. I put the bowl down on the floor and stretched my legs, careful not to make any noise. I was puzzled. Why did so many people help? Perhaps for a reason that was unknown to me. They gave me a chance to live for some purpose which Buddha only knew. Moving rats caught my eye—they were coming from the drain in the floor sink. They were scurrying around a bucket and squeaking angrily because the bucket was so tall they couldn't get into it. A huge rat came along. It appeared she was the mother of the little ones. She had something clamped between her teeth and she dropped it down on the floor near the little rats. The big rat made a sound like she was calling her children. One small one came and then another. They began eating their feast. The big one bent over the small trash can. Suddenly, the door opened and the light came on as I heard the heavy steps of the woman cook. The rat clan scampered about the floor looking for places to hide. I finished my food and told her I had to leave.

I walked out to the garden, just wandering around. I gave up the idea to search for Chu Tu since it was getting darker and I wanted to find a place to sleep for the night. The mosquitoes kept following me, buzzing in my ear, biting me as I slapped at them. I wanted to smoke so that the mosquitoes would go away, but I had no cigarette. They bit me on my face, and on my thigh where there was a hole in my pajama pant. Like a cow, I stamped my feet on the ground angrily, chasing the bugs away.

I walked onto a brick moss path, curious about where it led. On both sides of the path, two walls about a foot thick ran from the garden to the building with vines crawling over it. I stepped over the dead branches on the ground, making a cracking sound. Up in the sky, many stars looked down on me.

Everything was so quiet I felt lost in an empty space without anything living around me. I tried to locate the building. I looked back to where I was before and discovered this was the building across from the registration desk where I had sat this afternoon. It had a strange feeling about it. I stepped closer and closer to the building. Bats were flying around in front of my face and they made a swwwuuu . . . sound in the air. They flew up and descended downward from one place to another, searching for food. Sleeping birds woke when I lifted branches to walk beneath them. I came to the door, grabbed the door-knob and turned it slowly, not realizing it was open, ajar. Gently, I pushed the door open wider. It creaked like it needed oiling, as if no one had been living there for years.

It was blacker inside than out. I stood still before I walked any further. At the side of the door, I saw a little wooden bench with something on it. Further inside the room I saw a broken chair at the window and grass that grew between the cracks on the floor. A branch, which had grown inside the open window, moved up and down, scraping the frame of the window. Cracked wood beams dangled near the hole-pocked roof. One hole, about the size of a bucket, let in the sky. Fragments of brick formed a big pile on the floor. The mosquitoes began biting again, and I fled on into a hall that seemed to stretch on forever. I didn't want to look into any of the dark rooms I passed, so I walked straight ahead out of the hall. At the end of the hall, two other halls forked off in different directions. One of them opened onto a play yard. I crossed through the yard to the next building. A noise came from behind the door, then vanished into the distance: a rat or a cat, perhaps. Inside this room I saw more tables and benches. Though curious, I felt tired and wanted to sleep. I lay down on the table and fell asleep.

"Uncle, uncle, are you coming back home now?" one of my nephews asked me.

"No, I have to go away for a while. Tell your father not to wait for me."

"But uncle, grandmother is waiting and expecting you to come home." He pulled my hand and shook it like he didn't want to release it.

"I want to but I can't, I can't."

I ran up the stairs and left him there crying. In the wide, well-kept main room upstairs, I saw the altar; it was bright with candlelight. There was an incense holder in the middle of it. Both sides were lined with grapefruit, oranges, mangos, and plums, all nicely set up on plates. At the side of the altar, I reached for a stick of incense, lit it, folded it in my hands, bowed to the altar three times, and prayed. I placed the incense in the holder. Briefly, I glanced around the room. I heard footsteps running on the stairs.

"Uncle, uncle, they're coming." His voice was trembling with tears, his brown eyes wide.

"Don't cry, don't cry!" I held him in my arms, patting him on the back reassuringly. I looked into his innocent, childish eyes. He was so young, so tender. I let him go, stood up, and ran to the back door of the house where I heard a dog barking, snarling furiously outside the gate. I opened the back door and ran out. Bang, bang, bang, bang! I woke up with sweat pouring off my face and body. I didn't recognize where I was. I heard banging on the door. I jumped off the table and crept over to the next room and peeked in there. I saw a small group of people carrying a coffin in. They set it down on a stand.

"Do you want to put him in now or what?" someone asked.

"Later. Let's go and find something to eat." They walked out of the building and went to another side of the hospital.

The sun rose with its big red face at the end of the horizon. The air was cool, crisp. The palm and coconut trees seemed like they were relaxing, the leaves echoing softly like the early morning music. Inside the yard in between the two buildings, the grass grew wild; some of the weeds crawled up and followed the cracks of the brick wall. Whose coffin was this? Who were they? Why did they put a coffin here? Who was "he"? Were they talking about me? Was I alive or dead? I touched my whole body to see if I was really there. I touched the wall; I held the table and I noticed everything was real. What was going on? If I was alive, were they going to kill me or bury me alive in the coffin? How could I breathe in here? I felt something heavy on my chest. I needed space, I needed air, air . . . I drew back to the room where I had slept. I wanted to find a

place to hide. I didn't care where. Why were they after me?
What had I done? Would I have to run away and hide all of my
life? I saw some chairs that had fallen down; the whole room
was in a shambles. Next to my table was a small bench and another table twice the size of mine. A big cloth covered the
whole table and reached to the floor. On the top of it was a big
lump. I didn't know what was in there. I looked carefully at the
cloth, which seemed dyed with different colors in different
spots, from red to black and burgundy. It was in shreds at the
corner where the cloth was touching the floor. I felt cold all of
a sudden. I didn't know why this object so fascinated my eye.

I came close to the table and with both of my hands I lifted
up the cloth. There they were; two dead corpses lying opposite
each other. They looked like they were napping softly. I took a
deep breath, then let it out slowly. My chest was lighter. I tried
to see if I knew who these people were. I recognized one of
them; one was the northerner who had traveled with us to the
hospital yesterday afternoon. His chest had stopped bleeding,
but the stain was still there. He appeared to be relaxed, relieved
that he had finished his duty, his job, his love, his life. On his
collar was a red pin to let people know his position in the
army, but I didn't know which rank it signified. I wondered if
he was going to take it with him or leave it behind. He looked
young and energetic: too young to die. I looked at his lips, and
it seemed they wanted to say something, but had been silenced
at the moment of his death—a moment to dream, a moment of
happiness which I didn't know. He had kindly closed his eyes
next to the feet of the other dead corpse and he hid his nose
beside them. I didn't recognize the other dead person but it
seemed they were happy to share the table together. I heard
noise outside, getting closer. I walked out the front door,
heading for the main wing of the hospital, and ran into a small
group of people. They seemed to be ready for work, but did
not appear to be doctors or nurses.

"Hello, I'm looking for Chu Tu but I couldn't find him in
here. Do you know where I can find him?"

"Who is Chu Tu?" they asked me.

"The person who died yesterday."

"Are you sure he died? I don't know anybody of that name

on today's list to bury. Is he a northerner or southerner?"

"He's a southerner."

"You better come with us to make sure it's the right person."

"That's a good idea."

I pretended that I hadn't seen the dead yet, and went with the undertakers into the morgue again. They were middle-aged and seemed very nice. One had a mustache and beard. It looked shabby and dull. One was short and one was tall. Maybe he didn't have a razor to shave, or maybe he wanted it to grow wild.

"What are we going to do after we put him in the coffin, Nam?" one man asked the other.

"That's the easy part. Send him back home to the north. We don't need them here." His voice became softer like he was afraid someone might hear him. He laughed sarcastically.

"Do you understand what I mean?"

"Sure, how do we get rid of him?"

"We better get him ready because a truck will pick him up this afternoon. Our job is to put him in the coffin and to make sure the carrion doesn't give off an odor."

"Watch out what you are saying. This young man is a communist," One of them turned around and looked at me.

"No, I'm a prisoner. I'm not a Communist. They sent people like me and others related to the old government to what they refer to as a 're-study camp.' I think you all know about it."

"Yes, we're just kidding."

While we were talking we came to the dead bodies.

"Here, take a look to see if it's your friend."

They pulled the cover off and I looked at the corpse again and shook my head.

"No, not him."

"Nam, do you think we can go home early after this?" one man asked.

"Yeah. I would rather put more of these northerners in coffins and send them back home where they belong rather than let them remain here to bother us." He turned to me, his eyes flat. "What do you think, young man?"

"I agree. They'd better leave us alone." Before I answered I glanced around to make sure no one was there.

"It's safe here, don't worry. We like to have a chat now and then, but nothing ever happens. If they had caught us, we would have seen you at the place where you stayed as a prisoner a long time ago. Are you going to give us a hand?"

"I want to, but I have to go to the hospital to look for my friend, I'll see you around," I said.

"Good luck."

They began to do their job and I left for the hospital. The dew on the grass was gone and the damp air was dry, signaling the beginning of a hot day. I saw the sun shining down like a stove ready to bake meat. I breathed easily and enjoyed the morning sunshine. I saw the sun's rays beam their way through the hospital roof and shine on a battered wall. It looked like a huge person standing up looking at his shadow. The wind moved the tree limbs making the beam move up and down, back and forth like the lights at a discotheque. All the birds had disappeared for the day because of the noisy sounds of people working, and I couldn't see where the bats were hiding themselves to sleep after their long night on the prowl. I strolled down the path and climbed the brick steps to enter the hospital. Kids sat on the step with their sleepy eyes, too tired to play. Others ran into the street and yelled to each other to get their gang together for a new game. Some of the mothers began to hang the clothes out on the brick wall and some of them filled the basins and buckets with water. Some built a fire to cook on the porch near the hall next to the garden. One of the cadres, the female VC nurse, walked down the hall and glanced over at me.

"Are you the one who was looking for the comrade yesterday?" she asked with a pleasant, even-toothed smile.

"Yes, ma'am. Do you know where he is?"

"He is in the Intensive Care Unit. I'm heading that way. If you follow me I'll show you where."

"Thank you, ma'am." I walked along with her to the room.

"Make sure you don't stay in there too long."

"Yes, ma'am."

At the end of the hall we entered another wing of the building and passed the little park.

"There, go straight and it's the first room on your right."

I came to the room and saw the blurry sign on the door: "Intensive Care Unit." I opened the door and walked in. The seven beds were full. Equipment was hooked up to each patient: bottles and blood bags. A fan was running like it couldn't stop. The smell of blood and chemical odors made me feel dizzy and light-headed. Saliva accumulated in my mouth and I wanted to spit, but I swallowed it back.

I circled the beds, looking for Chu Tu. Finally, I found him at the corner of the room, sharing a bed with another patient. I gazed at him from head to toe, but his leg was missing from the middle of his thigh and there was a big, bloody bandage wrapped around the remaining half of his thigh. I could smell the dried blood as the strong odor rose to my nose like water evaporating. What had happened? Why did he have to end up this way? I knew the wound wasn't that serious, since I cleaned it for him; it had almost healed. Even though I was not a doctor, I still had the conscience and mind not to destroy people's lives this way. Why amputate it? Why amputate it! What was the reason? Was it because of a "genius doctor"? Was it because of a "communist doctor"? Yes. Under this government this was the only kind of doctor who could do this to human beings. They were proud of themselves and especially of the title "doctor." Struggling in the jungle for ten or twenty years or more, they had learned this kind of "work," this kind of "medicine" this kind of "quality" to carry out in the name of "helping people." Was it saving us or was it wasting us? They could do anything to us, even take our lives away without any reason. Where was their conscience, where were their hearts? Whether we loved or hated each other, we still had feelings toward one another and still revealed them. We were not machines. Only God knew. But look, look at him. He was still asleep; I listened to his childlike breathing, gazed at his face vigilantly, his cheeks pale, a little like a virtuous child who has made a mistake for the first time in his life. How could they take this life away and give him a half-life of combat, half a life of being disabled? The patient next to him tossed and turned around, and he saw me.

"Water, water."

I grabbed the cup on the stand next to the bed and walked out of the room to get some water for him. I came back with a full cup and held his bald head up and gave him a sip. He drank it like he was very thirsty. His face looked like a child just waking up, his eyes still closed. I took the cup away to let him catch his breath.

"More, more . . ."

I gave him some more water. Now he seemed to be awake. Maybe the cold water revived him. He opened his eyes and looked at me.

"You aren't my nurse, are you . . . ?"

"No, but I think I can help."

"Who are you?"

"I'm a friend of his." I pointed to Chu Tu, who was lying next to him. He turned his head around to look at Chu Tu and said, "Oh, my bedmate." He had just realized that he had been sharing a bed while he was unconscious. "Oh fate, oh friend, not only myself, not only one victim," he muttered and consoled himself. He looked at Chu Tu's leg where it was cut and wondered if he could bear this burden.

"How long were you asleep, do you know?" I asked.

"Two or three hours, I guess. I came in here about four-thirty in the morning."

I began to worry because Chu Tu had been here since yesterday and I didn't know how long he'd been asleep. The person next to him saw me fretting.

"It seems you're his close companion. I wish I could have someone like that."

I didn't know what to say to him. I kept quiet and thought about what he had just said. Was it really true? Was my friendship sincere, or did I only want to get close to Chu Tu so that I could draw him into a conflict with the northern man and they could fight against themselves? Now I saw Chu Tu crippled and all my hope was gone and my aim was broken. How could Chu Tu go back to work, how could he fight the northerners? How could he help me? It was over. I didn't know if I sympathized with myself or felt pity for him. What would happen to me if I went back there without him? Was my life folded into the northerner's hands? What was the matter with me?

"There's my small towel in that little bucket; soak it in cold water and apply it to his face so he can wake up."

"Oh, thanks." I took the towel, soaked it in the cold water and placed it on Chu Tu's flushed face. I took it off and put it on several times and he began to wake up slowly.

"Chu Tu, are you awake? Do you want some water?"

"What, what! What is it? Let me sleep." He was having a dream, his hands clenched and waving. I patted him gently on his face. I held his head up to let him have some water because his lips were dry and peeling. His eyes were closed, but he still took a sip of water. I used a cold washcloth and washed his face again.

"Chu Tu, wake up, wake up," I kept calling him.

"No, no I don't want to go home; I want to fight the foreigners. I don't want them to ruin my country. You better let me go, father . . ."

"Chu Tu, what are you saying, are you awake?" I grasped his hand and tapped it lightly, trying to wake him up.

"I know I love you, but I can't stay; maybe this is our happiness, to be apart from each other—or maybe I'll see you in the war. I don't know," he murmured. I felt scared, and I patted his hand faster and splashed more cold water onto his face. He began to open his eyes slowly.

"Do you feel better, Chu Tu?" He didn't answer me; his eyes rolled around and were blinking like the morning sun was in them; he rubbed the sleep from them and I gave him some more water.

"Oh, you. I thought you already went back."

"No, I was here with you yesterday. Do you remember?"

"When? Yesterday?" He bit his lip, uncertain.

"Yes, yesterday. I left you to call the doctor. When I came back, you had already left."

"Oh, I remember, I remember . . . yesterday."

"What do you remember?"

"Someone took me to the room and gave me some alcohol and I enjoyed drinking it and I went to sleep. That's all I remember. Oh, I remember I had a dream about my father. I wanted to run away to join the "regroup" organization to fight the French, but he didn't let me go. I talked to my neighbor, the young girl who helped me to get away. Yeah, yeah, I remember . . ."

The nurse came in and walked over to the bed and checked the person next to Chu Tu.

"You're okay now," she said to the other patient. "We're transferring you to a regular section of the hospital."

"Are you sure I'm okay? When will I get out of here? I hate it!"

"I'm a nurse, remember. Are you still asleep? I know what I'm doing," She sneered at him and walked away.

"I'm finally out of here, my friend, I'm out of here."

The patient tried to sit up and pat Chu Tu on his back but when his hand came halfway to Chu Tu's back he suddenly stopped, all of his excitement gone. He stared at Chu Tu's half-limb and glanced at him abruptly. He tried to open his mouth to say something, but nothing came out—just his breath. Chu Tu, uncomfortable after lying down for so long, grasped the edge of the bed and tried to move himself up, but his leg felt lighter than before. He wanted to lift it, but there was nothing for him to lift. Something was missing; he looked at his leg. He appeared to stop breathing and bit his lip hard for a long time. He turned his head toward me, and tears began to roll down his cheeks. He pounded on his chest.

"Why me, why, why me?" he shouted angrily with his soft voice. Restraining my own emotions, I held his arms back to stop him from hitting himself. I looked at him with sorrowful eyes to try to console him. So much pain—I wished I could help him carry some of it. What could I say, what could I do?

"I don't know, Chu Tu. I am one of millions of human beings like yourself. How do I know . . ."

I felt my heart pounding violently as if it was breaking my chest. I could feel the blood inside my body moving and flowing in all different directions, through my veins, from small to big, from tissues to muscles, from skin to meat. A cold chill came over me, waking me, like a storm descending on life's one peaceful day. I helped Chu Tu move, to make him feel more comfortable.

"Here, Chu Tu, have some water. You'll feel better."

I let him drink some water and he wolfed it down without any feeling. The nurse pulled the stretcher next to the bed to move the other patient.

"I wish you much luck, my friend . . . I hope to see you before I go home." He lifted his head up and extended his hand out to shake Chu Tu's hand as the nurse pulled the stretcher away and the door closed behind them.

"Are you hungry now, Chu Tu? I think I better go and get something for you before breakfast is over."

"I don't want to eat anything. Get something for yourself."

I knew he needed to eat something to keep his strength up, but I didn't want to tell him, so I quietly walked out of the room. He needed to be alone. He needed to be alone to face his loss, a loss no one could ever restore.

I went to see the lady in the kitchen who had given me food before. I saw her putting some vegetables in a big pot of soup then running to the water basin to wash the dishes, all in a hurry.

"Let me help you, ma'am."

"Sure, I need it. I need these bowls now to serve our comrades." She handed me the coconut skin to wash them. I began to do the job like an expert. She walked over to the table to get the ladle to stir the soup. She removed the lid of the rice pot and put it back.

"It's almost done. You know, I have to do all this work on my own without any help. I'm old and I need some help. They never hire anybody to work with me. Oh, looks like you know how to do good work. Where did you learn it? My son never touched dishes in his life. Boys are not supposed to. I'm very surprised!"

"I used to help with my family's restaurant, ma'am."

"Oh, that means you know how to cook too. I wish you'd stay here. Does your family still have a restaurant?"

"No, ma'am. The VC took it over when they came."

"It's sad. Sometimes we can't do what we want to do in life, son, like myself. I have a piece of land on which I want to make a garden and build a small house just big enough for my family; on the rest I would plow and raise some rice in order for us to have enough food. I want to raise some ducks, chickens, pigs; I love to watch them crowd around and hear their noises when I feed them. That is my dream, son. It's so simple, isn't it?"

"Why don't you do it? What happened to your land?"

"The land is still smoldering after they bombed the area and we had to flee for our lives. I came here as a refugee. I don't know when I can go back there. It isn't safe, even now."

After I washed the dishes, I set them up on the table for her to put the soup and rice in. She asked me to take them to the comrades. When I finished my rounds I came back to get more till I was through with my errands. I walked down the hall, looking around, and, not seeing anyone, I snuck food from different plates and bowls. The hot food and the aroma from the steam increased my hunger. Finally, I came back to the kitchen; I was embarrassed to see her. She walked to the window and looked out, then turned around to look at the door to make sure no one was coming.

"Here, eat it fast and don't let anybody see you."

She gave me a small bowl of rice with some soup. In the bowl was sweet potato, cabbage, onion, and one small piece of meat the size of my thumb nail. I ate it quickly, but choked, something trapped in my esophagus. I swallowed slowly and drank some water and washed the food down, all the while on the lookout.

She walked out of the kitchen in a hurry just as I made a sound to thank her from my full mouth. When I was done, I began to clean up the kitchen. I wondered where she had gone. Why was she treating me so nicely, like one of her family? Was she a wonderful person or was she pretending, in order to lure me into a trap? I hated myself for mistrusting everybody. If she worked for them faithfully she wouldn't have given me food to eat. Maybe she was testing me to see if I was a good person or not. Was she waiting outside the kitchen, peeping through a hole in the wall to see what I was up to? She could tell the comrades to capture me if I did something wrong, and get on their good side. I wondered what would have happened if I had tried to walk away and gotten caught by the comrades. They would have crucified me and killed me for sure. Would she have been happy to see me grieving while I was dying? Wouldn't she? What would happen if I was her son, she the mother who had given birth to me, but she hadn't seen her son for years, and now we had crossed each other's paths? Did she have any emotions? I didn't know, but I knew mine. What would you feel if you ran into your mother and didn't have time to greet her and then you had to bid her farewell and die? Oh, God, why would you arrange things for us this way? There was no time for her, there was no time for me; not even the time to call my own mother, not even the time to call her own son . . . What was I thinking? I didn't trust myself anymore, and I felt guilty for this thought. I smiled to myself, shook my head slowly.

"What are you smiling about?" She peeped over my shoulder. I jumped up like a spark.

"You scared me!" I said. "I just finished cleaning the dishes. I haven't cleaned the pots yet. Do you think you could finish them? I have to go see my friend. I don't have any money to buy food, but is it okay if I sneak a little bowl of food for him?"

"Yes," she smiled. "But be very careful because I don't want to get in any trouble. I have to live for my children."

"Yes, ma'am. I'll never forget your generosity." I mixed some rice with the soup in a small bowl to take to Chu Tu.

"Here, use this plastic bag. It's easy for you to hide it in your shirt."

I put the food in a nylon bag and hid it in my pocket. As I walked out of the kitchen, the cadre VC nurse walked over toward the kitchen door and glanced at me curiously.

"Thiem Nam, do you have the food ready for me to eat? Who just walked out of here?"

"Oh, just a person who asked me if he could buy food for his comrade." She put the full dishes down on the table. "Your food is here." She said, then wiped the sweat on her forehead onto her long, black sleeve.

The cadre ran to the door and caught up to me when Thiem Nam told her that.

"Are you the person who just walked out of the kitchen?" Her face was puzzled, ready to be angry.

"Yes, ma'am." I stopped, turned around, and answered her. She wore a white cotton uniform without a name tag.

"What did you come to the kitchen for?" She looked at me from head to toe with a detective's eyes.

"I came there to ask if I could buy some food for my comrade."

"Who is your comrade?"

"Chu Tu. He's still in the intensive care unit."

"Don't you know you're supposed to bring your own food to the hospital?" She grinned suddenly, her black eyes lively.

"Yes, ma'am, but my comrade came here for an emergency,

and we didn't have time to bring any food with us. I think I may ask him if I can go to the market to buy food for him."

"Cadre, are you going to eat your food before it gets cold?" Thiem Nam popped her head out of the door from the kitchen and called to her.

"I'll check your comrade later."

She turned around and walked back to the kitchen. I headed back to Chu Tu's room, feeling like I had just passed the college exam for my school.

When I came to Chu Tu, I saw him lying there as if he was half-dead and half-alive. His face appeared tired; his eyes were staring at the ceiling. I didn't know what he was thinking; he was somber. Only he and I were in the room. The sun shone down on me through the window; I guessed it was about ten or eleven in the morning. The room was getting hotter and I didn't know why they called this room *Phong Lanh*, "Intensive Care Unit." There was only a small air conditioner in the room, running as if it was out of energy while the fan kept circulating stale smells, disturbing the air. The coconut and palm trees stood still, their leaves drooping like a flag without any wind. Outside, birds weren't singing or jumping joyfully. It seemed like everything was gone, and not promising to come back. I felt empty.

"Chu Tu, how do you feel? Here, eat some of this to give you some nourishment." I sat on the edge of the bed and gave him the food.

"I don't feel like eating. My leg aggravates me. I feel sore, a throbbing feeling."

"But you have to eat something. Look, your leg seems as if it's still bleeding." I saw a small bowl and spoon on the nightstand on the other side of the room. I took it and put the food into it from the nylon bag that I had gotten before. I propped him up and fed him. He ate it slowly, staring down at his leg, so I pulled the blanket over it.

"Did you mail my letter to my wife yet?"

"No, you didn't give me any letter. Are you sure you gave it to me? Maybe you gave it to someone else."

"Yesterday, I wrote it in the registration room. Then I gave it to you."

"No, Chu Tu. Do you remember you borrowed the paper and pencil from the nurse? I went to call the doctor for you; so you couldn't have given it to me."

"Yes, I recall." He began to search his pockets and he pulled out a letter, which was all wrinkled up.

"Here it is, I found it." He held it and waved it to me like a kid who had just found his toy. I was glad to see this sign of enthusiasm, of life.

"Do you want me to mail it now?" I took the letter and put it in my pocket.

"Yes."

"But first you have to eat some more." I placed the spoon in the bowl and served him. He ate it without reluctance. After I finished feeding him, I went out to the fountain and washed the bowl and spoon. I got some water in the bowl for Chu Tu to drink.

"I've been watching you for a long time now. Instead of treating me like an enemy, you treat me as if I'm your friend. I want to help you, but I don't know how," he said.

"Do the best you can, Chu Tu. Don't worry about anything. Try to relax so you can recover."

"You don't understand; you don't understand. Sooner or later they're going to kill you. I wonder how I can save you."

He closed his eyes and thought for a moment; then opened them as if he had just thought of something.

"Go and borrow a pen and paper for me. Hurry," he said, his eyes busy.

I went to the nurse's station and asked for a pen and paper. When I came back, Chu Tu took it and wrote, saying that I had saved his life and asked the authorities to make it easy for me. On the bottom of the note he signed his name, assistant chief of the "re-study camp."

"Keep this paper and use it whenever you go." He handed it to me. I folded it and put it in my pocket carefully, as if it were a piece of jewelry.

"One thing—don't escape, because if you do then we're both in trouble, especially between me and the Communist Party. You see, I have a wife and two children. I have duties as a husband, father, and member of the Communist Party. I want to help you, but I don't want my family involved. I am like the person who throws the javelin. I have to follow it."

"I understand, Chu Tu."

He lowered his voice.

"Would you get me some water?"

I gave him a bowl. He drank it and began to speak.

"Let me tell you my story. When I was young I went to school like the other kids. I was fortunate and had more chances than others since my father was a teacher at an elementary school in a small town. At that time, he was working for the French government and he spoke French very well, so we had all kinds of benefits from them. Somehow, I got involved in the students' "secret group" at school, which organized activities against the French, from underground publications to demonstrations. I didn't know that the organization was trying to take advantage of me, using my love for my country to further their own ends. One thing was for sure: I hated the commando army that came to the village searching for VCs. They captured people and tortured civilians, especially those who didn't know how to speak French. They kidnapped young girls and raped them like animals. My hatred remains even now, when I think about the army that was hired by the French government to do these inhuman acts." He took a sip of water, took a breath and continued.

"I felt I had to do something for my country, for I was young and arrogant. I had to do what I had to do."

"If I were you, I wouldn't have had any choice either. Who was the leader at that time?" I said. "Was it Ho Chi Minh?"

"No, we had our own group. We also had our own local leader because at that time Ho Chi Minh was in the north. The real battle was between the French and the Vietnamese. We had a slogan: "Let's get our independence and fight the foreigners." We had to regroup and go to the north and struggle. After dinner one night I talked to my father about my idea to go north, but he told me that was not the appropriate way to go about it. He demanded that I complete school first and see what happened next, he said that way I could do something later when I was old enough to judge my actions. I pretended to listen to him and acted normally, as if nothing was happening. I left school, family, and friends, and went to contend with the war. On the way up north, there were so many things happened to me—but I'll tell you that later."

He settled back onto his pillow for a moment, recovering his breath. Then he leaned forward, grasped my wrist and gave it a squeeze as he looked into my eyes. "Now," he said, "Let me tell you about my love. On the road I met a girl whom I knew when I was little. I was from a prominent family and she was from a poor family. She was young and beautiful. I didn't expect to run into her on the way to war. We fell in love and we shared many pleasurable and many dismal moments. When we arrived in the north we had such a warm welcome from Uncle Ho. We had many meetings. Finally, Ho Chi Minh declared: 'This is the time we have to do something for our homeland; we have to sit together, united, hand in hand, to fight the French to get our independence back. We have suffered enough, especially the people in the south; our relatives, our brothers . . . I want to thank all of you who have already sacrificed yourselves and left your families behind, your wives, children, and lovers. But we have to share this kind of pain: no freedom, no democracy.' After this, the party arranged everyone's marriages. Northern comrades were married to the southern women who had just come over. Southern men were married to the northern cadres, female VC. Oh, my love, we're separated by two other people; she has to live with someone whom she doesn't love and I have to live with someone I don't love. After the training, the Party assigned us to different areas and we never saw each other again." Chu Tu paused for breath and continued, "I still love her even though I live with my wife now. I have a big responsibility on my shoulders whether I love my wife or not. Many things have happened in my life, but not the way I wanted them to. It is too complicated to explain." He sighed and his eyes dropped down to his half-leg like he was tired of life.

I looked at his pale face, wondering what to say.

"You have met your challenge," I said. "You have taken your chances. You did your best and you have to accept the way you are, whether it's painful or happy. You have to be proud of you, Chu Tu! I wonder, if I were you, what would happen to me."

Suddenly the door opened. The nurse walked in to check Chu Tu. She had a stethoscope around her neck. She looked at Chu Tu's eyes, checked his heartbeat, pulse. She pulled the blanket down to look at his leg.

"It has stopped bleeding. You're okay now, but don't move a lot as it will start bleeding again. I think I can transfer you out of the Intensive Care Unit."

"Can you pull the stretcher over?" she asked me.

I grasped it and put it beside the bed. I helped her lift Chu Tu onto the stretcher. I pushed it out of the room.

"Where are we bringing him, ma'am?"

"Follow that hall straight ahead to the last room on the right." She walked in front of me and I pushed the stretcher behind her as she shouted at people to move away. We came to the room. There were a few beds, some occupied, one empty. People looked at us curiously when we came into the room. I didn't know whether they were expecting their relatives or friends or another patient. The room was a pale color, like some of the patients' faces. On the top of each bed was a net, which was folded till the patients were ready to go to sleep. There was one fluorescent light about one meter long in the middle of the ceiling. Near the window, people had hung their clothes to dry.

Outside the window was a courtyard, with pebbles and stone paths that circled the garden and crossed over it. It was humid now and the shadows of some surrounding trees were shading the people from the hot sun. In a corner of a court-yard, an elderly woman collected wood for a cooking fire. By the fire an infant lay on a small mat, crying. Then, with one hand she fanned the baby and with the other hand she put the wood into the fire. She turned and called a child, who was scampering around with another child. The baby kept crying, so she patted his bottom to lull him to sleep. In the distance were two trees, and beside the farthest one was a bench. An old man who didn't care if the sun was shining on his face slept on the bench. Sometimes his jaw moved like he wanted to eat. His cheeks were indented and I could see the wrinkles around his mouth. A child was yanking his hand, trying to wake him.

I left the room and walked to the entrance of the hospital to mail Chu Tu's letter. Two guards were busy in the booth at the side of the road near the gate, watching and checking people.

I thought about Chu Tu, lying inside and how far I had come from when I first decided to be kind to him. Then, I thought only of using him as a means to spark a conflict among the guards; but he had touched something deeper in me, something more fundamental than any plot. I had came to understand that he was a victim, a human being caught in a stupid conflict of ideology, like myself, and I felt compassion for him.

But now I was in his hands and he still wouldn't let me go, even though freedom seemed so near, a real possibility. Instead, he clung to excuses, dodging the problem. The hardest thing in life is to learn to let go, I realized—for both him and me.

They had told me that if I escaped, the others would be punished. But surely Chu Tu would not be so stupid as to report to headquarters that I had escaped; he would lose face and dignity in front of his comrades. Considering the confusion which the Cambodian attack had brought to our camp, and the difficulty Chu Tu would have keeping charge of me in his medically weakened condition, I did not think they would punish him if he said that the best course of action seemed to him to release me. I hoped that Chu Tu would understand me as I understood him. I hoped that the Communist Party would let him retire, now that he was disabled and of less use to them. I wanted him to make his dream come true, to go back to his relatives, inherit a bit of land, and live in peace with his wife and children. Perhaps, by acting now, I could help him learn to let go.

But I had my own life to think of, too. "They never release any prisoner except by death," the cook in the hospital had said. In the end, I could not let their threats of what might happen freeze me, keep me from acting, prevent me from reaching for my chance to live. I wished Chu Tu and the prisoners I had left behind all the luck in the world, and I took a moment to appreciate them for whatever they had done for me in the camp, in spite of the cruelty, because it was a worthy lesson and the most expensive one I had ever learned. Buddha never abandoned his son, I thought, and prayed.

Slowly, I crossed the street.

Book III

CHAPTER I

I was free for the first time, without a guard watching me. Temporarily, I pretended to be a beggar, sitting on the filthy cement floor at the Chau Doc bus station, looking for transportation back home to my friend, Hanh, in Sa Dec town. I saw travelers rushing back and forth, getting off and on the bus. I felt I could travel like them to any destination: my world, my dream, my family . . . a place beyond my imagination. Am I really alive? Am I really free? Did I really escape? Yes, yes. I laughed, starting, almost afraid I might wake up. I touched myself to be sure. I saw an attractive young woman, carrying a grass bag, pass by. I grasped her bag and put my hand out, "Please, for the poor." She put a coin in my palm and I felt its coldness. I jumped up and bounced around the rusted iron pillars with my happiness. People stared at me, thinking I was crazy, but they didn't know that the crazy one was the happiest one on earth. I laughed loudly until my stomach ached. The abandoned children surrounded me. We shared our food like a big family. We could eat anytime we liked. We could walk anywhere we wanted and we were limited only by our imaginations. Suddenly, I saw a cowskin colored uniform; a policeman handcuffed a lady on the bus and took her away at gunpoint. What kind of freedom did my future hold, I wondered?

The last time I had seen Hanh was three years ago in 1975, when we had tried to escape the country. When he saw me alive again, our reunion was filled with tears, laughter, and embraces.

His family took me in, and in the next week I regained my health, put some flesh on my bones, and got to know Hanh again. He liked to dress up now, although his clothes didn't really create a better look for him. In any case, he didn't let his limp keep him from having a dashing style. He had dark skin and at first glance looked rather African, though his hair was straight. His nose was prominent, while his broad forehead gave an impression of intelligence and determination. He had a wonderful heart and a rare soul.

Hanh lived in Sa Dec, a small town about 100 kilometers from my hometown. His father, who died just before Hanh finished elementary school had been an English teacher at a local high school. Hanh spoke English well. His mother was a nurse in the community. Two older brothers were now in a labor camp in Dong Thap. Hanh had an uncle who had gone north to join Ho Chi Minh to fight against the French in 1945, and this uncle had returned to Sa dec to take charge of the secret police in the county after Saigon fell on April 30, 1975. Hanh's mother asked this uncle to register me with the police, telling them that I was her adopted son. Indeed, Hanh's parents did treat me like their own son. I had a temporary place to live now but I knew my identity was precarious. The government was very restrictive: every household had to report to the police whoever was in your house, who comes for a visit, where you go, for how long, and what purpose. The government watched us like a hawk. Maybe I would have to move on somewhere but I didn't know where or when. I couldn't go back to my family and I couldn't return to my relatives because most of them lived in the same village and the VC would recognize every resident.

Hanh knew I missed my family terribly and he tried to con-

tact them to pass the news that I was here and that I was okay.
My youngest sister stopped by for a visit on her way to volunteer at a youth work camp in Dong Thap. She had to work
there two weeks a month, in exchange for my parents remaining on the farm. We sat on a broken bench beneath a plum
tree, where there were hundreds of petals lying on the dusty
ground. They weren't like ordinary petals but were shaped like
delicate needles, white on the tip like tiny matches.

Kha looked at me with joy showing through her tears. "You
are so thin," she said, worried. She wore a grey blouse and
satin pants.

"I'm okay. How is our family?"

Kha began sobbing. She was still young like when I was at
home, but now she had the worried look of a mature woman
on her face.

"Anh Hai is in the labor camp. Anh Tuong disappeared
without any news. We think he's dead. If he was lucky, he escaped . . ." She stopped for a moment and sighed. I waited for
her to calm down and avoided looking at her. I held my stick
and poked the ground.

"What else happened?"

"Anh Sau vanished since Quang Tri fell. He was stationed
in Chu Lai. I thought you knew about it. It happened before
Saigon lost."

"Yeah, I remember."

"I think they captured him and threw him in jail somewhere."

"How about Lang?"

"He's in a labor camp somewhere. We don't know exactly
but we heard from his wife in Saigon."

"How about Baba? Is he doing all right?"

"When the government took our house and everything in
the city, they threw us into the new 'economy zone.' You
know Baba, he worries a lot. He lost a lot of weight, doesn't
eat regularly like he used to. He's always afraid we won't have
enough food to eat so we begged the authorities to let us move
back to our estate in the village. They let us move there. Then
they had a meeting in the village to execute Baba, but the
people told the VC not to because he wasn't guilty of any-

thing. He was rich because he worked hard. He ate with us from the same table, he helped us when we needed him . . . I don't know, brother, you know them. They called it a cultural revolution or whatever. Baba is still doing okay now."

"How about the rest of us?"

"Anh Lan is in hiding at Aunt Muoi's estate. Anh Tam is somewhere with his friends in hiding or in the labor camp. I don't know. The rest of us are staying on the farm."

"What happened to mama?" I asked.

"She cries a lot. You know her. She keeps talking about you, asking me what has happened to her sons. She talks to herself and I'm afraid she will lose her mind."

My eyes were stinging. I took a deep breath to regain my composure while I stroked my sister's head to comfort her.

I stood up and paced back and forth along the fence. A bird landed on the plum tree and petals flew down; another bird came and they began to chirp as my sister's voice echoed. Then Kha left for home. I wanted to help my family, but how could I when I couldn't take care of myself? I felt frustrated and powerless. My tears came.

little dust ball flew up in the air, spread out, then disappeared in the heat on the road. The green trees were exhausted. The voices of spring birds scattered away. Hanh and I walked into the backyard and came to the bench beneath the plum tree's shadow to sit.

"I don't think it's safe here," I said. "We must plan something."

"Yeah, if my uncle gets transferred or anything happens to him, then what will we do about you?" Hanh said. His eyes narrowed. "We should take advantage of him while he's here."

"But how?" I said.

We sat quietly and thought for a while. Hanh bit his thick lips and cupped his big forehead.

"I have an idea!" I exclaimed.

Hanh looked around to see if anybody was in the bushes.

"If you can steal your uncle's papers then we can make fake ones for ourselves," I said. "We can go to different places to find a way out of the country."

"I never thought of that. We are stuck here because we have no papers to go anywhere."

"See, if the police discover me they will take all your family assets and throw all of us in jail. Even your uncle won't help because he would lose the trust of the Communist Party," I said. "Do you know anyone who can make a duplicate seal like the stamp on your uncle's paper?"

"I don't know anybody, but we can try to do it ourselves," Hanh replied.

"I know I'm a burden for you and your family, but I have nobody to turn to. Besides, you're my best friend. I wish I had some money," I sighed. "I hope that someday I can pay you back."

"Stop it. We are lucky to be together. I'll steal my uncle's papers this week and figure out the money for our expenses later." He patted me on the shoulder to give me confidence. I had to laugh: Hanh seemed to figure things out before I even thought of them.

"We have to do it fast."

"I'm going to town to see if there is any news," Hanh said, hoisting himself away.

He hopped onto his bike and rode out of the gate. I came back into the house, chatted with his uncle, trying to get something out of him. My friend came back later but there wasn't anything extraordinary. Hanh began to observe his uncle closely to learn his habits.

Two days later Hanh stole the papers from his uncle when he was drunk. We used a raw banana to make the seal.

"Damn it. It's not working," Hanh said as he used the banana to stamp the paper.

"How about potatoes?" I said.

"No, I don't think it's going to work."

"I wish we had a copy machine. Do you know anybody who has one?"

"The government took everything, especially the kind of equipment that is related to publishing. They don't want any pamphlets around the streets. No new revolution, remember?" Hanh answered.

"Hey, why don't we try a cork? Wait here."

I ran out of the house to the side of the river and cut a piece from the cork trees growing in the mud and came back.

"I think this will work," I shouted confidently.

Hanh carved the cork into the shape of a seal with the words "Department of the Secret Police." We put the stamp in ink and stamped the paper.

"It's too much ink; give me the rag," Hanh said.

I gave him the rag, and he dabbed some ink off the seal and stamped the paper again.

"Look, it looks okay," I said.

I looked at the scrap paper. It looked unclear; I could barely see the seal.

"That's what we want. We don't want them to see it clearly because it would make it easy for them to identify the name on it."

"Yeah, I forgot about that," said Hanh.

"Where do you think we can get a typewriter and some red ink?"

"I don't know, but there must be a way," Hanh answered.

I used a piece of paper to copy the document exactly the way it looked, without missing a word, even a comma, a period or a dot. After I finished I gave the original to Hanh.

"Go put it back before he wakes up!"

He took it and went into the living room where his uncle was sleeping. I put things away and hid the seal we had just made near the stove. Hanh returned, smiling at me.

"It's all done. Not bad for a start, huh . . ."

We stepped out of the house and strolled along the river.

"Hey, I think Phuoc, the schoolteacher, has a typewriter. I'll go see him tomorrow if he's around," Hanh said.

"What is he doing lately? Do you know?"

"The government is letting him teach still but they're watching him very closely—he's a member of a Catholic congregation, after all," Hanh said. "They don't pay him enough so he has to use his bicycle for a taxi to make money. His two children sell cigarettes at the bus station."

"You gave me an idea—why not get him involved?"

We came back to the house in good spirits. His uncle woke up and drank some tea. The night came quietly. I could hear dogs barking from time to time on the road. Once in a while the dogs howled loudly because they were hungry. Next morning Hanh and I went to the bus station to find teacher Phuoc. We saw him sitting on his bike waiting for customers. We came to him.

"Hello, teacher."

He looked at us inquiringly, wondering what we were up to.

"Don't call me teacher," he whispered to us.

I pretended to be a customer. "I need a ride downtown. How much does it cost?" I got off from the back of Hanh's bike, jumped onto the back of Phuoc's.

"Twenty dong," Phuoc said loudly so all the other bikers could hear him, so that they wouldn't be suspicious.

"Okay, let's go. I'm in a hurry."

We pedaled out of the lot onto the boulevard to downtown,

while Hanh followed along, first behind and then beside us.

"How are things, teacher?"

"It's getting tougher every day. I don't know what to do with my situation anymore."

"Don't give up hope, teacher. I have something really interesting. We can help each other."

I pulled out the piece of paper that I had hand-copied yesterday and gave it to him. He looked at it while holding onto his bike with the other hand.

"Where did you get this?"

"From Hanh's uncle. But we have to type the whole thing again, and put our names on it. Then we can use it temporarily," I said. "Do you have a typewriter?"

"No, I sold it years ago."

"Do you know of anyone who does?"

He signaled to us to stop talking because there were some bikers passing by. The tamarind trees stood along the road as the sun peeked through them but the shadow wasn't strong enough to completely shade us. We could see our own shadows moving, chasing one another.

"I may contact my church. They may have something I can use." He asked, "How about the seal?"

"We have the seal at home." I said.

Hanh turned to him and said, "If you can ask them to do the whole thing we can pay them. That makes it easier."

"Okay, let me figure it out."

"We'll see you tomorrow then."

We stopped at the side of the road. I went back to Hanh's bike. The wind blew against us on the road, making it harder for Hanh to pedal. Few cars passed by. We rode away.

There were many more bicycles than scooters or cars now. The only cars or scooters on the road were operated by officers of the government. Everything was tightening up and resources were running out. We had electricity in the city only once or twice a week, forcing us to use oil lamps or candles the rest of the time. We couldn't travel anywhere without permission from the secret police. Even if they let us go, we had to have a very good reason, like the death of a relative; and when we arrived at a destination, we had to report to the secret police there. We could never say what we wanted to—we lived like deaf people, always pretending not to hear, not to know. You only speak the way the Party wants you to. We couldn't practice our own religion. They trained the children to sing the Communist song, encouraging them to report whatever their parents or relatives said at home. They could send the secret police to your home anytime there was anything suspicious. You had to be a good citizen in order to vote. A good citizen is someone who turns you in, kills your relatives, or makes you do exactly what they want you to do.

Suddenly a whistle blew, with someone shouting in front of us.

"Stop or I'll shoot!"

I saw a child running from the market with the police after him. He darted into the crowd and the policeman cocked his rifle, shooting in the air. We stopped the bike on the other side of the road, as three more secret police ran yelling after the boy.

"Let's go home. I don't think it's good to get into trouble," I said.

We climbed on the bike and headed back home thinking. When is this government going to change?

When the night came, Hanh's uncle had already left saying that he had to be at his office. Hanh's mother, sister, and the kids went to bed early. Hanh and I sat in the kitchen discussing how to get involved with the group that fights against the government.

"I heard there is a Hoa Hao religion group in Thot Not that is fighting against the government right now," I said.

"The VCs killed their leader; that's why the Hoa Hao have fought against them for years," Hanh said. "Where there are Hoa Hao then there are no VC. Where there are VC there are no Hoa Hao."

"I know that, but do they have a strong force? We don't want to be executed or put in prison."

"We can check it out," Hanh replied, raising his black eyebrows.

"Do you know any members?" I asked. "I'm out of luck since I returned from the labor camp. I don't know anyone anymore." I took a heavy breath.

"We can check with teacher Phuoc because right now they are having a religion movement." Hanh was excited. He said, "They are trying to unite all religions to fight back."

"Do you think it's better for us to stay and fight, or to escape?" I asked.

"It's much easier to escape than to stay and fight. We have no support and no troops."

"How about the people and our patriotism?"

"Nobody gives a damn anymore. If they really care, why don't they stay and fight?" Hanh answered angrily. "They just run away like cowards. Nowadays no one speaks about patriotism."

"Are you suggesting that we are a part of that? What happened to our youth and our dream?" I said. "I'm an idealist."

"This is our real life. Keep your ideals and morals in the closet and let's do what we have to do today," Hanh said. "If we escape successfully and get an education, then we can do something for our country. Isn't that much better for us than to run around hiding? Otherwise we will jeopardize our families," Hanh speculated.

"I agree. But why don't we try both things to see which one we can grasp, then we can decide."

All of a sudden we heard a noise that sounded like something falling down outside the house, with footsteps running in front. Hanh blew out the lamp. He went to the window; I went to the back door. It was about 11:00 p.m., but it wasn't too dark to see shadows moving along the bushes and on the road, making a clicking sound as metal struck against the wire fence. Someone leaped over the fence, scampering into our yard. The dog next door barked, snarling at the shadow. There was a hard rap at the door as if they wanted to break it in. Hanh tiptoed over to me.

"What's going on?" he whispered in my ear.

"Don't tell me our teacher betrayed us!"

My heart beat faster. I could feel it throbbing.

"Are we going to run away or pretend nothing happened?" I asked.

"It's too late now. They are all around the house. We will get shot if we run out. You pretend to sleep on the bed. I'll call my mother to open the door."

The rapping continued, stronger.

"Open the door!" a voice shouted. "Open the door!"

Hanh's mother came down the stairs, lighting a lamp and saying, "Who's that?"

"Secret police."

"Wait, I'll get the lamp."

She held the lamp and walked over to the door and opened it. They poured into the house. One of the secret police stood next to her and asked, "Where is your family registration paper?"

She walked to the cabinet near the altar, opened a drawer and searched for the list of family members, but she couldn't find it. While she was looking the other police used a flashlight to search in every room.

"I can't find the papers; let me ask my son."

"If you don't have it you will all go to the station."

"Hanh, have you seen the list of names that your uncle gave to me a few days ago?" she shouted upstairs. Hanh came down, rubbing his eyes like he had been asleep.

"It's in the kitchen somewhere, mother."

"Move out!" a secret policeman screamed, pointing his rifle at us. The children began crying hysterically. Everyone walked out the front door into the yard. Hanh and his mother walked into the kitchen, found the paper, and came also. She handed it to the secret police. Another kept searching the house while we were outside. The secret policeman who held the papers stood on the porch, calling out each name. One of the policemen inside the house came to the porch to report.

"We couldn't find anything, comrade."

"Did you look on the roof and in the ceiling?"

"Yes, comrade."

The policeman who was holding the paper turned to Hanh's mother.

"We have a report that you are hiding a soldier in your house. Where is he?"

"I am not hiding anybody, comrade. I'm a good citizen. Everyone knows me here. My brother is a secret policeman also."

"What's his name? Is he in our unit?"

"No, comrade. He works in the city," she said.

"I don't care who he is but if he stays here you have to report it to us."

He began to let us in one at a time, calling our names one by one. When he came to my name, he looked at my face.

"Why is your family name different from this family?"

"He's my nephew. I raised him since he was small," Hanh's mother answered.

"Why is his name recently on the list? The date shows it right here," he stared at me with his insistent eyes, beating his finger against the paper where the date was stamped.

"My brother took it down to the office to register for my adopted son to serve on the labor force in a 'new economy zone'."

"You come to see me at the station tomorrow," he said to me, giving the list back to Hanh's mother.

"You can all go in now."

We went into the house and got back in bed but I couldn't sleep since I didn't know what would happen to me the next day. The children were quiet now. The dog lay still on the floor. The police moved on to other houses. The roosters crowed at 12:00 a.m. A dog from the neighborhood barked in the distance. The night became restless, lasting forever.

I woke up when Hanh pulled my leg and the sun was shining into my eyes.

"Hey, time for you to go to the police station."

I got up, went to the backyard to wash my face in the bucket next to the river.

Hanh carried some water into the house so that they could do the dishes. I came in, wondering where everybody was. Hanh told me that his mother was at the black market selling goods. His mother had become a vendor when the VC had taken over the city, since she couldn't support the family with the salary paid to nurses. Hanh's sister went to get in line at the government commissary to wait and buy some food, Hanh was left in charge of the children.

"Where did you hide the seal yesterday? I thought we were finished last night."

"I hid it in the stack of wood in the kitchen. Even if they see the wood pile they won't think anything of it."

"Good."

He called his niece and nephew in to eat, then told them what to do, and to watch over each other. We got the bike out and rode off.

We arrived at the police station, which had been the house of a colonel in the southern army. I found myself wondering how many families had been executed since they had taken over.

"I'm going to find teacher Phuoc at the bus station to see what happened. I will come back to get you. Be careful what you say," Hanh whispered to me as I got off the bike.

"If I'm out early I'll walk home. If you don't see me here then don't wait."

I walked into the gate and asked the guard to let me in. When I came into the living room I saw several people sitting around waiting. I told the guard at the corner that I was here to report to the police because they told me to come here today when they searched our house last night. The guard said, "Come with me."

He walked in front of me, through the hall, and I heard laughing from the room across. He knocked on the door.

"Captain, there is someone here for you to interrogate."

"Let him in."

I had heard the same voice the night before. The guard opened the door to let me in. I stepped inside the room fretfully. I saw him propped in the wood chair next to the window, facing his desk. I bowed to him. He didn't say anything but looked at me from head to toe as if he was looking for something suspicious. This room had been a bedroom but they had converted it into an office. I felt like there was no air to breathe. He stood up, walked around the room for about two minutes and stopped in front of me.

"Are you sure your aunt told me the truth last night?"

"Yes, comrade."

"I don't think so. I know you are a liar," He walked to his desk, picked up a cane and tapped the desk, pausing. "Do you know how long you will be in the labor camp?" He wore the cow-colored uniform.

I couldn't stop my heart from bouncing but said, "I am telling the truth, comrade." And I tried to look innocent.

"No, I don't want this kind of truth. I want the real truth."

"I have nothing to hide from you, comrade. I'm an innocent citizen."

"But why haven't I seen you before?" He drilled into me with his eyes. "Your name is different from your aunt's family and you just moved in there recently."

I did not dare to look away. "My parents died when I was young, I have no family and my aunt took care of me since I was little."

"Oh, if your aunt took care of you since you were little, your aunt would have to fill out a birth certificate for you with the same last name as hers. So that means you are a liar."

The air was thick inside the room. I tried to be calm.

"No, comrade. She didn't change anything. She just kept my old birth certificate."

"So where were you from April 30th till now?"

"My aunt's family is poor. We don't have enough food to eat so she sent me off to Cholon to work for a Chinese factory. The owner volunteered to give the factory to the government. I came back to my aunt."

"That action is against us because you quit your job, refusing to work for the government," he said, and slammed his hand on the desk.

"I want the truth. I've had enough chitchat!" He glared at me furiously, his eyes deep red.

He pulled out a plain piece of paper with a pencil and gave them to me.

"Write your family tree and confession on this. I want to know your great grandparents down to you. And remember I don't want anything missing in there."

"Do you want me to write their occupation, where they are from, financial status, and relationship to the old government?" I pretended not to know what he wanted.

"Yes." He walked over to the window and closed the curtain, making it darker in the room. Then he walked out the door and slammed it. I picked up the pencil, began to write my name on the top, my address, and the whole history of my family. I had done this so many times in the labor camp that I had memorized every word to put down on the paper.

From another room I heard someone moaning. Once in a while a body was slammed against the wall, making the room shake. "I told you to tell the truth. I'm fed up with your lies. Where did you hide the gun and bullets?"

The northerner's accent grated on me. My hands shook and I began to sweat. The captain opened the door, came right over to me, picked up my confession and plopped into his chair as he read it in silence. Every time he ended a sentence he glanced at me, then looked at the paper again. The texture of the paper was very poor and I was afraid the words would disappear under the force of his eyes. He tried to find flaw in my confession.

"I want your aunt to be here this afternoon and I want you to be here tomorrow morning. You have to report to me every day until my investigation is finished." The captain said. "You can go now."

I bowed to him and left the room. When I got out of the building I felt as if my breath had been taken away from me and then returned again. The heavy rock was taken off my back. There was no sign of Hanh. The sun shone strongly. My legs seemed crippled because they wouldn't respond to my brain's signal. I sat down for a minute, then I rose and hurried down the road back home.

* * *

When I came home Hanh's mother hadn't come back yet. Hanh was chopping wood in the back yard.

"We need to go to the black market to find your mother right away because she has to report to the station this afternoon."

"Why do you look so pale?" Hanh asked. "Did they beat you up?"

I shook my head, out of breath. Hanh threw the ax down on the ground and took his bike out of the house. We darted away.

We talked as we rode along.

"I have to tell your mother the story I wrote on my confession, so she will know what to say when the police interrogate her. We have to stick with the story."

"Is that a lesson you learned in the labor camp?"

"Yes, a really expensive one."

"You have experience dealing with the police now," Hanh laughed, confident in me.

"You know, we are very lucky, because if the captain who interrogated me this morning had demanded that your mother and I report at the same time, we would be in big trouble." I paused, then asked, "What happened to teacher Phuoc?"

"We are all set." He pulled the paper from his pocket and gave it to me.

I opened it and it looked exactly like the original just a little unclear where we had stamped.

"It's very good. How much did you pay?"

"Never mind about the money. I had enough money to pay."

"Was there any luck with the Catholic group?"

"I talked to the teacher, and he said he would take me there to talk to them himself, since nobody would trust us to go there by ourselves."

"When do you plan to go with him?" I said. "I have to report to the police every day now."

"You have to report to them every day? How is our plan going to work if I'm the only one who does it?" Hanh said, disappointed. "I want to take you along to the meeting in a few days when my teacher contacts me."

"I report to them but I don't think I'll be there the whole day."

We rode a bike around the block, looking for his mother where the black market was located.

"You search this side. I'll search the other."

The little street was noisy with people walking around bargaining their goods.

"There, there she is. Stop the bike!" I shouted to Hanh.

He stopped the bike and I jumped off. We came to his mother, who was busy paying for a small bag of monosodium. I helped to carry the bag, put it on the bike, and the three of us walked away. I told Hanh's mother about the story I had written on my confession, and asked her to tell the same story. We came home and ate our lunch.

"It was a good day at the market since the police didn't chase us today," Hanh's mother said. "They want to control the black market. That's why they are always after us. Yesterday they captured my friend, took her goods, and put her in jail. I don't know where our future lies," she sighed.

After she finished lunch she left for the police station.

Hanh and I began chopping wood and carrying buckets of water from the river to fill the big barrels. The children were playing in the yard behind the fence, silhouettes on the playground, drawing lines on the ground to play hopscotch. The air seemed to stand still. At our neighbors', a funeral was going on, and mourners stopped in and out. Occasionally, you could hear a drum beat. The sound from a *dan co*, a string instrument, would chime when someone stood bowing. The music blended with the crying and lamenting, working its way into my heart. We waited for Hanh's mother to come back but it seemed so long.

"What do you think the police will ask your mother?"

"Same questions," Hanh said, showing concern on his face.

"You know the policemen's job. It takes them half a day to read a confession, another week to question you." I said, "Can you imagine, a bunch of illiterates running the government? What will our future be like?"

"Prison for sure."

"We have our papers but we can't go yet," Hanh said. "I hope there isn't much of a hassle reporting to the police."

"If teacher Phuoc contacts you, go by yourself if I'm at the police station," I instructed him. "Otherwise, suggest to him that we go in the afternoon because I will have more of a chance than in the morning."

"Yeah, I'll talk to him when I see him tomorrow at the bus station."

We heard the children calling their grandmother at the gate in front. They stopped playing hopscotch and ran to her. We went into the house through the back door.

"How was it, mama?" asked Hanh.

"Oh, it was nothing. They just put me in a room and questioned me. I told them the story you told me but they kept repeating the same questions over and over."

"Is there anything important that they asked, mama?"

"No, but I heard something about the killing of our neighbor when I was sitting there. I think they killed him in cold blood," she said. "Oh, remind me about the meeting tomorrow. The police will gather the whole district to talk about the new economy zone, about our responsibilities to perform duties at the work camp. I think some of us will have to go to the work camp to slave for them and we will even have to bring our own food."

We went to sit at the dinner table in the kitchen. Hanh's sister-in-law began to prepare dinner. She checked the green beans in the basket for worms, then went to the stove and gathered some wood to build a fire. I went to carry in some wood. Hanh's mother went into the bedroom; she laid down, worried. When I came back, the rice pot was already sitting on the fire. I heard one of the children yelling for their mother from the playground. She asked Hanh to go out to check on them. Hanh walked out from the back door, calling the kids in. The children came to her but one of them was still complaining, "You owe me one game, you better pay me back tomorrow."

Hanh stood next to the big water bucket near the river at the back of the house. He held a small can, scooping the water into it.

"Put your hands out and bend down."

One of the children would hold his hands out, rubbing them together as Hanh poured water over them. When there was no more water, he filled another jug, putting some on his hands to wipe the children's faces. After he finished cleaning them up he told them to go inside, and not to disturb their grandmother. Smoke came out from the window, from the side of the stove, swooping into the air. Dinner was served when Hanh's mother came into the kitchen. Hanh's sister-in-law gave each child a bowl of rice with some fish and vegetables, asking them to sit quietly to eat. The afternoon was gone. Dusk fell upon us. The fluorescent light came on. It felt good to have electricity even though we only had it once a week. It was not a necessity of life anymore, but a luxury. We didn't have to rush to prepare our dinner like the other days. We ate our dinner.

"Do you want some more rice?" Hanh's sister-in-law asked me.

I nodded my head and gave her the bowl. She scooped some rice into my bowl from the pot and gave it back to me. I held it up to my mouth, using my chopsticks to push it in. It was hot and good but I felt guilty that I had to live off others.

I hoped I could help them someday, but right then it was only a dream.

Dinner was over, and Hanh's sister-in-law was busy doing dishes. Hanh and his mother left for the funeral next door. After Hue finished cleaning up in the kitchen, she took the children upstairs and mended their clothes. I went out to the porch to sit, looking over to the funeral next door and thinking about home. I couldn't stand it so I went to bed.

I hadn't heard any news from my family since my sister visited and I couldn't return home because I didn't want to end up in a labor camp again. Hanh and I got involved with an anti-government organization; our mission was to transport pamphlets from our town to another. But the job was dangerous and we knew it wasn't going to accomplish anything so we quit, and began to focus on a way to escape. We had heard through Phuoc about the possibility of buying places on a boat leaving the country. It would be expensive, but Hanh and I were both determined to find a way to do it.

After I reported to the police a few times, wrote a bunch of confessions and self-criticism and learned more about hassles, Hanh bought a pack of Salem cigarettes and a zippo lighter from the black market; he gave them to me to bribe the police, since he had heard me say that the captain loved to smoke. Who would refuse a foreign product as a gift? The captain took our gift happily and told me that I didn't have to report to him for a few days. Hanh and I were riding home after my interrogation, and I told him what had happened.

"Hey, our plan is working. He loved the bribe."

"That's very good. But we have to watch out because when we run out of bait we'll run out of time," Hanh replied.

"Keep reminding me of that," I said. "Do you know that since they have taken over the south they have killed more of us than they did during the war?"

Hanh became quiet when we reached the avenue. It was crowded with people who were cleaning up the street. Some of them were sweeping the sidewalk. The dust blew up in the air. The trees on both sides of the avenue seemed suffocated with dust.

Hanh turned at the corner and rode into the bus station, where there were many people and vendors standing around. Because they were running out of parts, few buses were at the station. Several of the buses were just parked there. Some of them only ran once or twice a week since there was a gas short-age, but not many bus drivers wanted to do anything else, be-cause if they did, they would have to surrender their buses to the government and slave for them. After the north invaded the south, my whole country, once the land of waving palms, had turned into one of the poorest nations in the world; our people had become homeless beggars.

"Where is teacher Phuoc? I don't see him."

My eyes opened wide, searching through the crowd of people on bicycles.

"He isn't here. He's waiting near the public rest room."

"Watch out, watch out!" someone shouted.

A chill ran up my spine. I turned around to see what had happened. I saw another bike coming towards us with a pas-senger on back, followed by another.

"He's my customer. It's my turn."

"Nobody is your customer, if you move fast then you get them!" one biker shouted back and both of the bikes swooshed by us so fast that I could feel the wind. They were fighting over the customer.

"There he is," called Hanh.

I jumped off the bike, walked into the public rest room and pretended to use it. Then I came out to hold the bike for Hanh so he could do the same thing. Teacher Phuoc saw us and brought his bike closer. I walked over to him and sat on the back of his bike and we rode off with Hanh behind us. When we came to the boulevard we started talking about our plan.

"Teacher, are you sure we can trust these people?"

"They are Catholic, don't worry," he assured us.

"We have to protect ourselves. Our neighbor was killed yesterday."

"These contacts are close friends of mine."

"Do they know the right channels?" Hanh spoke up.

"Don't worry!" teacher Phuoc said.

We rode about twenty minutes and turned onto a dirt road with fences around. Teacher Phuoc signaled to us not to talk. We got off the bike to walk to the gate.

"Do you have some eggs for sale today?" teacher Phuoc

yelled at the gate. He was using code language; white eggs meant escape and brown eggs referred to a resistance organization. I saw a tall lady walk out of the house with a little dog to see who we were.

"We don't have many eggs today. We have about two dozen left. Is that all right, sir?"

"Sure," Phuoc answered.

"Come in then and pick up the eggs," the lady spoke loudly, as if she wanted her neighbors to hear.

We followed her through the gate. She closed it behind us and we continued past the house to the chicken coop. We left the bikes at the side of the house, and I saw a man in black pajamas like a VC uniform working in the garden next to the chicken coop. He took off his hat and smiled at teacher Phuoc.

"Hello there. I haven't seen you for so long. I asked one of your students to tell you to come and pick up the eggs but I didn't know if the message would reach you."

"Yes, I got the message," teacher Phuoc replied.

Phuoc introduced the man to us. We bowed and greeted him.

"Excuse me, I have to finish this furrow for my salad garden. If you don't mind."

He continued with what he was doing.

"Would you like some tea or something to drink, teacher?" the lady asked.

"No thank you, we just had some."

The lady nodded her head and left us there.

I picked up a shovel, helped the man dig the soil while teacher Phuoc began the conversation.

"Do you know for sure how many white and brown eggs you have?"

"Yes, I know, but it has been a while since I contacted them," the man said.

"Where did you get the white and brown chickens?" asked Phuoc.

"Not in this city. I bought them in Vinh Binh. Are you familiar with the city?" he asked me.

"Yes, I know the area," I chimed in. "I have some friends there."

He looked at me as if judging me. He dug the soil deeper. I could see the muscles moving on his sweating arms.

"I think it's best for you to go there to pick up your own choice," he told teacher Phuoc.

"How do we find the owner?"

"You go to Thien Duc District to the church, and ask for Ho Dao. The priest's name is Truong. Tell him I sent you. You can go there some time next month so I can have time to make arrangements."

"How about the cost?"

"He will let you speak directly with the owner about it," the man answered.

A small dog was running around jumping up and down, wagging his tail as if he recognized me as a friend. At the back of the vegetable garden were mango and lechee trees with young fruit dangling from the branches. A light wind blew, softly pushing the hot air away. I could feel it, like an air conditioner turned on low. I didn't understand at all what teacher Phuoc was talking about with his friends.

"We better go now to our meeting at the district before we get in trouble," Hanh reminded me.

Suddenly a dog ran to the gate, barking. The man lifted his head up, looked over, threw the shovel down and wheeled the wheelbarrow into the chicken coop.

"I'll see you later, Phuoc. Let me know what happens."

We nodded our heads and left.

On the road back home we discussed who would go to Vinh Binh to see the priest.

"It's better for me to go since I know the territory well," I said. "If one of you went then you would have to ask directions. People would be suspicious; you would get in trouble easily."

"But if you go, will police recognize you?"

"I don't think so because I won't get near my home. Thien Duc District, where our house is, is on the other side of the river."

"Don't forget, I have four places that you need to reserve for my family. That is part of our deal since I gave you connections," teacher Phuoc emphasized.

"Don't worry, teacher. We are on the same boat," Hanh said, to give him confidence. "We cannot do anything without you."

"Good. Just remember not to leave without me. Keep in touch."

He turned his bike to another street to go to the bus station while we went back to the police for a district meeting. When we arrived it was crowded in the front yard behind the gate. We came in and sat down on the ground like everyone else. There was a VC talking into a loudspeaker about the city project in Dong Thap, which involved digging a canal with human labor and no machinery. I volunteered to go in order to pay something back to Hanh's family and to distract the attention of the police. After a month of slavery at the new economy zone, I came back home.

CHAPTER 7

Hanh and I sat in the parlor and chatted, until I excused myself to get ready to go to Thien Duc District early the next day. Hanh's mother returned in the afternoon. She didn't feel well and complained about her health. Hanh's uncle asked her if he could borrow some money, but she said she didn't have enough. Dinner was served. The day faded; the night came. Hanh and I went to the backyard to talk about our plan one more time. He gave me three gold bars which he had stolen from a jar his mother had buried under a ceramic bucket in the kitchen; this would be the deposit to reserve our places on a boat. We went to bed, frightened because we were at a turning point in a new adventure.

Everyone was still asleep when I left the house the next morning, except for Hanh, who brought me out of the house and gave me his bike.

"Don't leave me behind."

"I won't disappoint you," I said. "If I'm alive, then you're alive."

I pedaled away while he stood in the dark, looking after me. The dew was still lying on the grass. The air was stagnant. Everyone was asleep. The dog barked when I rode by, and I felt so fresh when the air hit my chest that I pedaled harder. The street was tranquil with no street lights on. Occasionally I saw someone carrying goods on a bicycle to the early market. I came to the main road to go south. Vinh Binh was about twenty kilometers from here. I was enjoying my ride. I passed the Bac My Thuan ferry dock, a place people had to pass by if they wanted to go to Saigon. The darkness brightened. At the end of a range of trees was the sky, holding on to the big sun, slowly pushing it up over the top of the trees. The sun colored the surrounding clouds, its red face radiating stronger with each degree it rose above the horizon. I felt warmer and began sweating.

The highway stretched out ahead of me but I wasn't afraid

of the distance. A bus would pass by occasionally. I was thinking about the trip I would take to escape with my friend. It
gave me more hope as the sun rose. I rode by Vinh Binh airport, where my father had lost his twenty acres of land when
the U.S. built it. My brother used to land at this airport to visit
home. It was very close from here to my grandfather's estate. If
I stood at the end of the airport, I could see a clump of trees by
a village shrine. From there I could walk just two kilometers to
my grandfather's estate, where my family still resided. I wished
so much that I could go home. Suddenly I heard a horn blow.
I had been riding in the middle of the highway.

"Do you want to die, dammit?" a man with a heavy northern accent yelled.

I turned and rode closer to the sidewalk. The Russian
Molotova truck, transporting soldiers, went by.

The highway seemed like it had been in the old days but it
was more deserted than before, eroded in some spots. I went
past my uncle's garden near Tan Ngai market and it looked the
same, but the dirt path was empty. I usually carried gifts to
them every New Year, when my mother sent me. They had a
luscious landscape that consisted of topiary plant sculptures
with elephant, dragon, and bird shapes. Their cherry blossoms
had come out on time for the New Year, after being watered
and pruned so that the flowers would bloom at just the right
moment. Many times I had stopped at my uncle's house to eat
and hang out. I saw my fifth-grade teacher's children playing
in their yard, and my heart throbbed as I passed by. I wanted
to stop but I was too scared because beyond the Tan Binh
Bridge was my home, where I had lived as a teenager. I pedaled faster to get away from my memories but not fast enough,
it seemed, to stop them.

I pedaled harder up the bridge. When I reached the top, I
coasted down and there it was—my home on the side of the
road next to what used to be a Cartex gas station. Across from
my house was the police post, where they checked the passengers in the cars passing by. Next to the police post was a driveway to the navy base where my fourth brother, Tuong, used to
work as an interpreter for an American advisor. There it was,
my family's house: the same old look with the blue railings on

the second-floor balcony and all the windows in the same places. On the top of the third-floor, a *Bong Giay* ivy still crawled on the cement railing in shapes of stars and the moon. It was blossoming. The iron front door was closed. There was a little alley at the side of the house where I used to sneak in when I was late. The VC had invaded our house and kicked us all out as soon as they captured Vinh Binh city in 1975. Everything was there, but where was my family? Where were the old people who lived there? What had happened to them? What had happened to our laughter? Where were our conversations? It was still my family's home, but I couldn't get in, I couldn't find any of my loved ones here anymore. I had nowhere to go but ahead. Behind was so much happiness, yet even the good times were painful to remember. I pushed the pedals harder, trying to get myself out of this picture.

I turned at the intersection where Phan Thanh Gian monument used to be, and followed Le Thai To Avenue to go downtown, passing the big Catholic church connecting to Gia Long Avenue, which led to Thien Duc District. On both sides of the avenue there had been many thriving businesses, but now everything was deserted. The buildings were peeling because people couldn't afford to paint them. At the end of the street was my high school. The gate was closed and quiet. The sun rose higher, its heat stronger. It was around eleven. I came to Thien Duc District, where I had to pass the rickety bridge. The street was shaded by trees, and I felt fresh riding beneath them. I made a right turn at the dirt road where I used to come for my French lessons. There was the church, surrounded by a wire fence. I came to the gate; a guard was standing there watching people walk in and out for noon Mass.

"Comrade, is there a Mass today?"

"Yeah."

"Who is the priest here, comrade?"

"Truong. He's our suspect."

"I know that. I'm here to do the investigation," I said. "I'm from the city department." I pulled out my fake papers and let him skim them, then put them back in my pocket.

"Let me know if any strange things occur. I'm going in there now."

"Yes, comrade." He looked up at me with obedient eyes.

"Don't call me comrade. People will notice and it spoils my investigation." He nodded his head without saying anything, shifted his gun from one shoulder to the other, and walked out of the gate. It felt good to trick him. He was young, about fifteen or sixteen. I parked the bike in the back of the church and walked in from the front door. People were walking in, kneeling down in the middle of the aisle, and then sitting down on the benches. I went all the way up front, kneeled, and sat quietly as if I was praying. It wasn't too crowded today. The service began and ended. The congregation joined in, said amen and then the priest and the two boys served communion. The line ended and people went back to their seats quietly to pray. Some of them left. The priest went into the confessional booth and some of the congregation lined up for confession. I was among them.

I went into the confessional box and closed the door. The priest pulled a small panel aside.

"Hello, Truong. I was sent here by your friend in Sa Dec. He told me to pick up the white chicken," I whispered.

Truong was surprised when he heard an unfamiliar voice. He turned and looked through the small latticed window to see me. He smiled with a weary face and cleared his throat.

"I received the message from one of the neighbors last week. You are early." He paused for a second. "Is my friend okay? I heard he was sick."

"He's okay, Truong. God bless him."

"Are you a Catholic, son? You seem to know about Jesus."

"I used to go to a Catholic school when I was young, but I'm a Buddhist," I said.

"The chicken always comes home to roost," he coughed.

"Wait for me after the Mass. I'll show you where to pick up the white chicken. But watch out for the guard outside."

"Don't worry. It's already been taken care of."

I walked out of the booth and went outside to my bike to wait for him. People started to go home. The priest appeared, having changed clothes; only his white collar remained.

"Are you ready to go?"

"Yes, Truong."

"How do you know my name?"

"You used to be my French teacher. Do you remember?"

He paused for a second to recall. "I had so many students. I don't think I remember your name. However, I retired early."

"Do you remember the boy in ninth grade who was always on the top in your class?"

"Oh, yeah, yeah."

His face turned bright as if he had found an old acquaintance.

"You have a name that sounds like a girl's name."

"Right. It has been a long time since I saw you, Truong."

"Yeah, it has been a long time and a lot has changed. You have grown up now; I am getting old."

He cleared his throat, coughed. He was about sixty, his hair had turned grey and he looked tired for his age, his eyes no longer sparkling as they used to. We walked through the gate, not seeing any guard there. He stopped for a moment and glanced around, wondering if he should close the gate or not.

"They try to take over the church and they want me not to have Mass anymore, but we continue to have Mass. We have faith in God."

"I believe we have faith."

"How are you and your family?" Truong asked.

"It's a long story but I think you know what happened to all of us after they invaded."

He nodded his head and sighed as if he understood my circumstances. We walked on the dirt path as I told him my whole story. He made a sound which showed he felt sorry for me.

"I hope you pick the white chicken that isn't sick. Pray, son."

We arrived at the house in the district where one of the congregation had invited him for lunch. A stout man stepped out of the front door to greet us.

"Hello, father. Please come in." He smiled pleasantly.

We went into the house and they invited us to sit at the table in the living room. The family members came and said hello. Truong introduced me to the family, then we ate. The children were in the back room with someone trying to keep them quiet.

"When did you arrive?" the man asked me.

"About an hour ago, sir."

"He came to pick up the white chicken that I mentioned to you last week," Truong remarked.

"It's quite expensive now with the prices at the market. I wish I could sell it to you cheaper but I have no control over it. I have to get them from other people," the man said. He had fat cheeks and tiny eyes.

"It's a good lunch. I have an appointment to see another congregation member who is sick. I'll let you two discuss things. I have to leave now." Truong finished his lunch, making the sign of the cross in front of him. The man stood up and put out his thick hand for Truong to shake. He wore a short shirt which barely covered him. I stood up as the priest walked out of the house. I thanked him for his help and the lady called to him.

"Stop by more often, father!"

"Yes, I'll do that. I'll see you next Sunday in church."

He walked away in the midday sun. We went back in the house.

"How much does it cost for each white chicken?" I said. "I have to get back early."

"Three bars each. You have to give me half for a deposit. When you come to pick them up, you give me the other half."

"Does that include everything or is it only for you?"

"It includes everything. This season is a very good time for you to raise chickens. They won't get sick. We are planning sometime next week to sell all the chickens," said the man.

"What happens if the chickens die after I give you the first half of the deposit?"

"I will give it back to you."

I didn't know anything about this family. I didn't know if I could trust them enough to place myself in their hands. But Hanh and I were desperate. I looked at his stout, thick face, trying to find a sign there of whether he could be trusted, or whether he would rob and betray us. I pulled the bars of shiny gold out of my waistband, where I had made a hole for them, and put them in his hands.

"I want to buy two white chickens with this as my deposit," I said.

The man took them, smiling assuringly.

"Do you know this area very well?"

"Yes."

"Next week on Sunday there is a wedding in this neighborhood. We want to take advantage of that. Get your friend and come to the Gian Long Market across the river. From there take the passenger boat to the store where they sell coffins and ask to buy two. They'll know what you want," explained the man.

"How about the cage and food for the chickens?"

"Everything is all set. Just be there exactly at four o'clock. If you are not there, we will have no responsibility."

"What happens if our deal doesn't go through?"

"If an accident happens, everybody must take care of themselves. We have no guarantee."

"Are you going to take all your family chickens with you?" I asked.

"Yes. And since you are a friend of the father we will try to look after you," he encouraged me.

I wanted to find out about any resistance groups I might join if my escape failed, and so I continued our conversation in the code language.

"Do you know any other people who raise brown chickens?"

"Yes, but it's in Thot Not," the man said. "Do you want to know?"

"Yes, just in case, if I become sick."

"You have to go to Thot Not, where there is a pagoda on Highway Twenty that leads to An Xuyen. It's the only temple you can see from the road. I don't think you will have any problem finding it. If you go there, ask for the man who is the caretaker at the temple to tell him you want to burn incense."

"Thank you. That's really helpful. Do I have to pay anything extra?"

"No, since you do it yourself there is no fee. The reason

we charge for your white chickens is because we have to prepare everything for you. I wish I could give them to everybody
free."

I stood up and bowed to all of his family. The youngsters
were playing in the front yard and one of them was sitting in
the corner watching for strangers.

"Be there on time."

It was eight in the evening when I got back home. The sky was still hanging on to the light, even though the sun was already set. I met Hanh at the door.

"How was it? Tell me!" he exclaimed.

"Good. You want to hear the whole thing?"

"Every detail."

"Let me have something to eat first. I'm hungry."

He pulled me into the kitchen and added, "My sister-in-law just made some good sour chicken soup. It's been a long time since we had it. It's not easy to get a chicken these days. I had the feeling you would be back today so I saved you some." He kept talking as if he hadn't seen me for years.

He took a bowl and a rice pot out of the cabinet and set the table. I sat breathing heavily. He scooped some rice into my bowl, and I ate it gladly.

"Hey, where did you buy this good rice?"

"Black market. They have it once in a while. But forget that. Tell me the good news."

I slowly ate my food and told him the whole story.

"It's wonderful news. I hope we can leave soon."

"Only one week," I murmured.

"Yeah, one week."

"So what is going on at home?"

"Helping the family as usual, playing with the kids . . . nothing special has happened except the new policeman really has gotten on my nerves. We have to have a meeting every day now in the district."

"Did your mother find out about . . . ?"

"Get me the lighter and lamp, Hanh," his mother shouted from the stairs.

"Yes, mama." He made a sign to shush, lit the lamp in the kitchen, carried it to his mother, and then came back.

"Not yet. You say how much for each?"

"You have a bad memory. I already told you three for each," I whispered.

"We need three more then. And some money for transportation and food on our way."

"I think it's better for us to tell her because we can say we are borrowing it," I suggested. "We will pay her back when we have a chance."

"Don't worry. Let me take care of that because if I tell her the truth, she won't let me go and everything will be messed up. You know my mother. She couldn't keep a secret if someone threatened her," Hanh said. "Oh, did you have a chance to test our papers?"

"Yes, they didn't notice a damn thing about it! I think we will need to use them more in the future."

After dinner, I jumped into the river to take a bath and went to bed feeling anxious to live. Birds came back home to the plum tree to sleep. I hoped things would go well for us. I continued thinking until I fell asleep.

The days passed by quickly but Hanh and I kept looking at the calendar, anxious for Sunday to come. Hanh already had three more bars of gold with some money he had borrowed from his sister-in-law. When she asked him why he needed it, he told her I was the one who needed it, but that I wouldn't want to ask her. He said. I didn't know that he was asking her.

"Chu Ngoc, I don't have a lot of money but if you need some help you can ask me directly. I consider you just like I do Hanh."

She held the needle, mending some clothes.

"I know that but I don't have any right to ask you, especially since you have children and I don't. I have been a heavy burden since I came here. I don't know if I will have a chance to pay you back or not, so I try not to get anyone involved," I said.

She looked up at me with sympathy and regret. The youngsters ran in and asked her for some water to drink. I excused myself and went to the back door to the spot where I had put all my old personal papers, my diploma, my ID, my birth certificate, and the paper on which my brother Tuong, the pilot, had registered all of our family members for the U.S. evacuation plan. Before Saigon fell, my sister had given these to me on her visit. Some of these might be useful in another country, I thought; I could prove that I was not connected to the VC or the Communist government, and I could ask for political asylum.

On Sunday morning, Hanh was busy helping his mother carry goods to the market. Before he left, he signaled to me to get ready. We could take no clothes with us, nothing to make Hanh's family suspicious. Hanh came back from the market and ran into the house, as if he were afraid I had left already. He smiled at me when he found me. He went around the house, looking at it for the last time. He didn't know how to have a regular conversation with his sister-in-law. He looked at his niece and nephew, wondering if he would see them again. His sister came back to the living room and gathered the children around her. She told them a story so they would go to sleep as she mended clothes.

"Chi Hai, we are going to visit our friends for a few days. Would you tell mama I'll be back soon? If the police come, you could tell them that we are volunteering at the work camp in Dong Thap. They can check with the authorities there if they want." His voice was cracking. Her round face tilted as she looked at him.

"Okay, but you have to be home early because mama will have nobody to help her."

Hanh got close to the children and kissed them. I was afraid his sister-in-law would say something; she had never seen Hanh kissing her children in front of her before, and her big eyes looked puzzled. I gave Hanh a look; we left the house.

We walked a half hour to downtown, and tried to buy a bus ticket at the station, but there were too many people. I stepped into the ticket booth that was for government officials only. I pulled out my fake paper and gave it to the girl at the booth.

"Cadre, two tickets to Vinh Binh, please. I have a mission there."

She skimmed over my paper, looked at me thoroughly, then returned the paper. She tore off two tickets and Hanh paid her. She gave me some change back.

"How much is that?"

"Forty dong each, comrade."

"Everything is expensive lately. I just went down there three weeks ago; it only cost thirty-five dong."

"The gasoline and everything went up, comrade," she smiled at me, thinking I was stupid.

"Are you all done, comrade?" Someone with a northern accent shouted behind me.

"You have a nice smile," I whispered to the cadre.

She showed me her teeth again, called the next person in line. Hanh and I stepped out, laughing quietly.

"What a joke, huh . . ."

We got on the bus when the driver started the engine. It was exactly one o'clock; we had a three-hour ride to our destination in Vinh Binh. At each stop, Hanh would look at his watch. It began to make me nervous, but I didn't want to say anything to Hanh, didn't want to pass on my jumpiness. We arrived at the bus station in Vinh Binh at three o'clock. From there we paid a biker for a ride to Cho Gian's main market, where we could take a boat across the river to the coffin manufacturer. This spot was on the main branch of the Mekong River in Vinh Binh, where the French used to attack when Phan Thanh Gian wouldn't give in to them. We went through the market but there were only a few people left. We came to the dock and searched for a boat to get across. Standing there, we could see the coffin warehouse across the river. In the past, this area had been very crowded with many entrepreneurs, but now there was only a government-run restaurant; its original owners had been kicked out when the northerners came into the city. Some ferryboats were anchored at the dock. We jumped from one boat to another, asking people if they were going across.

When we came to a small boat that was anchored behind the ferryboat, the bargee asked us, "Are you here for the wedding?" The lady smiled.

"Yeah, we want to go to the wedding. We are almost late. Would you take us there?"

"Sure, I'm here to take people across the river for the wedding today. You came to the right place."

We got into the small boat as the short lady released it. We held on to the paddles and rowed.

"It's beautiful today, isn't it?" I said, trying to strike up a conversation.

"Yes, it's really nice. Especially since it's not hot anymore; the water is so fresh." I looked into the Mekong River. It was so big I didn't think I would make it across by swimming if the boat sank.

"Are there a lot of guests at the wedding yet?" interrupted Hanh.

"Yes, there are quite a few people." The broad-faced lady took off her *non la* hat and put it on the floor of the boat.

The wind blew while the waves beat the sides of the boat.

"Did the people from the groom's side come yet?"

"Yes, they came early in the morning. I think they are ready to pick up the bride."

"Oh, we are not that late then," I said, and winked at Hanh. Hanh and I laughed and the lady joined in.

We threaded our way through the river traffic. It took about ten minutes to get to the other side. The lady got off the boat and held it for us, and we walked up the steps onto a pebble path. We pretended to walk straight to the wedding, where we heard the music playing. I looked back to see if the lady was there or had gone back across. I saw her rowing the boat away from the dock. Then I signaled Hanh to follow me, and we turned onto the small road that led to the main warehouse gate; it was open, and we walked in. It was located half on land, half on water. We stepped onto the wood floor, where there were several empty caskets with their lids off. A man came to us, wanting to assist us.

"We need to buy two coffins."

"Yes, I have it. Come with me."

We followed him to the back of the warehouse, where a few boats floated. In one of the long, narrow, wooden boats, several people sat around a coffin.

"You are the last ones," said the man.

We got into the boat as the man untied it and pushed out into the dark green water. The small, two-horsepower engine started.

"Hello, teacher Phuoc. Did you just arrive?"

"Just a minute ago."

"If the police stop us, we will all say that we are going to have a funeral for our grandfather," the man who steered the boat warned us, cutting off our conversation. "If they don't ask you anything then let me do the talking," he instructed us.

We all nodded our heads. The boat picked up speed. We moved out into the river.

As we ran along the river to Cho Lach, I remembered they used this way to get to the ocean by Ba Dong. In the boat I recognized Phuoc's wife and two children, and the lady I had met at the connection family in Vinh Binh with her children, along with five other people. We looked at each other nervously because we had the same thoughts. We saw in each other's eyes that we might never return, or might die on the water. But at least there was a little hope in searching for our freedom. The children looked at us and felt something was wrong; one child cried out, then another, and then they all started crying. We watched them but didn't stop them. I wondered if it might be good to shed some tears for our ancestors, or maybe for ourselves.

Along the river there were small canoes that ran close to the shore where some of the people were fishing. There were many cork trees in the mud on the little island along the river. The wind blew the leaves, making them wave like someone saying goodbye to us. The afternoon was mild. I inhaled the fresh air, feeling as if I had been released from a tunnel under the water. We arrived in Cho Lach about two hours later. The ride was smooth but the children seemed sick. The clouds were clear up in the sky, red and orange shades that were scattered at the end of the water where the horizon met and the waves moved.

From time to time I saw a dead tree or some grass floating on the current. We passed some poles that people used to hang fishing nets on. When it was dark, we turned into the small branch of the river. We went on for another half hour and then heard the engine of a big boat running along the river. Our driver stopped the engine, signaled three times with the lighter, and waited. We saw a light in the middle of the river flash back three times. We paddled our boat quickly to the middle of the river. When our boat got close to the big boat Hanh and I jumped on, then began to help the rest of our group get on. The children were crying.

"Cover their mouths," someone whispered.

The crying was hushed, then loud again when someone released a hand from a mouth. The night was tranquil. We tried to be very quiet, but you could hear tiny voices here and there in the front and back of the boat. When our whole group was almost on, the captain of the big boat asked us, "Did you catch any fish?"

"No, we didn't. We prefer chicken."

"Wrong group. Go back."

Chaos broke out. Some people yelled to others to shut up before the police heard anything. We grabbed the children, passing them back to the small boat. I jumped off the big boat. I heard someone cursing because I stepped on them in the cramped dinghy. We pushed away, rowed our small boat back to the side of the river to hide ourselves in the thickets, and waited for our boat to come. Teacher Phuoc suggested, "I have some sleeping pills. Let the children take them so they can sleep. It will be much safer for us."

We passed the pills along to the adults to give to the children. About ten minutes later they all fell asleep. We kept our eyes and ears open but nothing came. Another half an hour passed. The taxi person kept demanding that we pay him in advance because he said when we saw the big boat we would forget to pay him and jump on. We told him to shut up. If he made any noise and the police spotted us, we would kill him. He was quiet but still mumbling. Hanh gave him a bar of gold.

"We will give you the rest when the big boat arrives."

He seemed satisfied and didn't say another word. The mosquitoes attacked us, and our slaps pricked the night air. Bats twittered, looking for cork fruit, and occasionally the fruit fell into the water, making a little noise, just enough to notice. There was no sound at all except the mosquitoes, birds, bats, water lapping into the bushes, and occasionally an unexplained rattle of leaves. High in the sky stars scattered about in different shapes, creating their own groups, beaming and dimming. There were no clouds. We waited and waited. Suddenly, from the middle of the river, the sound of an engine moved toward us.

"Don't be in a hurry. Watch out for the police boat," I whispered softly.

We waited for the boat to come closer. The taxi person signaled with his lighter, and was answered by a lighter signal on the big boat. We held on to the branches, pushed our boat out into the current. Everyone was paddling, some of us using our hands because we didn't have any paddles. The big boat turned the engine down low and stood still. We approached it cautiously.

"Do you have any white chickens?" I asked.

"Yes, we have white chickens!" a voice from the big boat called back.

We moved our boat faster in their direction as the taxi driver shouted.

"Give me the money now! It's the right boat!"

Some of us pulled out the money and gold and gave them to him. He didn't say anything more.

"Give me your hand," someone on the big boat whispered.

We began to climb aboard the big boat. The children were still asleep, and we passed them up. It was packed on the boat. When they placed the children on they split them up, away from their mother or father; since it was dark, people didn't recognize one another and there was no one spot for an entire family to settle.

"Teacher, give me your money. You haven't given it to me yet," the bargee whined, trying to squeeze some more money out of us.

"I'm the middleman. I arrange the customers and owners. So I get my family's fare free," teacher Phuoc answered while I climbed onto the boat.

"That's right, taxi!" a voice shouted from the cabin. I recognized this voice as my connection, the fat man to whom I had paid the gold.

The bargee pushed his boat away from the big boat and started his engine. I could hear the propellers churning. We filed down below the deck, into the dark hold of the wooden hull. Hanh and I sat near the engine room where several plastic containers of food and water were located. They revved the engine louder as the boat moved off. I heard the captain ask the organizer, "Are they our last group?"

"Yes. We can go now. It's all yours now. One hundred twenty-four people."

The unwieldy boat moved like an old man. People squatted on the leaking wooden floor, on the deck, on the cabin; every inch of the boat packed.

It was very hard to breathe because there were only two holes on the deck above us where the air could get in. Besides the engine's odor, gasoline fumes from the exhaust also circulated, making us nauseated and lightheaded. I couldn't see any stars or breathe the fresh air anymore. I began to vomit and pass out. I woke up with a heavy head, like a bad hangover. I felt the boat slapping against the water, shaking it like a huge wave. We were on the ocean. A little light came in and I saw vague human forms everywhere, sitting, lying, and breathing. We were squeezed in like so many flowers in a small vase.

"Is it safe to come up yet?" I shouted. "People are dying down here."

The cover from another hole was removed and more light came in with a little air. I crawled over people, climbed up on the deck. When I speak of a big boat one may think it was a ship, but it was not. It was a shabby wooden boat, four meters wide by fourteen meters long. It had to carry 124 people including food, water, oil, gas, and the engine. But it was amazing how valuable a small piece of wood was in the big ocean. We began to help people crawl up onto the deck to breathe some good air. The scent from the water drifted in the wind like a miracle medicine to cure all of us. How wonderful an ocean mist is on a hot day! Just like fresh coconut water to drink. The children were still knocked out with the sleeping pills. Someone asked for water. The engine ran smoothly and all around us now was water. Further away there were some dinghies scattered about. I looked ahead and saw the sun rising slowly. There were no obstacles between us. The water, rippled with the sun's reflection in a crimson background. The sky was like a huge canvas on which were painted many bright colors on this clear, blue day. I was thinking about my family, wondering if I would have a chance to see them again. I remembered this kind of morning when I was in Vung Tau waterfront on my school vacation. It was totally different now as I looked back. Was I really free now? The boat kept moving farther away from the shore, the water becoming a darker blue. The surface of the water was gentle now, like a cotton blanket that my mother used to put over me on a chilly night. The seagulls began flying back to the land, no longer circling us in the sky. I looked in front of the boat to where it crushed the water, creating a foam mass running along both sides of the boat and disappearing at the end. Suddenly I saw some kind of fish diving in and out of the water in front of our boat. Someone shouted.

"Come on, race with us, *ong nuoc!*" we all clamored in excitement. Everyone forgot about their sickness as the whole clan of fish jumped up and down ahead of and alongside our boat, their fins glimmering.

"It's very good weather. It will be an excellent day today because we have had some *ong nuoc* show up," the captain smiled. The fish flashed on, their silver jumps leading us into the dark blue sea.

The children began to recover from the sleeping pills, and cried now for water and food. The people in the cabin started to pass out food and water for each person. It was only a few teaspoons of food and one teaspoon of water. I looked at Hanh as if to ask him, "Do we have enough supplies for 124 people?" He shook his head, not knowing. Our course was for Thailand, which was over 4,000 miles away. Families tried to get together in one spot with their children, but it was so cramped that it was hard even to straighten our legs, let alone move. After people had something to eat they were happier but still had a little doubt in their eyes, wondering where they were going. The heat became more powerful; people started sweating. Some of the men took off their shirts, made little umbrellas over their heads for their children. The day went by.

When the night came the waves were stronger and the sky seemed dark, without any stars. I tried to locate the *sao hom* star. This was the star used at night to find directions. But I couldn't find it. People got inside beneath the deck because we knew a storm was coming. An hour later the boat was tossing up and down in the water, riding with the waves. Every time it went down I felt it would sink all the way to the bottom, like a little fish in the big ocean who couldn't struggle but let the current carry it away. I held on tight to the deck like everyone else; the water poured over us as if we were taking a shower. It was so loud that I couldn't hear if the engine was running or not. The storm went on for half an hour, then flattened out. I felt chilly, exhausted, and dreamed about a new land. The sky turned bright as the stars came out. We could see a little phantom boat in the dim night, the engine groaning like a sick person. Dawn came, and I found the *sao mai* star. It only shows up at daybreak; we used it for directions. It hung in the sky beautifully, outshining the other stars. The night turned bright, the sun rose, and another day passed with a little food and a little water. People were seasick; the children were crying and vomiting. The parents couldn't help them because they were sick too.

"Where are we now, captain?" People gathered their last energy to call into the cabin, but there was no answer. The boat kept putting along in an ocean of nowhere. Another storm struck in the afternoon before the sun went down. This time it was more violent; one of the children fell into the ocean. The captain couldn't stop to look for him. The parents yelled for help, but there was no hope. His mother wanted to jump off the boat but people held her back. I heard the water pump working harder; there was a lot of water in the boat. The engine broke down, the mechanic labored to fix it. Finally the storm ended. The ocean was so gentle after its anger. The engine began running again. One more night passed but there was no sign of land anywhere. The food was running out and the water was all gone. We had used up all of our energy. We realized what was going on around us but could do nothing to prevent it. The boat moved on. The heat came again and the engine broke. People were losing hope. In the afternoon, we saw a fisherman's boat coming closer to us. Our spirits lifted when I saw a sign on the boat that said, *Tau Danh Ca Quoc Doanh*. It was a government fishing boat. Men stood on the deck with machine guns and AK-47s aimed at our boat.

"Where is your captain?" they shouted.

The captain came out from his cabin.

"I'm the captain."

"How many people are in your boat?"

"I don't know, comrade. It's over 100."

"Tie the rope on your boat. We will tow you back. If anybody tries to escape, we will shoot."

"We don't have any more food or water. Can we have some for our people?"

"I'll send someone over."

They got closer to our boat, and one man carried a jug of water over.

"Captain, why don't we negotiate with them; maybe they'll let us go?" people shouted to the captain.

The captain spoke with the other man, but he didn't say anything and went back to his boat. Then a northerner came over. After the Communists invaded, they took over all the fishermen's boats and put one northerner and one VC on each boat every time they went fishing on the ocean. They carried machine guns with them.

"How much do you have?" the northerner asked the captain. He was thin, wearing an army-colored shirt.

"We have only thirty bars of gold left. Would you take that?" the captain pleaded.

"Over 100 people for only thirty bars. Too little. I'll take fifty in exchange for food and water."

"We don't have that much, comrade."

The northerner pointed his AK-47 as he turned around to inspect us. The captain asked all of us to take off all our jewelry and give it to him, plus the thirty bars of gold.

"That's all we have, comrade. Please let us go."

"I don't think it's enough, but I'll take it and think about it."

He took the bag, went back to his boat, and started its engines. The line stretched tight, towing our boat back toward the shore. A VC stood on the deck with his gun, watching over us every minute. People started to argue, saying why didn't we try to fight back when they came onto our boat? When we arrived back on shore they would execute us or put us in a labor camp. We had a chance to escape if we fought back.

"Do you think you can win with that machine gun?" said the captain. "It's lucky for us that they towed our boat back since our engine broke. We ran out of food and water. We would die in the middle of the ocean anyway. We may have a chance if we come back to shore."

"I think it's our captain's fault because we were on the ocean two days and two nights and we didn't get anywhere. That's enough time to get to Malaysia. I think he was just driving in circles."

"Yeah, I think he's right!" someone yelled. "The captain's on their side!"

"Why don't we throw him in the ocean?" someone called.

"He let them rob us and we will be put in jail when we get to shore."

People were muttering but they weren't doing anything. I still felt sick, but better for having drunk some water. Hanh and I looked at each other without saying a word because we saw our future. They towed us about half a day. Then we saw a boat just like our boat with many people sitting on the deck. Suddenly the fishermen's boat released the rope, turned around and chased that boat, calling to them to stop. The boat kept running and the shooting began. The government boat went after them for about twenty minutes but the small boat ran faster. Finally they gave up and came back. The man shot at the water near our boat to threaten us, to show us that they dominated the ocean. He ordered us to throw the rope back to them. Our boat followed their boat under the fiery sun without resistance. I saw a little line showing up at the end of the water—the land, I guessed. The seagulls were flying around in the air and landed on one of the poles that had a string on it. They made their own sound, pecked at each other, then flew up in the air. They seemed so carefree, looking down at us like we were prisoners. I wondered if they had any sympathy or felt the way we felt. I wished I had wings to fly. The kids were bawling because of the sun and were asking for food but we had nothing to give them except some water. The line at the end of the horizon became clearer, a shoreline. The VC still held on to their machine guns and stared at us. From my pocket, I pulled a small plastic bag in which I had carefully folded all my papers. I opened it, took them out one at a time and slid my hand along the side of the boat to let each one drop into the ocean. I kept only the fake police paper, folding it back into the plastic bag, which I handed to Hanh.

"Save it for me, so we don't have to buy it again."

He took it, and put it into his pocket.

"What are you going to do? Are you going to jump off the boat now?" he murmured.

"It's better for you to stay because you have nothing to lose. You are handicapped; you have the police papers. You can fool them, saying that these people forced you to escape with them.

Then just take a ride back to your grandfather in Cho Lach. I think they will release you in a matter of days when you get on shore. Go back home and wait for me."

"Don't tell me you are going to jump?" He looked at me like he was shocked.

"No, you think I'm stupid or something?"

Hanh looked at me.

"What else can you do?"

"Wait for the dark."

He nodded his head as if he understood.

"After three weeks, if you don't see me come back, I'm finished. Burn some incense for my cold soul."

His eyes were watery, looking to the side.

"Don't let my family know. I don't think my mama could stand it if . . ."

The afternoon came to a close. The breeze was nice, carrying a little mist as if it were baptizing a new life. The sun was gone, but Hanh kept watching the guard holding the machine gun on the back of the towboat. I spotted a large plastic container which I planned to use. I saw a light flashing on shore. I waited a little longer for it to get darker. I squeezed Hanh's shoulder, held on to the side of the boat, and slipped into the water gently. I held on to the plastic container, then heard a sound as if someone else had jumped into the water. The waves pushed me away from the boat as it moved on its way. I didn't know where all my energy came from, but it felt so good. I took my shirt off and tied it to the buoyant container. I couldn't see anything in the dark, only the waves, with a flicker of light in the distance, bobbing up and down.

I held the container for about ten minutes, but I felt like I was struggling with its bulk, rather than getting much benefit from it. I opened the lid and let some water in until it sank down just enough for me to stay on it comfortably. I kicked my feet slowly to save my energy, drifting with the current. The water was warm; I didn't know how far it was from there to the shore, but I didn't want to think about it. Once in a while I felt a little fish nipping me as if I were bait. I was scared but pretended not to be. I wondered what was going to happen to Hanh. I hoped he would be all right. I thought it was much better for me to take this risk rather than stay on the boat holding onto the fake papers and trying to persuade them to believe in me, only to end up dead. Water babbled and whispered in my ears as if someone was chanting along with the echoing gong of a temple. I did not know which way the current would take me. I thought of my parents and family and remembered that the Buddha would help me, for I had my hidden virtues from my past life. I said my prayers.

I changed my position on the container. I saw a light move up and down. It got clearer. I knew I was getting closer to the land. The night sky was darker. I kept floating on the water until I hit something in front of me. I extended my arm like a blind person feeling his way in the dark. I touched something cold that I had never touched before, especially in the water, but my curiosity kept my hand moving along the object until it ended at the head. I knew it was a dead body. I pushed it and swam fast away from it. Then another hit my back. It felt slippery. I pushed the can harder and harder, breathing heavily. The waves seemed like they were rolling over me, like someone rolling a carpet. I slowed down; my whole body was falling apart, my energy was gone. Suddenly my feet touched the ground. It was a wonderful feeling; I was on land. I stumbled, stubbed my toes on rocks. When I reached the sand I couldn't stand up anymore. I fell down, blacking out.

CHAPTER 11

I woke up under a dim oil lamp and felt some warm juice in my mouth. I swallowed it gradually. A weathered old man held a spoon, looking at me calmly as if he had done this many times before. I didn't know where I was. I wasn't wet, but wrapped in a torn blanket and lying in the middle of a big wooden plank in a hut with no walls. The old man's eyes looked at me tiredly. His thin grey hair was in a bun as he smiled at me with mercy showing in his wrinkled face.

"How do you feel, son? You are on an island called Hon Khoai."

"Do you know what time you found me?"

"At around one o'clock last night, when I went to the ocean to check my fishing net. You were unconscious. I found another three bodies washed onto the sand, too."

I lifted my head and tried to sit up, but was unable to.

"Don't move, son. You are still very weak. Let me feed you."

He scooped the rice soup into the spoon and put it in my mouth. I swallowed thankfully and wondered why he was by himself. I didn't see anyone else around, or any houses either. After he finished feeding me he said, "Get some rest, son." He hopped up from the side of the wooden plank and smiled at me, his gums showing. "I'm going to the shore to check my nets again to get some fish. I will take them to the village to have someone sell them for me. I'll be back in about an hour."

I nodded my head. When he shuffled out of the hut, the sun hadn't fully risen yet. He didn't wear a shirt, just shorts with a bamboo bucket on his shoulder. In the corner of the hut I saw a little stove with a small pot on it. The fire had settled down but it was still red. The lid on the pot was popping from time to time as the steam escaped. There was a little mud partition surrounding half of the stove, built at a ninety degree angle to prevent the wind from blowing out the fire, and on the floor there were some paddles, a fishing net, and buoys lying around. I felt much better after drinking the soup but my head still felt heavy. The birds landed on the branches, making morning songs. Surrounding the hut were trees, and a little sand path that led somewhere. Beyond, I could hear the tide drawing in and out. A pale wind blew, bringing in mist from the ocean, making me feel refreshed. I slept again until the old man came back.

"Are you doing okay now, son?" asked the old man.

"Yes, sir." I sat up to prove it.

"That's very good, but you need more food and rest."

He went to the stove to get me another bowl of soup.

"Eat it, son. It's good to eat little by little because if you eat a big meal all at once you will get sick. How long were you without food on the ocean?"

"Not that long, sir. Only one day and one night."

"Did your boat sink?"

"I jumped off the boat when they captured it and towed us back."

A chill crawled up my spine as I remembered being in the water—the coldness, the empty silence in an ocean of night and nowhere.

"I will need some people in the village to help me bury the bodies this morning. Maybe their boat sank or maybe someone robbed them, then threw them in the ocean. Do you know that I bury dead people every day? This spot is right for the current and that's why it brings all the objects here," he sighed.

"How long have you lived here, sir?"

"All of my life."

"Where is all your family?"

"I never had a family, son. My parents died in a storm when they were fishing. I have lived by myself until now. Before, I lived at the head of the village. Later, I moved here since I like it better. I have seen so many young people dead in the water, and I never know where they come from."

He seemed like he wanted to talk more, as if he hadn't spoken with anyone for a long time, or maybe just felt comfortable talking to me. He pulled a rock over for himself, squatted on the ground, sharpened his knife, and started to mend his net.

"My occupation is fishing but since I moved here, I have become a grave digger. Life is so funny somehow," he grinned at me, showing some of his teeth. His mouth looked like a young child's, when the teeth were first coming in.

"Did you catch a lot of fish this morning, sir?"

"Half a bucket, including some crabs."

"How far from here to land, sir?"

"A half day or maybe closer. Depends on the wind. Do you plan to go back this early, son? Stay for a few days until you get well. I will arrange a trip for you."

He seemed to understand what I was thinking.

"That's a wonderful thing for you to do but I don't have any money or anything to pay you back."

He set down his fishing net, stepped over the stove, took the pot off, put a kettle on, and fed the fire. His thin hands reached for the bucket with water for washing the dishes, and dumped it out.

"Money doesn't mean anything, son." he said, his eyes watching the fire. "It means something if you know how to spend it right, like a vehicle to take you places. But I don't need any. I think it depends on each person, on how you look at things."

"Are there any police around here, sir?"

"They come to the village once in a while to check on us, but it's easy to hide in these parts."

Three bare-chested boys about fifteen years old came out of the trees holding their shovels.

"Ong Bay, are you ready to go? My father cannot help you because they already went fishing, so my mother asked us to come," they called to him.

"Yes, I'm ready. It's good that you help me because it would take me the whole day to dig three graves," Ong Bay said. "I have some fish here. If you feel better you can cook something with it. I'm going to bury these people and then come back. Oh, there is rice in a jar beneath your bed," he told me as he stopped mending his net. He took his shovel and padded out of the hut with the children. I heard the kids asking about me as they all disappeared at the end of the narrow trail. I got up slowly, standing for a moment to make sure I had enough strength to begin making lunch. I cooked the rice and made some fish soup, first chopping some small branches and poking them through the fish mouths to bake them.

After I finished cooking I walked around to familiarize myself with the area. I followed the sound of the ocean and came to the water, where the sun shone vibrantly. Even though it was hot, the wind and the air were active, making me feel cooler, like someone applying ice to my forehead for fever. I looked along the golden dunes with their grass blowing in the wind like hair. How had I made it here? Far off, a line of trees ran along the water to show me land existed there. The ocean was so gentle now; I walked on the wet sand, letting the water touch my feet again. I saw hundreds of tiny crabs making little castles for themselves everywhere, only to have the water move up and sweep them away. They ran back and rebuilt their castles after the water withdrew, and then the water came again, over and over, endlessly. I thought of the *Da Trang Xe Cat Bien Dong*, a story about life as this tiny crab knew it: no matter how hard you struggled and fought for life, you would have nothing when you died. It was a story my mother used to tell me, and I thought of home. I wanted to die at home. I saw the old man and the children walking towards me. I met them halfway. They threw their shovels down to wash them in the ocean. The youngsters were laughing and the water rippled on the sand. The old man walked over to me.

"It feels good to breathe this air. I wish people could realize that. It's so simple but it's hard for people to know."

"I understand what you mean, sir. I just don't know what people want anymore."

"Are you from the city?" one of the boys asked me. "Is it big? Are there a lot of stores and people?" He slapped his smooth face into the water and shook it like a wet dog, then looked at me, dripping, his eyes wide.

"It's not a big city, but it's bigger than your village," I said.

"Are there a lot of cars? I have never been in the city. I grew up here in this fishermen's village and I come to the dock every day to watch the boats come in and out, but I don't know where they go," the boy said. "I asked the merchants where they were from; they said they were from the city. They brought a lot of candies and a lot of stuff to sell. But now I don't see the merchants come here anymore."

"Yes, there used to be many cars in the city but not anymore. It's much better for you to live here than in the city," I said.

They looked at me with surprise.

"Why is that?"

"It's hard to explain to you, but when there are fewer people then there are fewer problems."

"What do you mean, problems?" asked another boy.

"Like myself."

"You mean they threw the city people in the ocean?" he asked.

I didn't know how to explain to him so I said, "Something like that."

"Are the dead people your relatives? Are they from the city too?"

"No, they're not my relatives, but they were in the same situation I was."

The old man began to walk along on the rippled sand in the hot sun. We followed in his footsteps along to the path, where coconut trees danced in the wind, throwing their shadows over us.

"Why didn't they swim like you?"

"Maybe they didn't know how to swim or it was too far from here and they couldn't swim any longer. They never reached the shore."

The kid dragged a shovel on the sand, leaving a track behind him.

"Are you a good swimmer, then? Do you want to swim with us tomorrow?"

"Sure, but I'm not a good swimmer."

He ran ahead, yelled to the other kids walking with the old man and said that I would swim with them.

We arrived at the hut and ate our lunch, and then the children went back to their village.

"It's good to have the children come here to keep us company," I said to the old man.

"Yes, they come often and help me with a lot of things around here," Ong Bay cleared his throat and said gently. "Tomorrow evening they will come to help me set the net up when the current rises. At that time there will be more fish looking for food near the shore." He looked pleased.

"We can catch a lot of them."

The afternoon sky was clearer, the air mild. The trees and shrubbery seemed very content with the weather. Ong Bay took out two buckets and a yoke.

"I'm going to water my garden. Do you want to come?"

"Yes, I can help. I used to do this when I was in the labor camp."

I carried one bucket for him as he walked through the garden to the well. He threw a small container with a rope down the well and drew up enough water to fill two buckets, which he then carried on a yoke slung over his shoulders. With the two buckets dangling, Ong Bay walked into his garden and began to water the greens, cucumbers, hot peppers, and beans, which were growing there in little furrows. He shuffled between the green rows, tipping both buckets back and forth so that water sprayed from their spouts, just enough for each plant. The sound of the water as it touched the dry soil was like someone drinking, the soil cracking, smacking its lips. The odor of soil rose in the air like rain on a hot day. He walked so gently, even though the yoke was heavy on his shoulders, and his body was very flexible as he stepped. He finished the first half of two furrows just as the water ran out. He came back to the well where I stood without showing any sign of fatigue. I threw the buckets into the well to fill them up for him.

"Let me help you to water this time."

"Sure, go ahead." he smiled at me and gave me the yoke. I did it exactly the way he did: lifted it up, walked about three steps, and collapsed, dropping the buckets. The water splashed everywhere.

"It's not easy, huh, son?" Ong Bay said. "Maybe you are still weak."

"It's too heavy."

He took the yoke with the two buckets from me and hoisted it back onto his shoulders to continue watering his garden. I saw his dark skin and muscles, alive and healthy. The sun's beams became weaker as it went down slowly, the shining rays disappearing in the afternoon sunset. I stood in the middle of the garden, looking out onto the sea, and at purple flowers blending with weeds and tall trees, and I wished that I could live here. After we finished watering the garden, we stood at the well and filled the buckets, then took a shower. The water was a little chilly but the afternoon was beautiful. We came back to the hut and lit up the oil lamps. Ong Bay gave me some of his clothes to wear, and we made dinner and ate together. At dusk, he told me to sleep on the wooden plank while he slept on the fishing net, which he fixed into a hammock. I blew out the oil lamp.

The next day the children came in the evening when the sun had just settled on the horizon. We carried the fishing net to the ocean and placed it on the sand as the water began to rise slowly. The sun went down, reflecting beautiful color on the quiet water. We jumped into the water and swam while Ong Bay checked the net, sitting on the sand watching us. He puffed the cigarette that he had rolled himself, enjoying it. When night came, it didn't seem so dark and it was still easy to do things. The water was at high tide. We carried the net into the water, one of the boys holding one side of the net, and Ong Bay the other, walking further and further out into the sea until I could see only the top of his head. His head shook as he held the net, keeping himself afloat with only his strong legs. We followed him out but when my feet couldn't reach the bottom I felt like I was falling into an abyss.

"This is too deep. I'm going back to the shore," I shouted to the boy.

"Are you scared?"

"Yes. Do you want to go out there with Ong Bay or come back with me?"

They swam easily; nothing bothering them.

"I'm coming back with you," one of them said.

"I'm going with Ong Bay."

We separated, going in different directions. Ong Bay was moving further and further out until I couldn't see him. The net kept moving out; finally it stopped. We waited there about forty-five minutes until Ong Bay came in about one hundred meters away from us. We held the bottom of the net, pulling it in while Ong Bay did the same on the other end. One boy held a bucket, running after us. Finally we pulled the net up onto the sand. There were fish and crabs caught in it.

I shouted, "Wow, you caught a lot of them!"

We began to pick them up, putting them in a bucket. Some crabs bit flapping fish to fight for a space, as they jumped all over the bucket. After we finished emptying the net, Ong Bay swam out again, working on in the night. We had quite a catch of fish, and so we went back to the village, to one of the children's family, so that Ong Bay could ask them to sell the fish for him when they went to the dawn market. We spent the rest of the evening there with the family, drinking tea. We talked about the fish season and I learned a lot about the weather: when was a good time to set out on the ocean to avoid a storm, what month was best for fishing and what was the most peaceful month on the sea. I stayed with Ong Bay for four days, helping him with his daily activities. On the fifth day, around noon, one of the kids ran to our hut with news.

"The police just arrived at the village. I just came to let you know."

"Okay, boy, go home. If anybody asks about anything or if you see any strangers in the village, tell them you haven't seen anyone."

The kids ran back to the village. Ong Bay, his eyes showing his concern, told me to follow him. He guided me to the shore, then to a rocky area too steep to climb. He showed me the entrance to a small cave.

"Stay here until I come back to get you. I'm going to fish close by."

"Yes, Ong Bay."

I climbed into the rough, dark hollow.

He went back to the hut to gather his net and got one of the boys to help him, then came back to the spot to begin fishing again. The tide was getting low. Soon, a group of police came down the beach in their yellow uniforms, and approached Ong Bay. They were close enough that I could hear their voices.

"Did you see any strangers around here lately?" one asked.

"Yes, I saw three strangers about five days ago but I don't know their names. Do you want to arrest them?" answered Ong Bay.

"Where are they? What do they look like?" The VC were excited.

Ong Bay cleared his throat. "I buried them in that stand of trees," he said. "Why don't you go in there and take a look."

Ong Bay held his cigarette on his lip while he talked, puff-

ing it in and out like an old train. He pointed to the direction
where he had buried them. Five policemen looked at him with
doubt.

"Oh, you are talking about the boat that escaped five days
ago, which we sank."

"Have you seen anybody alive?" all the VCs chimed in.

"No, I didn't see anyone. Maybe if you stay here longer you
might meet some more dead people."

The policemen shook their heads with a look of disgust and
walked away in the direction of the bush where Ong Bay
pointed his finger. They thought he was a crazy old man, but
they wanted to check the spot where he had buried them to see
if it was true. They came to the spot, searched around, then
walked back to the beach on the opposite side, disappearing at
the verge of the tree range. I considered the conversation between Ong Bay and the police and thought about myself. It
seemed like being on the run had become my life. When could
I settle down and live a normal life like other people? Would I
ever see my family again? Who knew? I sighed. I would only
visit. I stayed in the cave until evening, when the boy came to
tell me everything was all right, that I could come out now and
go back to the hut to have dinner. The next day, Ong Bay took
me to the dock to ask the passenger boat captain to give me a
lift back to the mainland when he went to the market.

"It's better for you to go back now, son."

He put some money in my pocket. I didn't know what to
say, I knew I would miss something wonderful here, even
though I had known him for less than a week. The tide was going out; the boat had to leave the dock before it got stuck.

"Let's go, let's go!" the owner shouted, releasing the rope
from the pole.

I stepped down into the boat without saying anything. Not
even a "thank you" to Ong Bay. He seemed very understanding about my situation. He never asked about my family or
background. Suddenly the children ran over yelling.

"*Thang Chong, Thang Chong!*" A dead body floating on the
water.

Everybody turned and looked at the river to see the body
drift against the current. It was a pregnant woman.

"If you can hear me, stop right here. I will bury you!" Ong Bay muttered.

Indeed the body seemed to hear him, for it quickly made its way directly to the bridge where he stood, stopping right beneath him. Suddenly, from the mouth of the body, a cloud of blood spilled out, a silent "thank you" to the old man for helping her.

The owner pushed the boat out and the engine started. I stood on the deck waving to the old man and the children. Their picture blurred in the distance. A tear rolled down my cheek as the boat chugged further away from the dock, slicing into the ocean.

CHAPTER 13

I arrived in Kien Giang city, South Vietnam around noontime. The boat stopped at the dock near the market. I went to find something to eat and to figure out how to get back to Hanh's family. The market was crowded, so I had no problem blending in. I guessed that Hanh was home already; his family probably knew everything about both of us, and I was afraid we wouldn't have a second chance to escape. I decided to stop by Thot Not town to meet the contact I knew about the Hoa Hoa religious organization and wanted to join them in the jungle to fight against the government. I wandered around the city to get to know the area. Maybe I could use this city later, for a second escape, since it was on the Mekong Delta on the ocean route. I was disguised as a farmer as I walked, wearing black pajamas that Ong Bay had given me, the shorts old and stained. I tore the pocket halfway off on my sleeve when I went to use the public rest room, then bought a cone-shaped hat, soiling it with mud before putting it on.

I spent the afternoon in the city, and then found a bus station at the edge of the town. I noted that each time the bus left the city it had to stop at the police post, where all the passengers were checked. I walked slowly past the post since it seemed they weren't asking for papers from passersby, thinking they were local people. Still wary of the buses, I continued for five kilometers out of the city on the road to An Giang. I waved at people to ask for a ride, and finally a motorbike carrying kids on the back pulled over and stopped. I told the driver I would pay for a ride. He agreed and I sat down behind him as he put his children in front of him. We traveled for three hours. When I knew we were almost in town, I asked him to stop so that I could pay him and we said goodbye, everyone smiling and waving in the dark.

I walked on the road into town; everyone was asleep by now. I went to the bus station and found a place to sleep among the homeless. It was easier to stay here than any other place in the city because you could pretend you were a bum or

a passenger who had missed a bus. I found a corner on the cement floor where several children were asleep, and joined them
for the night, all of us struggling with the mosquitoes. The
smell of urine, the smell of gas from the dirtiest puddle of
water stuck in my nose like the smell of a public bathroom.
The night wasn't cold but mist fell, dampening my senses, and
I coughed occasionally. Sometimes one of the kids would wake
up and go outside next to a car to urinate on the tire. It was a
good way to do it, not waking anyone up. Finally, I fell asleep
from exhaustion.

"Wake up, wake up!" the youngsters called to each other
as they walked outside. They began to disperse, looking for
people who would pay them to carry things. The place was
noisy now under the dim neon light that hung above us on a
pole. They didn't know who I was but one of the kids kicked
me and called out.

"If you want something to eat, you better get up to find
some work. If you stay here the police will kick you out."

When I heard the word "police," I felt a chill, and instantly I
jumped up.

I was famished because I hadn't eaten yesterday. I began to
search for a vendor selling something to eat; I spotted one of
the carts near the well in back of the bus depot. Under the oil
lamp, a lady was busy feeding the fire, making soup, slicing
something on a wooden cutting board. I went over to ask her.

"Are you open now, ma'am?

"Yes, how can I help you?" she said.

"How much does it cost for a bowl of *Pho* noodles?"

"350 dong."

"May I have one bowl?"

I sat on a bench next to her table where she displayed some
dishes and chopsticks.

"Sure, coming right up," she said.

She put the vegetables and noodles in a bowl, scooped the
broth from the boiling pot into the bowl with a big ladle, and
then placed the steaming bowl of soup in front of me. The fire
from the small stove was crackling, a little smoke spreading
out. I felt warmer as the noodles reached my stomach. I was
full when I finished all the noodles and a small amount of soup

was left in the bowl. I gave her the money. After I put my chopsticks down on the table and stood up, three youngsters suddenly jumped over, grabbed my bowl, and drank the water I had left, sharing it with each other. I stood watching for a moment. There were so many homeless and hungry people now. I knew these youngsters used to be in happy families of soldiers or officers connected to the southern government. But after the north invaded the south, the VC had thrown their fathers into labor camps, broken up their homes, and shipped them to the new economy zone. Now they were wandering around, looking for food, and struggling for their lives. I pulled money out of my pocket and counted it. I had just enough for my trip home. But I thought I could walk the thirty kilometers and I bought the three children some noodle soup. They looked at me as if they had never had anything to eat before. I walked away and felt like I had done a wonderful thing today, even though I suspected I might be one of them soon. The night was over, the sun was just coming. I left for Thot Not town.

I met my contact at the temple in Thot Not and he told me that the organization wasn't interested in recruiting new members. I left disappointed; my best chance had just turned out to be a dead end. I noted sadly that the temple no longer flew its traditional religious flag. I turned away. I walked back to the main road trying to find transportation to Sa Dec, the only place that might accept me. The heat over the black tar shimmered in the air, and my sweat rolled down. I didn't want to take the risk of going through Can Tho city, and so I went north towards Cao Lanh to find some backroads home. It took me another day to arrive in Sa Dec.

I went back to Hanh's house in the afternoon. The VC had put Hanh in jail for two weeks, but released him and the whole boat-load: one of the comrades had complained to a higher officer that the money hadn't been split up equally, and the VC let them go to avoid an investigation. His family was happy to see me alive but by now his mother knew about our escape and the money that Hanh had stolen from her, a sum that could have fed the whole family for a year. I felt uncomfortable staying at the house because I felt guilty. Besides, Hanh and his family were quarreling about money these days. It was time to leave. But for where? The police had come and questioned us. There seemed to be little I could do. Finally, I decided to go to my aunt Muoi on Con Cat island; maybe I could borrow some money to pay Hanh's family back. But my aunt was supporting her two sisters and three children along with my older brother Lan, who was currently in hiding, and I hesitated to ask her.

I was happy to see them and I stayed there for a few weeks. And, though my aunt sympathized with my situation, she couldn't afford to feed one more person. She did, however, dig up some gold which I had asked her to keep for me when I was young. I told my brother that I would help him escape with me if I had a chance. I returned to Sa Dec and gave the gold to Hanh's mother, keeping four bars for my own use. Hanh had met an escape organizer while in jail and we began to arrange for a second attempt, but it turned out to be a con. Luckily we were able to get out before we lost any money or got captured. We began, again, to plan.

I had been in a hurry when I had left before, and hadn't had a chance to say goodbye to my family, who didn't know I had tried to escape from the country again and again. But my determination only deepened—I could see no other choice. I went to a city on the coast, about 250 kilometers south of Saigon. Hanh, myself, and some of our friends hid in the jungle preparing food and supplies for a sea journey. There were constant patrols of secret police searching around for people like us on the rivers and on the roads—everywhere. We had to disguise ourselves as local people to avoid suspicion.

On the appointed night, I walked into the jungle and followed a trail leading to a small creek where a canoe was hidden. We got in and started rowing slowly away from the site, the dark moon shining down on us.

"Who's there?" shouted the VC, as I heard metal clicking. A flashlight moved from side to side across the surface of the water.

We stopped rowing, remaining silent. A low hum buzzed over the water, a boat moving in our direction. We sat quietly, feeling powerless. A man in our canoe grasped some branches near the water and pulled our canoe to the side of the creek.

We waited there patiently for the police boat to pass. The moon was sparkling through the leaves at the side of the brook, and I saw our silhouette printed on the water. Our canoe began to move slowly. Our shadows were moving along with the paddles, stirring the water, making whirlpools and then disappearing.

At the side of the canal named *Kinh Hai Muoi,* we came to the big boat which was hidden, waiting for all the taxi canoes to come. My brother Lan was among our group to escape. The boat owner arranged for everyone to get on board at different times. I was excited to see him again. The big boat was about twelve meters in length and three meters in width, carrying twenty-four people. After the taxis delivered all the people, we began to follow *Kinh Hai Muoi* to get to the ocean. It was dusk, and I couldn't see a thing, but felt the boat hit a pole in the riverbank.

We arrived at the ocean around four o'clock in the morning. The moon had set slowly and yielded to the bright light, ready for the day to come. Our boat drifted smoothly on the water. I heard the waves splashing at the side of the boat and the early morning air cooled my nerves. I was at ease.

There were many small boats gliding back and forth. The shore appeared to be getting further and further away. We began to share food and water for the first meal at the beginning of the day. People were relieved to be free. Above, the sky became clear; below, there were many fish swimming by our boat, and we were clapping our hands and yelling happily to them to race us. Sometime during the first day, we saw a communist Vietnamese boat chasing us. The boat had guns. We turned our boat in a different direction, and after a tense chase, we lost them. We turned several times, trying to find our way by the sun, moon, and stars.

The day passed and a storm pushed its way in, trying to sink our boat and steal our lives away. Most of the people on our boat became sick, vomiting miserably. The boat swayed from side to side and almost capsized. People's groans mixed with the tired engine's noise. I labored to breathe, my eyes blurry, my head heavy. I didn't know what was happening anymore.

We drank water by drops instead of by the mouthful. There

was nothing in sight except for the watery horizon ahead of us. The ocean was a bottomless blue and it was getting darker and darker the further we drifted out to sea. I didn't know when our journey would end—I saw the same fear, the same uncertainty in everyone's eyes.

The boat began to leak; we plugged the hole with our clothes. Some started to give up hope and wanted to turn back; we told them we had to go on or die. We spent three days and three nights on the ocean. Our boat almost sank many times. The children were almost dead and we were desperate. The engine was broken, food and water were running out. We floated on the water for one night and two more days, and then our boat landed back in Vietnam. Of the original thirty, there were fifteen of us left, the others dead of starvation and illness.

It seemed that I could not betray my country: every time I went out on the ocean, the shore pulled me back. My brother went back to my aunt's to hide again. Hanh and I came to Sa Dec and began to discuss seriously with Hanh's mother the whole escape issue. We were running out of time and money, and we were under increasing pressure from the police, who watched us very closely and ordered Hanh's mother to report to them every week. And finally, we worried that if one person from the family escaped, any remaining family members would be executed. We decided to look for a boat to buy to escape with the whole family.

About this time, one of Hanh's relatives stopped by on his way to Saigon, where he was bringing his sick mother to the hospital. He told us about a boat he owned, in Soc Trang, which he hadn't used in years. We asked him if we could take a look at it to see how big it was and if it was still usable; he told us to go down there to do whatever we wanted with it. This serendipity seemed to have the marking of fate—once more luck had come. Hanh and I departed for Soc Trang, going by way of the countryside. As we approached and left each town, we had to get through checkpoints along the road, with a new set of local authorities. Each time, we would pull out our counterfeit police papers and tell them we were on a mission to follow some spy.

After a day of walking, we arrived that afternoon in My Xuyen, outside of Soc Trang city. There were a lot of coconut trees in this area, with creeks and rivers. We had to walk four kilometers until we arrived at Hanh's relative's house in the village. The house was built high over the ground with steps up to the porch. The walls were made of wood with red tile on the roof. It looked like a wealthy family's house. The dog ran out at us from inside, barking loudly, showing his white fangs in front of the gate, which was fenced by bushes. There was a pleasant old man sitting on the step, shouting at the dog to keep quiet. He stood up and walked slowly in our direction.

"Uncle Hai, Uncle Hai," Hanh called in a happy voice.

"Who's that?" he hesitated.

"Hanh, your nephew."

"Oh, I haven't seen you for so long now—come in, come in," Uncle Hai smiled, and opened the gate with his hospitable manner. The dog stopped barking as he ran back and forth, wagging his tail.

"How are your mother and family? I heard your mother, my sister, was selling things at the market," said Uncle Hai. "Now, is that right? It is harder to travel these days. I haven't seen her this New Year. With my age, it's better to stay home."

"We're doing okay, uncle. It's just that a lot of things have changed so we don't have the time to visit like before," Hanh answered politely.

Uncle Hai looked at me inquiringly.

"This is my friend Ngoc, uncle."

I bowed to him to say hello. Uncle Hai went to the steps and yelled into the house.

"Come, come, children. Hanh is here with a guest."

We followed Uncle Hai up the steps and into the house.

The children ran out with an elderly lady, Uncle Hai's wife, I guessed, and two girls about our age. We all greeted each other. Hanh went inside with his cousins to talk, while the children withdrew from the living room. Uncle Hai asked me to sit down. There was a long table with eight chairs around it in the middle of the living room. There were two big closets against the wall and one big altar in the middle. In the corner was a very old wooden sofa. Along the wall were beautiful plaques and portraits, all of black lacquer with shell. Uncle Hai asked about my family while a girl brought some tea into the living room for us. Hanh came back out smiling, as if he had good news. The dogs sat on the front porch now.

"Uncle, do you want to go with me to visit my mother?" Hanh asked Uncle Hai.

"It would be nice, wouldn't it? But I think it will be better for me to stay here. Who knows when I will die." He broke out laughing.

"How about if I take my mother to visit you, uncle?"

"That might be better. Nowadays, it seems the old go to visit the younger. Not like the old days when the younger visited the older," Uncle Hai said.

"What can you do, uncle? All the younger people are in labor camps, in jails. The older have to help to take care of them," exclaimed Hanh.

"I don't know. Life is upside down these days. I remember, when my parents were old, I took care of them, but now I have to take care of my children in my old age. God can see it." Uncle Hai took a deep breath as if he were disgusted.

"Uncle, can we get some coconut?" Hanh asked.

"Yes, sure."

We walked out to the back of the house where the river ran through his land. Along the side of the river, Uncle Hai grew coconut trees. Some of them were twice my height, four meters, and some were ten meters or more. The fronds of the shorter one slumped down, reaching the surface of the water like someone opening his arms wide, ready to caress. Uncle Hai picked up a knife on the way out.

"Which one is sweet and ready to drink, uncle?"

"Try that one," he said, pointing to a tree about my size with pink-colored coconuts where we could reach them. Hanh stepped over to pick one, breaking the stem off and handing it to me.

"Chop it."

He picked another one while I got a knife to cut through the husk of the coconut until I touched the shell. I made a hole, then offered the shell to Uncle Hai, but he declined. Hanh drank it all at once. I chopped one for myself. The sky was clear with many different colors of light blue, yellow, gold, and white, and layers of layers of thick clouds like cotton. The sun sank slowly at the end of the land behind the river. The air was fresh, a cool afternoon breeze lingering in the village. The grass was green in part of the garden, mixed with many different kinds of fruit trees. Beside the river was a little coconut-leaf roof which covered the boat from the weather. Next to it was a net hanging on bamboo sticks, which could be lifted up and let down into the river to catch fish.

"Is that your boat, uncle?" Hanh asked.

"Yes, we haven't used it for years."

We all walked over to it. Hanh climbed on board. It looked old and had some water inside. I jumped on the top of the deck to examine it carefully. We knocked on the wood to see if it was rotten, checking from side to side all the way to the stern. It had no engine and was about two and one-half meters wide by fourteen meters long.

"It's still okay but you have to fix and wax it," Uncle Hai said.

"How long do you think it will take to finish fixing it up, uncle?"

"Maybe a month or so. You have to pull it on land, scrape

the old wax with all the caulking. Then, you boil some new wax, paste it on, and let it dry at least a week."

"Ong Noi, Ong Noi, come in for dinner," a little girl called Uncle Hai.

"Leave it. Let's go and eat something before everyone starves!"

We went inside the house and dinner was already on the table. Uncle Hai sat down, offering us our meal. The children and others were sitting at another table. Uncle Hai's wife sat with us, rising periodically to bring more food.

"Have some more, we have plenty for the children." She put some more fish into my bowl, pouring some sauce into the rice.

"I'm okay, ma'am," I said.

"You have to eat it all. If you don't, she will get upset," Hanh warned me.

"It was a wonderful meal, ma'am. I haven't had this kind of family dinner for a long time," I said.

The lady smiled at the compliment. Tea always came after dinner. The girls were busy cleaning dishes. Through the window, I saw a clothesline moving. A small girl was helping her sister to hold the clothes as she took them off the line. A dog walked around as if he were an inspector. The oil lamps were lit, and dusk fell. The air was clean and fresh. Sometimes I heard the leaves rattling outside, mixing with the sounds of insects chanting in different voices and tones in the night. Uncle Hai kept us company until late with stories about his youth, as we sat in a circle with his grandchildren. We didn't realize how late it was until some of the youngsters fell asleep. His wife was working all the time on this and that, then went to bed after everyone was asleep. She would rise again before anyone the next morning. And so I spent a peaceful night with a good-hearted family.

Hanh and I decided to stay and begin work on the project immediately without wasting any time. We chopped some banana trees down, placed them on the ground in front of the boat, and hauled it ashore. Hanh scooped the water out and scraped the wax off, while I went to find a place where they built boats in order to buy some wax. The wax resembled tar but was a lighter color, and was made from tree sap. I boiled it for days.

"It is okay now. Take it off," Uncle Hai told me. "It looks like a liquid now, but after you let it sit for a half day then it will be a perfect softness to apply to the boat. If you have some yarn, dip it in, apply it as caulking to the joints of the hull. When you finish the whole boat, boil and paste it again, and then it will be done," he added.

We followed his instructions carefully, knowing he had more experience than any of us. I had three pieces of gold along with some other money, plus Hanh's gold. I told Hanh to let me hunt for an engine. He agreed and I searched all over the city but couldn't find anything. I would have to go all the way to Saigon to get one, with papers from the police saying I was buying an engine for a government company, according to papers we had obtained by bribing the boat authorities. I arrived in Saigon and walked around the government stores until I found a Japanese-made F-10 diesel engine. It was not very powerful, but it was the biggest engine left as they had imported nothing recently. After 1975, when the northern government had taken over from the businesspeople, many sorts of trade had come to a halt. I felt somewhat lucky. I knew from experience that if we went on the ocean, we would need a compass and some sleeping pills for the children. I went to a flea market to get them—all sorts of items were available there, even guns and grenades.

After buying everything I needed, I headed back to Soc Trang. On my way, I stopped to tell my brother Lan about the trip. He was excited, and I told him that when the boat was completed I would put him on board as a sailor. I came back to the village just in time, for the boat was done. I borrowed a small boat from a neighbor to transport the engine from the bus station in Soc Trang city to Uncle Hai's house and I had papers from the local government to show to any authorities that I purchased the engine for government use. We hired a carpenter to place the engine in it, asking him to make a little compartment along the side of the boat where we could hide rice and gas without anyone noticing. He agreed to do it and keep quiet, for extra money, and it was done in two days.

Uncle Hai was busy looking at the calendar, choosing a good day to put the boat in the water. I spoke with Hanh about my brother, and we registered the boat at the police station and the government business office. They put our names down, what route we would do business along, and the kind of material we would sell. I wrote down that the route would be from Soc Trang to Chuong Thien, along with the U Minh jungle, Vinh Binh, Sa Dec, and Saigon. We would sell wood, ceramic barrels, and coconuts. As always the authorities asked for their personal tax, some kind of bribe each time we did business with them. But since we had some money we got what we wanted. Chanh, Hanh's relative, returned from Saigon with his sick mother. We asked if he was interested in our journey; if not we would pay him for the boat.

"What do you think?" Hanh tried to convince Chanh. "We can't do anything here. We don't know when we will be drafted into the army. We don't know when they are going to arrest us while taking our assets. Your mother is sick with a gallstone. She needs treatment," said Hanh.

Chanh thought silently.

"Okay, I'm with you, but I have to talk with my grandfather."

"Speak with him to arrange things now while we look around to familiarize ourselves with this area," Hanh said.

Monday to Sunday, week by week, another month passed.

anh, my brother Lan and I launched the boat on a day that Uncle Hai had recommended as a promising one. We bought food and diesel from the local authorities, who sold us just enough for the first part of the trip. We would have to stop again at another place for the second half of the trip. We started at Can Tho and moved along the Hau Giang Mekong River to Soc Trang, and then onto the ocean along the coast. It was good to smell the breeze from the sea. I felt as if I was tasting my first freedom when I saw the waves and the boats moving back and forth at the mouth of the ocean. Sometimes we would stop the engine and row ten or twenty kilometers to save gas, which we hid in a small bottle in the compartments the carpenter had made.

We lifted our anchor, not knowing exactly where we were going. We kept going and stopping at different places, different cities, where there were boats anchored on the docks. We talked with the people about our new business, learning our trade: selling wood, ceramic barrels and coconuts. We went to U Minh jungle to chop wood, pretending to be lumbermen, then took the wood to Chuong Thien to sell. There we bought some ceramic barrels, the kind people used for holding water, and transported them to Bac Lieu and sold them along the way. Occasionally we stopped in Soc Trang, where we bought coconuts to sell in Can Tho.

We stopped by my aunt's to pick up my brother. Hanh's family was ready to go, but his mother would stay behind. No one could change her mind. I asked Hanh to contact my family for me, but my father said he would leave only when all of his children came back from the labor camp. Otherwise, he said, the children wouldn't know where to find our family and no one would be left to take care of the temple. My sisters couldn't leave because they had to take care of my parents. They told Hanh to help take care of me. My father prayed for us to be fortunate on our journey. This was the last I saw of my family, of my loved ones. I knew my mother would weep every time someone mentioned our names or whenever she heard someone call children with names similar to ours. Maybe she would weep until her last breath. How long would she live?

The New Year had passed by more than a month before. We knew our trade and route very well by this time. We discussed leaving during the New Year, when people were so busy with festivities that they would pay little attention to us. But during this season, the ocean still had violent storms. We waited for the season to change. Sometime in March, we would be able to go. We collected enough gas, food, and water, but we didn't have a captain yet. We knew how to operate our boat on the river, but not on the ocean. If we got lost on the river we could find our way and find food and water to feed ourselves. But if we were lost on the ocean, our lives would end. We had two families altogether for this trip: Hanh and Chanh and my brother Lan and I, with children and women.

We tried to go onto the sea once more to practice before the actual trip took place. But we made the mistake of heading straight for the sea, instead of following the channel when we reached the ocean. The boat ran aground at the mouth of the river where the water was shallow. We asked another boat to pull us out from the sandbar, having learned a lesson about this submerged island.

We noticed that the police checked traffic usually only during daylight. The guard boat ran along the river at night once in a while. They stopped several times to check our boat, but we had nothing to hide. They were familiar with our boat now. We gave them some gifts from time to time to make it easier for us to travel between Rach Gia, Can Tho, and Soc Trang.

We decided to use the Rach Gia city route since the security there seemed loose. It was close to the sea, and it would be easy to find a place to board. We had a big debate about this because it seemed easier to leave from Soc Trang as this was closer to the ocean than Rach Gia; but Chanh's family and Hanh's relatives were local people, and would be instantly identified if the police caught us. We put some of Hanh's family members on board first along with my brother Lan, before our boat reached Rach Gia. My responsibility was to help transport Chanh's family to the place we had agreed on, while Hanh transported his family to Rach Gia. Hanh's uncle, the secret police officer dressed in his uniform, helped. People could see that it was just a nice communist family moving into town. I didn't know how Hanh persuaded his uncle to help him move, but he told me later that even this powerful bureaucrat was fed up with the communist government. Also, he had his own plan to move in with Hanh's mother and inherit the house after she died, so helping us leave worked to his advantage as well.

We arranged small canoes as taxis to move two groups to our main boat, which we had hidden in some woods. We agreed to leave at exactly eleven o'clock on March 3, 1978. If for some reason people got lost, we would wait until midnight and then leave without hesitation. It was especially dark that night. The current would rise until midnight, recede until four o'clock, then rise again. The sky was clear with no sign of storms. I thought it was our time, our last chance. We had put all our money, hope, and energy into it. I prayed for our trip, believing our future would be decided now, one way or the other.

I went quietly to Soc Trang, to the village, to move Chanh's family. At the last minute, his grandparents decided not to go. Chanh's family and I arrived at Rach Gia bus station at 8:00 p.m. We had two hours to spare so we wandered around the market and ate, disguised as local people to avoid any suspicion. We hung out, acting as if we had missed the bus. We sat at the platform where other people slept at night, while the police walked around smoking with their comrades. Chanh and I didn't talk to each other, and let the women and children stay together. Whenever we needed to speak I signaled Chanh to come to the rest room to converse there, much as we prisoners had done in the labor camp. I walked down to the river from time to time to see if our taxi had come yet. In front of the dock was a police gate, but they didn't check anyone. On another side of the river a funeral was going on, and I could hear people moaning. I wondered whether, in some way, the funeral might be my own. People got on the boat that crossed the river without being harassed.

"Do you have a match?" someone asked me over my shoulder. I was startled, turned back, answering hesitantly.

"No, I don't smoke."

The man winked at me but I forgot about our signal until he walked about ten meters away. I ran back to the bus station to signal my group to walk down to the dock. There were two canoes for us. One had a woman to row it. We divided up our group and boarded both of the canoes, about seven of us in each one. Suddenly, a policeman came to the man who rowed Chanh's canoe.

"Give me a lift to the other side, would you?"

My heart seemed to stop and it felt like there was no air to breathe.

"Sure, comrade."

"Where are you going?" the VC asked.

"We're going home, comrade," the taxi man answered.

The policeman got on board and pushed the canoe off of the dock. Everyone was silent. I was planning how to run away if he discovered our secret. We were out about four meters when another policeman ran out from the booth.

"Stop, stop!" he shrieked.

I jumped into the water and the canoe tilted. A gush of water came in the boat, and people yelled, afraid the canoe would sink. The taxi man moved the boat closer to help me, thinking I had fallen off the boat. I tried to swim, but the policeman held my hand and pulled me back on board. He asked the police on the side of the river what he wanted, and ordered the taxi man to go back to pick up his comrade. I sat on the canoe trembling because I was scared.

The man paddled the canoe back to pick up the VC and carried them across the river. When they got off I felt like a great weight had been lifted off of me. I had come so far, but so much still depended on chance. On both sides of the river, dim lights shined weakly on the water. I saw people walking along the road and chatting inside their houses. Each time I paddled, I heard muffled voices and the light was getting weaker, disappearing in the distance. The crying from the funeral vanished. I asked the pilot woman if she had another paddle that I could use to help her move the canoe faster, but there was none. Everybody seemed exhausted from the trip. Bugs attacked us; slaps rang out. It was late and there was little traffic on this riverbank. The woman turned the canoe into another small branch, and continued on. The dim light of houses had faded some time ago, yielding to the darkness. One of the children, bored, put his hand out to play in the water. The woman began to speak as if we were a family to avoid suspicion in case anyone was listening.

"How's your grandfather?"

"He is okay, aunt," I answered.

"Did they say when they would come and visit us?"

"I don't know but they asked about you," I said.

Our conversation went on and then she called her husband, who rowed Chanh's canoe, asking him about what they were going to get tomorrow at the market. I couldn't see far, so I used my hearing and touching senses to determine our surroundings. I knew our canoe moved into a wilder creek with weeds, trees, and bushes because the sides of the canoe rattled against them and some small tree branches scratched our backs.

"Put your hand inside and bend your head down a little so that you don't fall into the river," a man's voice whispered from the front of the canoe. Birds burst from the leaves as we passed them. I heard an engine roaring along. The woman stopped our canoe, pushing it to the side under a big tree.

"Keep silent. The guard boat," a man's voice said gently.

We held our breath and tried to be numb but the louder the engine ran, the faster we breathed. Every adult put a hand over a child's mouth, just in case they shouted or sneezed. The police boat moved a searchlight from side to side on the river. I could see a beam flash on shore, bushes, trees, like a laser cutting through skin. The mosquitoes had a feast, as no one could chase them away. The waves rattled our canoe, sloshing it up and down on the surface of the water. The guard boat passed.

After a minute the woman pushed us out into the current to follow the canoe ahead. We released the kids' mouths so that they could breathe more easily. We came out to the big river again. In total darkness, I could hear the wind blowing and the waves splashing at the side of the canoe. We went on for one more hour, until we reached our spot. Our big boat was hidden in the middle of a small creek, surrounded by jungle mud. I saw the man puff his cigarette three times then put it out. The flashlights flicked on and off two times in the distance. We rushed our canoe in the direction of the boat. Chanh and others got out of the man's canoe. They were on one side of the bank and we were on the other.

"How many?" I heard my brother's voice.

"Nine."

We were all silent. The only sounds were of the canoe hitting our boat and of people moving around in the dark.

I climbed on board last while Hanh pulled some gold out to pay the taxi, counting under a small light inside the cabin. Our group was the last group. The canoe moved out. We pushed our boat from the mud and began to row to the big river. We put some of the children under the deck in front, giving them sleeping pills as the women watched over them. We passed a signal: we would break out to fight for a last struggle if we heard three knocks. We agreed that we would either die together or live free. All of the men helped paddle or row without any rest until we reached the gate near the ocean for the checkpoint.

We started the engine and posted our usual crew, as if this was just another business trip. The rest of us climbed into the ceramic barrels, closing the lids. We left some barrels empty so that if a VC asked to check them, we could open one of the empty barrels for him to see. Before I closed my lid, I saw a light from a booth near where the VC walked around on the side of the river. The engine stopped and our boat slowly came to shore.

"What are you carrying today?" one of the VC asked.

"Ceramic barrels, comrade," my brother answered.

"I know you are going to get wood on the way back, right?" the VC said.

"Yes, comrade, you know everything!" Hanh tried to flatter him.

He laughed cleverly and stepped onto our deck. I heard his footsteps on the wood, creaking from the bow toward the cabin where we hid in the barrels.

"Have some cigarettes, comrade," my brother insisted.

I heard the lighter sound.

"This is good," the VC coughed. "Is your engine running okay now?"

"Yes, comrade. Thank you for your rescue last time," Hanh answered from the cabin.

"Do you know how to fix your engine now?"

"Not that well, comrade."

"Those barrels are big. Can you give us some next trip? We need to have some at our booth," the VC said.

"Sure, comrade." Hanh agreed to the bribe.

The VC used his hand to knock on our barrels on the way out. He knocked twice on the lid of mine. If he had knocked one more time on my barrel, I would have pushed the lid off and jumped out: three knocks signaled that we were to come out and fight the VC until our last breath.

He got off our boat and my brother pushed it out.

"See you next trip, comrade."

"Yeah. Throw me a pack of cigarettes, would you? I forgot," the VC called from the shore.

I heard a sound like something dropping to the ground, and then our engine started moving us on our way.

CHAPTER 16

W e got out from our barrels and breathed the good
misty air of the pre-dawn. It was 4:30 a.m. on my
watch, but it was still dark. We hung a little light
on the cabin for the other boats to see, for the traffic was picking up. All of a sudden, I fell down, people shrieked. Our boat
had collided with another small boat.

"Can't you see where you are going?" a woman's voice
yelled at us.

"It's okay, no harm done. I'm sorry ma'am."

We pushed our boat away from them and turned our engine
to a higher speed. At about 5:30 a.m. we arrived at the open
sea. The sky was brighter but I could see light scattering from a
fisherman's boat. The moist air filled my nostrils. I felt as if the
light was seeping into me, showing me a new space, a new horizon. Life had just begun, maybe.

"Water, water leaking," a woman's voice came out from under the deck.

My brother and I rushed to check the situation before dark.
The flashlight in his hand went to the direction of the woman
calling. The children were still drunk in their sleep with the
sleeping pills.

"Where is it?"

"In front here."

We crawled all the way to the head of the boat, moving our
light slowly from spot to spot. Some water sprinkled on my
face.

"Anh Lan, right here," I called to him.

He turned the light on a little hole that had a crack around
it. Whenever the waves slapped outside, the water leaked and
sprinkled inside. I took off my shirt and held it there.

"Brother, ask them if they have any wax sap left?"

My brother passed my message to the cabin, reporting our
situation.

"No, we don't have any. Try to hold on till the day comes so that we can figure out what to do with it," Hanh's voice came from above the deck.

Both of us took turns holding the hole until daylight. Some of the children began to wake up, vomiting and crying out with their seasickness. I felt dizzy with memory in this tight, cramped place where everybody lay upon each other in their own urine, suffocated by the smell of smoke, gas, and oil.

"Is it okay to take some people up to the deck to get some air? We are suffocating in here!" I shouted.

"Okay, pull them out," someone in the cabin said.

We broke all the ceramic barrels and threw them into the ocean, then moved the children and women out from the compartment to get some fresh morning air. Everyone seemed to have recovered after a few minutes.

I let my brother hold the hole while I climbed into the cabin.

"Do we have any plastic cans and some nails?" I asked.

From the engine room beneath the cabin someone yelled out.

"Hold on, we found something."

Someone pushed up a carpenter's toolbox with wrenches, sockets, hammers, and screwdrivers. I picked it up.

"Don't drop it into the ocean. We desperately need it to fix our engine if it breaks."

"Okay," I said.

Hanh was our captain now. Whether he really knew where we were going, I wasn't sure.

"Is the compass working all right?" I asked.

"Yeah," Hanh said. "I guess."

"Which way are we going?"

"180 degrees east."

"How do you know that?"

"I learned from different people. Remember I have a cousin who was a captain in the southern navy."

"I didn't know if you were just making it up."

"Yes," he said, winking his clever eyes at me, his bold features looking bigger, somehow, out in the free sea air.

We laughed, looking at each other in appreciation.

"Go and fix the hole before we sink," he said.

The atmosphere was less tense now, even though we had a hole to take care of. I looked around the cabin to find something to plug it.

"Why don't you cut a piece of our poncho on the deck and use it?" suggested Hanh.

"But we cannot hold it all the time," I joked.

I looked at a small wooden door from the cabin, pulled a hammer out and broke off a piece of it, which I passed down to my brother.

We put two shirts into the hole, folded a piece of the poncho into a square over the hole, nailed it down, and hammered a piece of wood over it all. It looked okay to me, for now. We came up to the deck and put the toolbox back in the engine room.

The children began asking for food and water as the women started distributing our first meal at sea. The sun was red, just over the water. It looked so close. The air was clear in the high blue sky; clouds of pink, rose, orange, and red danced around the sun. The sky looked like a painting hung above the glistening water. And so our journey on the open ocean began. The waves were very gentle, the air was fresh, people in our boat started speaking all at once, lively after our meal. I saw the shoreline fade further from us. A flock of seagulls flew together in the air, gliding back and forth. In the distance, some dinghys sat on the water, fishing. The air patted lightly on my face, and I inhaled and exhaled in high spirits, enjoying my freedom at last. Two inches of mist above the water scattered, dissolved by the sunbeams that slowly began to warm us. Some of the children and women started their new day sitting along the side of the boat, searching beyond their thoughts. Maybe they were taking a last look at their homeland. It was a quiet morning except for the noise of the engine.

"Look, look, mama!" a child shouted, pointing a finger to the back of our boat.

I saw a gang of fish jumping up and down in the water, chasing us. Everyone clapped and cheered, excited.

"Come on, *Ong Nuoc*, race with us!"

The louder we got, the faster the fish moved. Soon they caught up with our boat, came closer to us, the water splashing against the boat and sprinkling us. When they were ahead of us we were excited for them. Every time they went too far from our boat, they slowed down as if waiting for us, then moved on again when we got closer to them. By now the fish seemed to know me as a family member; each time I escaped, they welcomed me. "Come with us, we will escort you," they seemed to say.

"We're going to have wonderful weather for at least two days," one smiling middle-aged woman said as she held a rag over the heads of the children, shielding them from the hot sun of the open deck. Our journey went on until the afternoon, when we saw a big boat appear from the distance.

"I think it's the government boat. It's moving toward us!" I yelled from the front deck.

Hanh and some others came out from the cabin to spot it if it came in our direction.

"Hanh, what degree have we been going for the last two hours?" I asked him as I jumped on the back cabin.

"350 degrees east. Never mind. Turn our boat to another direction to run away from this monster!" Hanh bellowed.

We lost our course from then on. But two days and one night passed without any problems. We were in the middle of nowhere and could see nothing but blue water, boundless sky, and hot sun.

The storm struck during the second night. The wind whistled and roared while the rain poured down harder and harder. Waves as big as a house pushed our boat from side to side; water came into our boat from the sky and from the hole I had mended, which now poured like a broken pipe. My brother and I took care of the hole, scooping the water out while the children cried and the women moaned. Hanh and Chanh tried to keep the engine running. The boat pushed against the waves. Waves pushed the boat higher, and then we'd fall into the abyss with more water gushing into our boat. Everyone struggled, but our seasickness made us weak. The kerosene lamp fell off from the side of the cabin onto the deck, broke,

burst into a blaze of oil, then drowned when a big wave splattered our deck. It seemed that life was going to end at the cruel
bottom of the ocean.

But all of a sudden the rain stopped, the howling of the
wind slowed to a whine, and the waves diminished. Calm
returned. Our engine stopped because too much water had
flooded it. We rested there for a while, helpless. Our men began to mend the leaking hole again. We got up and cleaned
away our defeat by nature. We scooped the water out, cleaned
the engine, made an inventory to see what had survived. The
storm had lasted for only half an hour but it seemed the night
would never end. We were lost in the middle of nowhere. We
moved on in the early dawn, not knowing where to go. We
searched for the *Sao Mai* star to locate our direction and went
east. Some women and men were begging us to go back but
Hanh told them to shut up. Hanh said that if he heard one
more word from them he would throw them into the ocean.
We lived free, or died, but would never return.

Another day passed. We hung a white rag as an SOS flag from the pole at the top of the cabin, hoping for a friendly rescue. We had no more food, no more water, but luckily we could squeeze our wet clothes for water, drinking water given to us by the storm. Another night passed. The hot sun came, pouring down heat as if to barbecue us. We drank our own urine to help us bear the heat and used it to dampen our clothes. The children fell down on the deck and into the bottom of the boat, where oil and excrement lay everywhere. The men lay about the boat, collapsed from exhaustion, starvation, and hopelessness. Two women who still had a little energy left collected urine. The children were groaning "Water, water." But no one responded, not even their parents now. I felt like I was walking into the sky, dizzy, wanting to move to a different place, but I couldn't move my body. I was a big rock stuck on the wood. I could comprehend everything happening around me, but I couldn't control my body. After a while, the engine stopped, out of gas. Yet even if it were running no one would have been able to steer, because nobody had any strength left.

We floated on the water like a ghost boat, carrying a bunch of wandering, innocent souls. I kept looking at my watch; sometimes I saw it was twelve and sometimes I saw it was two o'clock. Then our boat lurched off to one side while the water slapped harder against it. I saw a huge object appear and heard a loud noise. I was on the bottom of the deep ocean looking up at a giant on a hillside. The giant became clearer. It was a wooden boat painted red with some kind of picture on it. People stood up, looked down at us, moved away. Then another boat came, circling closer. Everything disappeared for a while. Finally, I heard people shouting in very strange voices, using a strange language. Our boat moved as if someone had jumped on it.

I opened my eyes and saw an old man with grey hair and skin darkened from time and hard work. His kind face looked

at me sincerely, worriedly, his eyes steady. He held a teaspoon
with water, putting it on my lips.

"*Ap nam, ap nam.*" Water, I guessed.

I sipped it, feeling the cold energy running all over my
body.

The old man called gently to the others. I heard people running. They surrounded me, smiling. They fed me some soup
from time to time, little by little, until I could stand up and
walk around.

A Thai fishing boat had rescued us at last. They towed our
boat on the back of their boat and sent a young man to fix our
engine. We scooped the water out of our boat once in a while.
My brother Lan, Hanh, Chanh, and eighteen others on the
boat were okay, but we had lost one child along with Chanh's
mother, who had been overcome by her sickness. She had died
just a few hours before we were rescued. They had already
been buried in the ocean.

They fed us as if we were their guests. I found out that the
old man was a cook, so I went to help him in the kitchen cabin.
He taught me *Kawpkoon krap* (thank you), and *mai* (doesn't
matter). I began to learn a new language and loved the sound
of it, especially when I heard a girl's voice.

For two days, our group helped the fisherman sort out fish,
and then we headed back to Thailand. The fisherman had already fixed our boat when we arrived in Thai territory. At sunset we bowed and said farewell to our saviours. Every one of us
wept tears of appreciation and wondered when we would meet
them again, since we couldn't get their address: the Thai government would punish them for helping us. The Thai captain
spoke to us in broken English, saying that he couldn't take us
all the way to the dock. The sky was a golden color over a tree
near a small mountain range at the end of the water. Seagulls
flew in the air, landed on a pole and on the deck to search for
some leftover fish. They made happy sounds whenever we
passed them, jumping up to another spot without hesitation,
continuing their hunt. They were free to fly while we enjoyed
our freedom. The water was clear but not as blue as it was farther from shore. We got back in our boat. They gave us water,
food, diesel, and showed us the direction to go.

"There, *Chanthaburi,* go there," they shouted.

We held our hands together, bowing them our respectful goodbye. We started our engine. They waited until they heard our boat run, then left us. We waved until the boat disappeared. The chilly wind blew, the sun sank. Lights gleamed from here and there, far away. Black smoke came out of our engine, because it hadn't run for some time, making us cough. We moved in the direction of Chanthaburi until eleven o'clock. But it seemed we weren't getting anywhere. The stars shone restlessly and I saw that Chanthaburi was brighter than any spot I had seen in a long time. I guessed the city had more light than other surrounding areas. I saw a boat with many lights coming our way.

"We are safe, we have help coming!" everybody shouted happily as they stood up, looking forward to the arrival of the boat.

When the boat came, the crew carefully looked us over, pushing their boat closer to ours. The boat was as big as the boat that had saved us. We held the side of their boat to stop it from hitting ours, while waves shook it back and forth.

"Please help. We are refugees," Hanh said in English.

Ten young men jumped onto our boat.

"Police, police," one of them said.

I thought they were police who came to help because the group was talking in Thai and broken English. Each one of them searched each one of us. They pulled my watch off, collected all the earrings from the women and girls. They searched in every corner, in every bag, and every little spot. Something seemed funny: if they were police why weren't they in uniforms, why did their boat carry no sign, and why were they taking our belongings? Before I could do anything the man searching me jerked a knife to my throat and yelled something to another in Thai. To our surprise, they held us hostage and we didn't know for sure what was going on. The children cried. Maybe it was a police search. They threw our utensils over to their boat, disconnected one essential part from our engine, and began to force all the men to one end of the boat, the women to the other. They turned all their lights off and I heard the three girls yell loudly for help, despair in their voices.

"Mama, help me, Baba, help me!"

The mother grasped the legs of the pirate who held her daughter, but he kicked her to the deck floor. We couldn't signal each other to fight back with our eyes, because it was dark. I shouted in Vietnamese as loud as I could.

"Fight for our last battle!"

My left hand grabbed the arm holding the knife to my throat and pushed it away while I used my right elbow to punch the chest of the false policeman with all my strength. He struggled with the pain and tried to press the knife harder into my throat but I grasped his hand with my two hands, bent down, and threw him over my head. He fell off the boat. The boat shook with our struggle and the waves, rocked from side to side as if it might capsize. I jumped in to help Hanh since with his polio he could not fight back. The pirate who held him pushed Hanh down on the floor and turned to me. He yelled something in Thai which I didn't understand, and the light from their boat turned on. Their boat was revving and gave our boat a strong push. I lost my balance and slid into the water along with others. They turned off their light and stopped crushing our boat. I swam to keep my head up for air, kept at some distance from the boat, unable to climb back on it.

The women and children cried out louder and louder, but who could help them? I heard the girls' voices become weaker and weaker as they struggled against the pirates. These girls were no more than seventeen years old. I was powerless and my eyes were stinging. Maybe I cried or maybe it was the salty water of the ocean, but I knew for sure that I had lost the last fight. I called out to my friends in the water to see if they were okay, but there was no response because the wind pushed the waves up and down and turned my voice into a whisper.

The pirates took turns holding the girls as they satisfied their animal thirsts. An hour later, I heard their boat revving louder, moving away into the dark, leaving only their laughter behind. They turned their lights on again. I swam back to our boat and got on board.

The women helped the three naked girls to find some clothes to wear. They were moaning, withdrawn to one spot, shaking like dying people. I saw tears drenching their faces, filled with hatred. Everyone became silent. Hanh had a bleeding wound on his head. My brother Lan had a cut on his chest. I had a small cut on my throat. The father of one of the girls was wounded on his arm and back, but not seriously. The wounds aggravated deeper hurts in our hearts more than our bodies. We started to paddle the boat ashore, thinking about what kind of freedom we would have.

At 5:00 a.m. we arrived. We made more holes in our boat to make sure that, if the authorities pushed us back to sea, we wouldn't make it, and they would have to rescue us. A big wave washed our boat onto a clean beach. We got off our boat and sat on the sand, but the drunkenness of the sea stuck with us. I saw the whole world go around in my head, the palm trees along the road, houses, streetlights, and cars spun in front of me. I vomited and vomited till nothing was inside my stomach and I tasted bitterness in my mouth.

The police discovered us in the morning when the chill was still in the air. We were shaking with our wetness, our clothes drying on our backs. The palm tree leaves rattled in the wind, lining the street along the shore. The lights were off now. A policeman came to check our boat, looking at us very strangely, cautiously. The police isolated us in one spot, not letting anyone go anywhere. We asked for permission to go to a temple, to beg for food. People gave us some bread and soda once in a while. They tried to talk to us, seeming to feel sorry for us, but the policeman wouldn't let them.

A few days passed as we bathed in the ocean every day and ran around until our clothes dried under the sun. We had to wait until dark to go to the bathroom, finding an isolated spot in the sand to do our business, or pretending to swim far out in the sea and do it in the water. A policeman would beat one of us up once in awhile, for some trivial reason. The three girls were terrified of all men. They sat in a corner with the old women without speaking to anyone, always in tears; I feared they had lost their minds.

We were stuck there in these conditions for a month. Two more boats full of Vietnamese refugees arrived in that time. They were in good shape morally and physically. They told us that they hadn't had any problems at sea.

On the first day of April, a reporter with a Vietnamese wife spotted us. The wife came, spoke with us, and then devised a plan for us to escape from the police and go to a refugee camp the reporter knew of. At midnight that night three journalists came. All of us swam to the two boats anchored outside the dock. We left Chanthaburi.

We arrived at Leamsing Refugee Camp on the night of April 2. The police didn't let us ashore, shooting in the air to threaten us. We stayed put on the boat, anchored about fifteen meters away from the dirty mud beach. Refugees rushed to the rock shore from their huts, standing upon the hillside, welcoming us, and asking about the news from home. Some of them identified relatives on the boat. Refugees threw bread, water, sodas, and cookies on board while the police tried to order them to go back to their shacks. It was becoming a tradition to greet new refugees, I learned.

"Hide any valuable things because tonight they will rob you before letting you ashore," someone in the crowd shouted to us.

"Where are you from?" they asked. "What is the situation at home?"

"Sa Dec," Hanh replied.

"It is horrible at home," I said.

"Break your engine just in case they pull you back to sea," another suggested. "Is there anybody from Phu Quoc island?"

We talked as if we were all relatives who hadn't seen each other for years. The refugees coached us on what to say to the police and how to fight back against intruders. Some people on the second boat gave one of the refugees a few letters to send to their loved ones in Australia; they would wait eagerly for the response.

We shared and enjoyed the food they had given us, celebrating our first chance to taste the air of freedom. At night we were alert on our boat and sometimes we heard pots and pans clanging, warning us of a robbery attack, but nothing happened. We were stuck on the boat as it lay at anchor for days, and then the United Nations High Commission for Refugees commissioner came to let us land.

On shore, we received rice, water, and several meters of plastic, which we fastened to an unfinished hut on a hillside, facing the ocean above an abandoned cemetery. This would be our place to rest, to settle for a while, and to begin our new life as a people without a country, as wandering souls who had lost their home just as surely as those lying beneath us had lost their lives. A gong sounded from the temple behind the bushes on the top of the hill. The wind hummed and whistled on bamboo leaves. Tides drew in and out, like an inner voice calling me back to the time when I was a young child, but the day went on without stopping. I sat down on the ground, inhaled the fresh air, looked further into the ocean, and wondered what was beyond.

CHAPTER 19

My brother Lan and I filed the papers with UNHCR for resettlement in any free country that would have us, and stayed in Leamsing Refugee Camp to wait for our release.

There were about 3,000 boat people in the camp and the refugees kept pouring into this dirty, tiny place every day. Because of its location, there were mudslides whenever it rained. On top of the hill was a brick cremation house where the villagers cremated the dead and held their funeral ceremonies. From time to time the smell and smoke of the dead floated into the air over the camp, making me nauseated. Next to the crematorium was a small office where the police who ran the camp were stationed. Beyond the office was a gate leading to the "problem world"—so called because if any refugee wandered beyond that gate they would be beaten by the police. It was a place we often came to in order to say farewell to refugees boarding buses for Bangkok or departing for resettlement in another country.

I had waited endlessly for this moment and sometimes I stood there watching refugees and dreamed until the red dirt from a departing bus flew up into my face. I dreamed of a wonderful world, my third country, wherever it would be. I would have a chance to go to school, to work, to do what I wanted. I would write home to my family to let them know I was alive after all. What had happened to them since I'd left, I wondered? I often wished I could be home, but how could I? I saw many refugees who escaped with their entire families and I envied them.

Lan was elected to be a head of the refugee camp, to help run the place and to deal with the officials. He divided people into working groups: interpreters to receive consulate officers who showed up at our camp, security, food and water, senior, youth, cleaning, health, and recreation. Lan himself headed the security group that patrolled the camp at night, since young Thai men had broken into our camp to sneak in girls' huts, raping or kidnapping them even though the Thai police were around. At night when we heard the pots and pans clang, everyone rushed for a wooden stick or whatever we could grab to guard our area while the security group sent someone to the police office to report.

We had only one well for the whole camp for baths, washing, and laundry. Each week a fire truck came to our camp to deliver drinking water. We waited for hours to receive a can of ten gallons or so, depending on the size of the family. Occasionally, they skipped a week or two. I could see desperation on people's faces at the well, waiting for each drop of contaminated water, but even the well would be empty for days. I received fifteen kilograms of rice a month for two people. It was enough for us and I gave some to bigger families with growing children. The mothers would grind the rice into flour and make treats, cakes, and soup to last until the next delivery.

Lan brought several young men to the shore to retrieve a disabled boat. We turned it into a library and entertainment center, filling it with magazines donated from overseas, so that we would have someplace to read. Our youth group met there and entertained the children while the waves ground against the shore, leaving debris behind.

While Lan helped to run the camp, I worked at household jobs. A truck dropped tree trunks off in front of the gate in the courtyard and I brought wood home to chop for cooking. I owned a couple of shirts, a pair of trousers, and one pair of shorts which Lan and I took turns wearing.

Every two or three weeks a supplier brought food to us, fish or chicken. I waited in line for hours to take home three pieces of rancid chicken about the size of my toe—I cooked them even if they were rotten since we had nothing else to eat with our rice.

There were a few Vietnamese-Chinese refugees in our camp who had escaped with gold which they could sell to live comfortably. Others saved rice to exchange for sugar or salt with the Thai people who lived around the area.

The pastor at the Baptist church near my hut handled all our mail. Every Sunday he held services, then called people to receive their letters. I used to come and stand around with the crowd in front of the church to listen for the roll call, even though I knew I would have no mail. People smiled and laughed when they received letters from their loved ones in other countries, and talked excitedly about the new life they would have when they joined their families. We would organize a game of volleyball, or set up an English class to pass the day.

When my brother became the chief of the camp, he changed a lot of things and was a very aggressive leader. He asked the police to do something when we caught the Thai men who invaded our camp at night. But the police did nothing and the same characters intruded again. Lan asked the UNHCR contractor to deliver water and food on time because we always received spoiled food, but they seldom kept their promises. The tension between the police and the refugees increased: they began to hate my brother for nagging them for this and that. Lan was twenty-three then but tall and strong; he wore a concerned and intelligent expression. Because the police hated him they also hated all the young men in the camp. Sometimes a police officer would pretend to be drunk and wander about the camp. If he saw a young man he would grab him and beat him up. No one could do anything about it, not even the UNHCR. Whenever the UNHCR officers came to the camp, the police were nice to them; but when the UNHCR left, the police returned to their cruelty.

After a few months, a Canadian consul came to the camp. Lan and I applied to go to Canada. After the interview, the officer admitted us, since we knew how to answer a few questions in English: "What is your name? When is your birthday? Where do you come from?" We were excited about the prospect and anxious for the day to come. I had heard people saying that after the Canadian consul interviewed and admitted you, you would depart for Canada within two months.

After the Canadian consul left, the water truck came and people gathered for water. A short police officer with small red eyes and alcohol on his breath was on duty that afternoon. I walked down the steps to my hut on the trail to get a plastic container for water while my brother cleaned up the Canadian consul's table. I heard people shouting at the cremation house in different languages—Chinese, Vietnamese, Cambodian, and Thai.

Suddenly, someone pushed me and I slid on the dirt. A Vietnamese boy my size swerved by me; there was a terrific boom. I looked up to see my brother push the policeman's gun aside and yell to the boy, "Run, run!" A middle-aged man standing by the side of the cremation house fell down on the ground and I saw blood dribble from his back. People ran away while I moved to help the wounded man lying a few steps from me, but my brother shouted, "Run, run and get a Thai interpreter!" So I dashed into the camp to search for the Thai interpreter. Ten minutes later I came back with him to the cremation house. He timidly asked the police what had happened and said he wanted to see the boy. My brother helped to bandage the wounded man, and asked the interpreter to tell the police to call for an ambulance to the hospital. Five minutes passed; a taxi came and took the bleeding man away.

I went home while my brother, the interpreter, and the Vietnamese camp advisors met with the police to resolve the matter. The police officer was angry and held his shotgun tightly. The afternoon silence was gone; the wind brought a fresh breeze from the sea into our bay. The waves pounded into the rocks, pushing a few exhausted fishing boats to the dock after their long hunting trips on the ocean. I heard their engines sputter in the water. Bamboo leaves rattled on top of the hill. The kerosene light made from a coke can was lit and I looked into the dark trail, asking myself why I couldn't have stayed at home in my country. I could not understand why a guard would shoot a young man just because he didn't like helpless refugees.

Two weeks later, a nurse who worked for the UNHCR came to the camp to take me and Lan along with other refugees, to the hospital in town to have a health checkup as part of the resettlement process. They gave us shots, x-rays, urine and blood tests. We received the results a week later, it indicated that Lan and I had no diseases or health problems. I began to hope we would leave the camp soon. Some of the people in my boat had already left for France a month before and I asked them to send a letter home. Hanh went to Italy to resettle and Chanh's family went to Australia.

A few weeks passed and the U.S. consul came to Leamsing Camp and called Lan and me to their table. I didn't know what was wrong. A Vietnamese woman who worked for the embassy held a letter, pulled forty dollars out, and gave it to me.

"You have a brother in the States who sent you some money," she said, and smiled at us.

Lan and I looked at each other. We thought our brother, Tuong the pilot, had died when the war ended on April 30, 1975. We had heard a rumor that he was in Canada, but I didn't believe it. I was elated and wrote him a letter that night, sending it to his address in Corinth, Mississippi. I told him that we had already applied to go to Canada and were waiting for the date to leave the camp. A few days later, I received a telegram from him advising us not to go to Canada, but to come to the States to reunite with him. Then another letter with a picture of himself, his wife To, and four of my nephews in front of a trailer park. He said he missed his brothers and sisters, and that living away from home was difficult. He would be happy if we were all together. Lan and I applied to go to the States when the U.S. consul came to the camp again; we told them we wanted to be reunited with our brother in Mississippi. The Canadian consul and the U.S. embassy argued with each other about us and we were stuck in the camp for eight months while my brother kept sending money from Mississippi to help us, along with a promise to pay for our airplane tickets.

In November, we got our names on the list to go to the States. A bus came to the camp to take us and two other families on the seven-hour drive to Bangkok. We said farewell to friends and refugees standing at the gate who waved to us. Finally, I was the one on the bus. We arrived in Bangkok, and a few days later an International Catholic Migration person took us to Bangkok International Airport for our departure. He gave us a white plastic bag with the ICM trademark, containing all our documents. When people looked at us they would recognize that we were refugees by the bag we were carrying. We flew Air France to Manila and stayed at a hotel for one night. They didn't let us out of the room; I felt like I was in jail. We continued our trip to Osaka, Japan, for refueling and then flew directly to Chicago.

About fifteen Hmong people travelled with us, most of them children. One of the flight attendants didn't know how to serve dinner to them. She asked me if I could speak to them to see how many trays they wanted. I didn't know how to speak the Hmong language but I took my ticket out, showed it to them, and asked for theirs, then told the attendant how many trays to serve according to the number of tickets. She was happy and thanked me. We had a chicken dinner with salad and cookies for dessert. It was good but I didn't feel like eating because I was anxious to see my brother and his family. After dinner they showed a movie but I didn't understand a word. I walked back and forth in the aisle to stretch my legs. I felt uneasy, and came back to sit in my seat. I covered myself with a wool blanket and went to sleep in the strange cool of an air conditioner.

We arrived at O'Hare International Airport the next afternoon. Two Vietnamese working for ICM met us and brought us to American Airlines for our final destination of Memphis, Tennessee. We waited five hours at the airport, exhausted. It was the longest trip of my life. I felt uneasy not knowing whether I would ever have a chance to return home. We departed, and arrived in Memphis around 11:30 p.m. As I got off the aircraft my heart bounced inside my chest; I walked through the gate. I saw my brother, my sister-in-law, and four nephews. We ran toward each other and embraced; we cried. For a few minutes we couldn't speak. Then Tuong asked me about home and I told him some of what had happened a year ago when I left. He rubbed my head and kept saying, "How big you are now! Who can believe that you escaped." He was shorter than me and broader, wearing a big white shirt. My sister-in-law asked me about her family but I didn't know much about them. She tried to look calm but could not hide the emotion from her smooth face. She still wore the jade earrings that she had worn in Vietnam.

My nephews tried to speak with me in Vietnamese but it was hard to understand them. Then they spoke in English with each other and their father explained to them who Lan and I were. They had been babies when they were in Vietnam but they were big now. They hesitated before approaching me but a few moments later they held my hands and pulled me away to a machine against the wall, put coins in it, pulled out some candies. We shared the sweets. Tuong asked us if we had any luggage and I told him, "Hey, we're refugees, you know." We all laughed. "You talk just like when you were young," he said.

The drive home on that foggy night took two hours. It was beautiful along the road, houses scattered about with faint light shining from front doors here and there. The air was fresh. People were asleep but our conversation never ended. My two younger nephews fell asleep.

We arrived at the trailer around 2:00 a.m. My sister-in-law put the kids to bed, showed us where to sleep, and asked us if we were hungry. Tuong showed us how to use the toilet, the lights, the television, and the phone. They went to bed so they could get up for their early-morning jobs at ITT. Lan and I could not sleep because of jet lag. We ate at night and slept during the day.

On the weekend, we all went to the supermarket. Tuong taught us how to buy food and his wife explained how to get better deals buying large quantities and using coupons. I could not believe all the stuff the supermarket carried, and how cold it was inside. Tuong bought beef to make steaks and beer for us to drink, even though he never drank. My nephews ran around to get toothbrushes for us and bought cookies. I felt as if we took a whole market home and the bill was $80.

We celebrated our reunion and talked more about our family and the situation back home. I told Tuong that if he had stayed behind, the VC would have executed him the minute they captured him. He was silent for a moment and said, "It's fate." We didn't have any news from home but Tuong had sent a letter to my parents through a cousin in Paris. He told us how hard it had been not receiving any news from home for years, until we had come. We missed home and our loved ones but we did not want to endanger them, so we never wrote home after our arrival. I got drunk that day and fainted in the bathroom. I was happy to be with my family.

Tuong told us to relax and put some flesh on our bones for now, but I couldn't sleep at night. The trailer was small even though it had three bedrooms. Lan and I stayed in one room, but I liked to sleep on the couch in the living room. My four nephews were in the second bedroom and Tuong and his wife in the third. November was a cold month in Corinth, Mississippi. The trailer was heated but I felt a new kind of cold that chilled my bones. I put some sweaters and blankets on and walked about. My nephew made a joke about me, "You look like an old man, uncle!" We laughed and I chased after him. I loved to watch television even if I didn't understand a word. Tuong questioned me in Vietnamese to see how much English I knew.

"Do you hear everything they say?"

"Yes, I hear everything." He looked at me with surprise, "But I don't understand a word."

My sister-in-law broke out laughing and we joined her. Tuong patted my shoulder. "It takes time." When some of their friends would stop by to say hello to us, the house grew merry.

One Sunday while we all sat in the living room watching Clint Eastwood in a Western movie—I was excited to see how he shot the bad guy—suddenly my two nephews Tuan and Long rushed to hide behind the sofa, nervous. I didn't know why they acted this way and I looked at Tuong to inquire.

"What's wrong?" I asked.

"They still remember the war." He stood up, looking sad, and walked into his room.

I held my two nephews telling them it was okay and it wasn't real. They got up slowly to sit next to me. I turned off the television and the gunfire subsided.

Tuong took a Monday off to take us to apply for a Social Security number and make an appointment to take the written exam for a driver's license. He drove us around Corinth, a small town of less than 5,000 people. We went to the local high school to register for English classes, but the counselor told us that we were too old.

"I think what you need to do is get a job, not go to school," he scolded Tuong, who translated the English for us. "Why do you want to study English?" We thanked the counselor for his lecture and left. I was disappointed, and knew we could not find a job if we didn't speak any English. I did not know what I was going to do with my life, because the dream of going to school was gone. Yes, I was too old, twenty-two already.

Tuong had spoken with his boss at ITT to see if they had any openings that he could offer us, but there was nothing. Tuong taught us how to read the newspaper for job ads, but there wasn't anything in this small town that we could do.

Lan and I stayed home, watched television, babysat the kids after they got out of school, and did whatever we could to help around the house while Tuong and my sister-in-law went to work to support six of us plus themselves. We barely survived on their salaries. I felt depressed and helpless; I didn't want to live off my brother's family. I felt that I was strong enough to take care of myself but I didn't know how I could in this situation.

Lan had a friend who had just arrived in California. He had received welfare and vocational training and English before getting a job. Lan planned to move there. We discussed the idea with Tuong and his wife. Tuong said, "It's better for us to stay together; we don't have many loved ones around. Besides," he continued, "you just came and you don't know much about life in the States. It makes me worry, especially if something were to happen to you. What would I say to our parents?" I looked over at Tuong. He was looking down at the brown carpet, crying.

"It will get better after the winter," To said softly.

Lan decided to stay for a while, and asked Tuong to take us to apply for welfare assistance, Medicaid, and food stamps like his friend in California. But the welfare department rejected us; I didn't know what the reason was. I felt humiliated and insulted because wherever we asked for help, everyone turned us away. Tuong explained to us, "We have to make it on our own; no one is going to help us if we cannot help ourselves. If we survived the Vietnamese War, we will not die here," he sighed. "Besides, using welfare is like putting ourselves down. We have dignity, grace, and we're proud to be Vietnamese. Welfare programs were not designed for us. It's lucky that they turned us down."

Tuong took us to a college about two hours away to talk to someone in the admissions office about our situation, to see if we could go to school there. But we didn't have any money to pay, and our English wasn't good enough. Lan and I planned what we would do when we had jobs and a car; but we had neither for a while in that cold winter.

Tuong taught us how to drive whenever he had time and when the weather cooperated. He and my sister-in-law tried to do the best they could to help us cope with our new life, and they cheered us up by taking us to see movies and to visit places in Memphis.

One day Tuong and his wife came home after work and called us.

"Come, come outside."

We went out and I saw that everything was white, cold, tender. "It's snow!" one of my nephews shouted. I scooped some off the bush, put it into my mouth, let it melt. I ran about to catch the snowflakes pouring down like cotton in the air. My nephews taught me how to make a snowman and we had snow fights. My sister-in-law brought gloves and jackets out for us so that we wouldn't catch cold, and went in to make dinner. At the range of the pine, oak, and birch trees, I saw a round-faced sun which radiated a beautiful red-pink vermillion. It was quiet and no birds sang. The snow slowed, I stood still to catch the last flake and took a full breath of air before I came in for supper. It was the first snowy day in my life and it stayed with me.

Lan and I ate like pigs since we had nearly starved at the refugee camp and in the labor camps back home. As we stayed on I noticed Tuong and his wife starting to work overtime to manage our circumstances. Their savings were dwindling and they didn't have enough money to buy a pair of shoes for my oldest nephew, Tuan, who wanted to participate at the gym. They had done better when they first came, they told us. I wanted to do something but there was nothing for me to do.

At last Lan and I received $500 from the United States Catholic Charities for our resettlement. Having a little cash, and seeing the strain my brother's family was under, Lan came to a decision: he bought a Greyhound bus ticket for California. He would go and look for an opportunity for vocational training. Tuong and To were against the idea, but they understood how circumstances were against us; plus, ITT was facing hard times. We helped Lan pack some clothes and my sister-in-law prepared sandwiches for him to eat on the road. Tuong asked for the bus schedule and where they would change buses, then explained it all to Lan carefully. We took him to the bus station on a spring day when the flowers were beginning to flourish.

"Call us right away when you arrive," Tuong said, and approached the driver to ask him to watch my brother on the road for him. Lan didn't say anything but nodded his head. I saw him holding back his tears, but he was determined to go.

"If you find things are okay in California, I will come," I said. "It is too much of a burden for our brother."

Lan boarded the bus. We stood there waving to him till the bus disappeared down the lush green road. We went home, feeling empty.

CHAPTER 21

I wanted to go to a Buddhist temple to pray but I could not find any in Corinth. I went instead, to a Catholic church where I met a stout, middle-aged man who owned a McDonalds in town. He offered me a job, flipping hamburgers, for which I received $1.90 an hour. A black woman who was a cook taught me how to make pancakes, Egg McMuffins, hash browns, Quarter-Pounders with cheese, and Big Macs, and how to fry french fries and make apple pies. With a heavy southern accent she pronounced the names of the food, then she made me repeat them in my Vietnamese accent. For the first time I learned how to clean a toilet. I liked her and enjoyed working with her but the supervisor didn't like me because I didn't speak English fluently. He always made fun of me and spoke behind my back, calling me names. I understood him very well but I didn't let him know. The supervisor made me work longer hours when he wanted me to, without paying overtime, and sent me home when he didn't want me. I knew this job wasn't suited for me.

Tuong helped me find an English tutor at the Adult Education Center. I went to the center once a week and a teacher gave me a tape to listen to along with a textbook. I didn't learn very much from the tape so I began to pick up English from people off the street, bit by bit.

At this time, ITT began to lay people off. Tuong and his wife now worked only a few days a week. We fished to replace meat that we couldn't buy. We went into the lush woods, chopped bamboo shoots to make fishing rods, and dug worms for our bait. If we didn't catch fish, we went to a local fishery to fish at the pond, paying for the fresh catfish—still much cheaper than buying fish at the supermarket. Once in a while we went to the farmers market to buy fresh produce like onions and potatoes.

One day a small boy from our neighborhood pulled out a beautiful kite to fly. My nephews wanted a kite, but their father had to say no to them. I used a trash bag and bamboo to make a two-by-six-foot kite for them. I tied a fishing line on it and told my two nephews to hold the kite wings while I ran against the wind, pulling it up into the air. My nephews proudly told the neighbor boy in English that I had made the kite for them with a flute on it; it chirped every time we pulled the string. We tied it on the trailer to let it fly free day and night that summer. My nephews laughed and I smiled while their parents worried about the job situation, wondering where the next meal would come from. Our neighbors came to ask me to make kites for them. The community grew more friendly and we had a wonderful summer together.

Lan called from California and told me he was making progress, learning to become an electronic technician paid for by the CETA program. He urged me to come join him, saying we had more of a chance to succeed there than in Corinth.

"I just received a letter from home through Hanh in Italy," he said over the telephone's static. "It was terrible. We have to find a way to help our family survive."

"Yes, I understand. I'll let you know exactly what day I will arrive."

I hung up the phone and was lost in thought. I knew I had to leave here even though I loved my brother's family a lot. But why was it that I had to leave every time I met my loved ones or the one I loved? I had to be strong since my family was calling for help. I consoled myself by remembering that I could come back to visit and that I could call them. This was America and not Vietnam. I told Tuong and his wife that I had to move. They accepted the idea, but I could see in their faces that they were growing more lonely. I quit my job at McDonalds and left the next day for San Jose, California, waving goodbye to my brother, his wife, and the children I had come to know so well.

Lan and his friend met me at the bus station. I applied at the Job Corps for machinist training and English classes. When I finished my training a year-and-a-half later I found a job as a machine operator earning $4.25 an hour in Santa Clara. I worked from 5:00 p.m. to 5:00 a.m., every day including Saturday, to make a living, and saved money to send home. In order to save money, we shared an apartment with others and ate together. During the day I went to a farm to pick strawberries for fifteen cents a basket to sell. If I had time, I would help refugees arriving in the region with paperwork, school, and hospital visits for health checkups. Even though my English wasn't good enough, I still knew my way around and I understood more than I spoke. I did what I could to make the transition easier for them because I knew what it was like to be a displaced person.

Whenever Lan and I had a few hundred dollars, we sent it to our cousin in Paris to send to my family in Vietnam. My cousin knew someone who had a lot of gold back home, and wanted to transfer their money out of Vietnam. He would collect our money, then telegraph it to his family in Vietnam, who would then give the same amount in gold to our family. This was how my family survived.

My cousin told me that my parents had to report to the secret police every day, or else my two younger brothers would be forced to go to the labor camps in Cambodia. I knew I had to do something for my family. Through an underground connection, I somehow succeeded in arranging for my older and younger sisters plus my two younger brothers and a nephew to escape from the country to Indonesia in 1980. They came to America in 1981, leaving my parents and two older brothers behind.

Time passed as I worked hard day and night at a machine shop factory.

One day I took my sister and her frail, skinny daughter Khanh to the WIC office on Tully Road to apply for the Women, Infants, and Children Program. I asked the receptionist for an application and an appointment to see someone who could assist us, and she called the manager. After speaking a few seconds, she put the phone down and looked at me sadly.

"The manager said she doesn't want any Vietnamese."

"What?" I said, not believing my ears.

The receptionist repeated what she had said very slowly, as if I hadn't understood. I was frustrated, insulted, and humiliated but didn't know what to do. I felt defeated. Sorry, niece, I thought, I cannot help you to receive a few free gallons of milk a month to help you grow. Why did I come here in the first place? I wished I could go home, to a place where at least my skin and culture, my morals and values were the same as others'. A place where I was born and spoke the language. I wished I could die there someday, coming back to my roots, to the taste of the water and the air.

In the next weeks I grew determined to do something to change my situation in this society. I knew the only way to get out of my present predicament was by going to school, by getting an education. But where was the money going to come from? And how could my English become good enough to handle classes? I didn't know. I signed up at the community college and started taking classes. I started to do well in math and basic courses; but the atmosphere was strained—there were many Vietnamese who had signed up for classes just to receive money, since California residents didn't have to pay tuition. The lack of seriousness of a few Vietnamese students and difficulty with racial politics made me decide to move on, for the time being.

In the summer of 1983 my nephew, Phong, fifteen, and my two younger brothers, Minh and Nick, ages eighteen and sixteen, moved to California from Texas. I knew they had to go to high school here but I predicted that they would not make any progress in this environment. If I could not make it in this world, I wanted them to; besides, they were young and I was not married, so I felt a responsibility to try to give them what my parents had given me, since their parents could not be with them.

I decided I had to move away from our community in San Jose to find a good place for school and a better place to call home for them. I asked my brothers and my sisters, who by this time had jobs, to help my parents back home in Vietnam, while I began an adventure into an uncertain future. I hoped someday to settle down to have a family like any human being; but I had became a displaced person, a wandering soul who had no home to begin with. I wondered what my parents would say if they knew I had moved like a gypsy from place to place. I quit my job and closed my bank account. I had $1000 and only a few words of English. I loaded Minh, Nick, and Phong into my 1967 Pontiac Firebird—our old buffalo— together with sleeping bags, a bag of rice, dried food, some clothes, and other necessities. We said farewell to my family members, and headed north. Where to, I didn't know—but I had a good feeling about our journey.

We left San Jose on a beautiful July day, and headed out Interstate 80 East along the hilly highway. The grass had already turned brown in California's summer heat. I took a back road, passing Sacramento, the state capital. Everywhere I looked I saw farmland, and every breath brought the smell of cow dung into my nostrils. From here and there, the dirt blew up like small tornados as tractors plowed the fields endlessly, back and forth, in squares and rectangles. We were coasting down the road and talking excitedly about our trip and their other trip from Texas to California. The scenery reminded me a little of home but I didn't mention that to them. Sometimes, a tractor got on the highway from a field, emergency lights on and signals flashing.

"Uncle, slow down!" my nephew Phong said. "Watch out for the tractor!"

"Hey, who's doing the driving?" I laughed.

"Yeah, I know, uncle but you're old," Phong fought back, giggling.

"Look at my old buffalo," I patted the steering wheel. "It runs and looks beautiful. It's a classic. I'm old but I'm a classic one, boy."

"Okay, uncle, keep your eyes on the road," he said.

We laughed and our conversation grew merry. We traveled into the Nevada desert, through Salt Lake City, deep into Utah and then past Casper, Wyoming, down to Cheyenne. We stopped at a highway rest area, where we found a beautiful spot to have our supper. We slept under the clear skies that night. We moved on, traveling from one city to another, seeing what life was like in each one, and deciding whether to stay or move on. We came to the land of the good life, Nebraska. It was flat and had vast wheat fields that ran to the end of the horizon. It was a hot afternoon when we pulled into a rest area. It was clean and pleasant, the air warm. My nephew read a bulletin board and got a free map to share with my two brothers on a bench beneath a tree. I went to the bathroom, and bent over the sink to wash the road-dust from my face.

"Hello," an old man greeted me.

"Hello, how are you?" I said, looking up from the basin.

"Nothing to complain about at my old age," he said. "But something isn't right, you know."

I stood up, and looked at his wrinkled, long face.

"What's that, sir?" I asked.

"I travel with many women in my car and look how many boys are in your car. That's what's wrong," he smiled.

He shuffled out of the bathroom, I followed. Taking me by the elbow, he brought me to his wife and four beautiful granddaughters, and introduced me. My nephew and brothers came to the table where I was and said hello to them.

"Are you ready to go, uncle?" Phong asked.

"Where are you going?" the old man inquired.

"I don't know. We're just driving around the country to find a place to live," I said.

"Why don't you follow me to my home town?" the old man suggested, looking at us with sincerity.

"Where is that, sir?" one of my brothers asked.

"Valentine, Nebraska." He gave me a wink. "Valentine sounds like a good place for you boys to meet wives, don't you think? And there's plenty of work to be done."

I smiled, wondering how life would be there. "Sounds nice," I said, "but we haven't finished our travels yet. Maybe next time."

The grey-haired old man said goodbye to us and left. I hoped we would meet other hospitable people like him on the road, but who knew? The tangerine sun kissed the golden wheat, as we walked to the car. The sky was clear, the air fresh with the fragrance of the wheat. Here and there I saw a tractor moving through the middle of a field. Some places were bare, the soil plowed into furrows. Maybe a new planting had just began for another new crop. I felt peaceful driving my old buffalo out of the rest area, and moved onto Interstate 80 East, into the vast prairie cornfields of Iowa. When we stopped at a Burger King, I went up to the counter and ordered four

Whoppers, two apple pies, and a few drinks. The young lady who took my order forgot to give me forks for our apple pies.

"May I have a fa-a-a-r-k?" I asked.

She looked at me with big eyes.

"What?" she said.

"May I have a fa-a-a-r-k?" I said again louder, afraid she couldn't hear me.

Everyone stopped what they were doing, and looked at us.

"Um, sorry, but I'm busy," she said, and giggled. Everyone broke out laughing and I didn't understand why. My brothers and nephew looked at me and smiled too. I waited for the lady to stop laughing and used my hand to describe what I wanted and pointed to my mouth.

"Apple pie, apple pie."

"Oh, you want a fork," she said.

"Yeah, yeah!"

They laughed again and the girl's face turned red. She gave me what I wanted and I went to the table to eat with my brothers and nephew, feeling good about what I had just accomplished and wondering what they were laughing about. I wish I could have understood what I said then. Perhaps I missed my chance to settle in Iowa.

We kept driving east, not knowing where we were going or where to get food for the next day if we ran out of money. We traveled up to Wisconsin. In Ann Arbor, Michigan a policeman threw us out of a city park. I met a student at Michigan University who tried to help us settle, but it was expensive around that area. While looking for an apartment, I asked a pastor if we could sleep in his church basement for a night. That night I had a nightmare, and didn't feel good about myself, or about staying there. I asked Minh, Nick, and Phong if they wanted to go on or stay, and we agreed to move on. I drove through Ohio and took Interstate 90 to Buffalo, New York. The old buildings discouraged us, so we drove on, through Rochester to Albany, the capital of New York. It was August 23 and we had spent more than a month on the road without finding any place that seemed right for us. The end of the country was near: Vermont, New Hampshire, and Maine would be our last stops.

We spent a day in Albany. The city was okay but we weren't happy about it so we took Route 9 East to Vermont. Along the road, houses were settled and a few streetlights shone through the trees. It was countryside, rural, and I smelled fragrances in the air that were different from the Nebraska farmland. The trees, the grass, and woods seemed relaxed and easy. The further I went the more I noticed and felt a change, something that reminded me of my home back in Vietnam.

It was 10:00 p.m. when we approached Bennington. On the top of a hill overlooking the town, my buffalo coasted. The town slept in its valley, as we steered along the mountain hilltop between the generously spaced houses and streetlights. We rolled into the silent, empty street. I felt like a thief invading a convent, disturbing the scene with my car's noise. We rolled down Main Street to an intersection where yellow traffic lights flashed. I saw motels and a few stores that had closed hours earlier. I drove to the end of Main Street—about 500 feet— then turned around, to another road, and made a right and then a left turn to finish my inspection of the town. I saw a few pedestrians walking on a sidewalk, laughing.

"It's a nice little town, isn't it?" I said.

"Yes, yes," Minh, Nick, and Phong shouted excitedly. "Look at the downtown, it's so tiny!"

My nephew popped his head out of the window of the car.

"Stop, stop, uncle. Let's walk around!" Phong said.

I pulled the car over and parked on the deserted street. We went over to the sidewalk and walked down Main Street, stretching our legs, peering into shop windows. A car passed by. Moths clustered around the streetlights as if they held the vibrance of life, their shadows mixing with ours. We rented a room at the Catamount Motel for a night and took our first showers in ten days. That night, I slept like a baby.

We checked out of the motel before 11:00 a.m., went to Burger King for lunch, then drove around Bennington again. Downtown grew crowded, with more traffic everywhere. I parked my car in front of St. Peter's Church and walked along a sidewalk, looking at the people. I struck up a few conversations with local people and they seemed nice. We found a laundromat next to an auto parts store and did our wash, talking to the attendant. I picked up a copy of the *Bennington Banner* and called about a few apartment ads but nothing was available. A woman putting her laundry into a machine suggested that I call the school superintendent to see if he had anything available since he had a lot of properties to rent. I called him and explained our situation.

"Why did you bother to call when you don't have any money?" he said on the phone.

I thanked him but he hung up the phone before the words came out. I drove my brothers and nephew to Willow Park. We hung out for a few hours, looking through the telephone directory and at a stack of newspapers. I was nervous because I had $250 left in my pocket after paying for the motel, but even so the scenery excited me. From the top of a hill we looked down at the town; a lush green mountain range rose behind us into the clear sky. A few maple trees on the side of the road had already begun to change color from green to umber, orange, and fiery red.

After calling some realtors to no avail, I decided to head back into town, and started down the long hill. There were thousands of flowers blossoming by the side of the road, on hills, on plateaus, everywhere my eyes drifted: orange wild flowers, black-eyed susans, white daisies, crimson and purple cloves, stretching through whole fields. Suddenly my car hobbled and pitched. I pulled over to see what it was, but couldn't find anything wrong. I started the car, continuing down Route 7A back to Bennington. The car rolled uneasily, so we pulled over in front of a big furniture store with a huge chair displayed in front. I got out of the car and opened the hood for a second inspection, found nothing, and turned the ignition a couple of times. The car wouldn't start. I asked a salesman at the furniture shop if there was a garage nearby. He directed me to Mr. East, saying he had a lot of experience with American cars. I walked to his house, a block away from my car. In the driveway, a young man was sitting on a motorcycle.

"Hello," he said, smiling at us.

"Hello," I said timidly.

"What are you guys up to?" he said, friendly, and got off his motorcycle, walking closer.

"Not much. We're looking for an apartment to rent but it's hard to find one," I said.

"Where are you from?"

"Vietnam," my nephew Phong chimed in.

"No, I mean in the U.S.," he said, moving a toolbox with his muscular arm.

"California," I said.

"Oh, yeah. I see your license plate. Maybe I can help," he said.

He asked Mr. East if he could use the phone to call his uncle, a local realtor, to see if he had apartments available.

"Hey, my uncle has one on Benmont Avenue but it doesn't have a stove and refrigerator. Is that okay?"

"Sure," I said.

We met Mr. East, a calm, older man, and he told me that it would cost about $500 to rebuild the car, which needed new parts.

"I don't have any money now but would you fix it later?" I asked.

"Sure," he said.

I left the car and we went to see the apartment. It was more than a little run down, but we decided to rent it. I was happy to have a place to live—and it seemed that perhaps my fate was supposed to be here in this town where my car had broken down. I made a $230 deposit including the first month's rent, and promised to pay when Minh, Nick, and Phong had welfare and I had a job. We moved in that afternoon. I went to the Salvation Army and bought an electric stove for five dollars and a few pots, pans, and dishes to start a new home. I took Minh, Nick, and Phong to the welfare department to apply for food stamps, cash assistance, and Medicaid. And I tried to look for a job. I had ten dollars left in my pocket.

On Monday we went to Mt. Anthony High School to register my brothers and nephew for the 83-84 academic year. Here I met a friendly counselor named Joan Costin. She had grey hair and a benevolent face with sparkley eyes. In the next weeks, Joan got to know us and began to help us set up our lives. Kenneth, her husband, gave me a job as a part-time janitor at his church. I registered for vocational training in nursing and at the community college to study English. It was a wonderful, adventurous summer. It seemed that, with a lot of work, some of my dreams might come true.

* * *

I usually came to Joan and Ken's house to study English, to have dinner with them, or just to talk about life and the challenges of raising my two brothers and nephew.

"I have to be a father, a mother, a brother, a sister, and a friend for them," I said. "Sometimes I don't know who I am anymore."

"You have to have your own life, too, Jade," Joan said, touching my hand. Tears came to my eyes. My life seemed so full of constant uncertainty; but now, at least, there was someone who could listen to and understand me.

Joan asked me about my family back home in Vietnam and I told her many stories about the war, what my life and my family were like, how it was when I was a child. I spent hours with Joan reading English poetry. I loved "The Wasteland" by Eliot, "Dover Beach," by Matthew Arnold, and many others. I could recite them without opening the book, just like I did with Vietnamese poetry.

"You're a good storyteller and a good poet, Jade," Joan said while chopping carrots. "It's not only because of your voice but the way you tell it, and it shows in your writing. I don't know how to explain it to you, but there's something there."

She poured the carrots into simmering water. I stood up from a chair to help her set the table for dinner.

"I'm learning English, mom."

"You're doing all right, kid."

She laughed and smiled at me. I called Ken for supper. Our conversation was light and cheerful while the evening wore on. Joan asked me what I wanted to do with my life and I told her that I wanted to receive an education. That week, she gathered applications for Bennington College, Castleton College, and the University of Vermont, and helped me fill them out and send them in. Bennington College called me for an interview. I came into the office to see a counselor.

"Why do you want to go to college?" the counselor asked me with a friendly smile.

"I love to study and I love school. I feel there is something missing in my life if I miss school for a day," I said.

"But why school and not something else?" asked the counselor.

"School is a tiny part of life and life is a whole big school," I answered.

The neatly-attired counselor paused for a second to think. He smiled at me.

"What do you plan to do at Bennington College?"

"I plan to study English first, then get into British and American Literature."

"Why literature?" the counselor asked. "That would be very hard since English isn't your native language."

"I used to study Vietnamese literature which is older than British and American literature. I think we are only limited by our imagination."

"What do you want to be then?"

"I want to be a Vietnamese novelist," I answered with all of my heart.

The counselor gave me a firm handshake and thanked me for an interesting conversation. He told me that if I had any questions I should feel free to call him. I was happy that day and slept well that night, confident that maybe the college would admit me.

The October wind blew into my room, waking me up early in the morning. I listened to the shade rattling against the window pane. The sound increased and slowly faded away like the footsteps of a person walking with a wooden leg. Within me I felt that autumn had finally arrived but I did not know for sure. It was a lonely sort of feeling, as if the whole world was devoid of meaning. Memories flashed in front of me and I tried to cry out but the sounds got stuck inside my throat. Outside the wind kept on whistling roughly like an asthma patient trying to whisper. The night became clear, yielding to the sunrise.

I went downstairs to boil some water for a cup of hot tea and to prepare breakfast for Minh, Nick, and Phong, who were getting ready for school. Behind the apartment, a field of yellow wildflowers stood in tatters. Dew had dampened them overnight but now it melted under the sun, I could see pollen whirl like millions of atoms. Birds chirruped on a maple tree next to the house. Bees and tiny butterflies began to get busy for those last autumn days, while ripened maple and oak leaves changed color. They would fall to the ground one by one, layer by layer, shaking and dying, leaving only their bare-chested natural skin to get ready for the coming winter.

Christmas arrived in that cold winter of 1983. Joan brought us many gifts, especially books. She gave us Webster, Oxford, and Longman English dictionaries, the basic book of synonyms/antonyms, *Immortal Poems of the English Language, the Harbrace College Handbook, Roget's II The New Thesaurus, The Elements of Style*—anything she could think of for school. She gave us wool sweaters, scarfs, gloves, anything for winter to keep us warm. Kenneth took us to the shoe outlet to buy us winter boots. We greeted the winter well prepared, and we could not have done it without my adopted parents. I loved them dearly, but though I never said so, I knew that they understood my heart.

A friend of Joan's had a daughter who worked at the Killington ski resort. He promised to take me skiing but he was sick that day so he asked his daughter to be the temporary host for the trip. Kala took me to where she worked and told me to rent ski equipment and gave me a day-pass ticket.

"I have to go to work now. Come and meet me when you're finished skiing."

"Okay, I'll see you later."

She left. I sat there and looked around, putting my skis on. I just did like everyone else in the room. When they walked out to get on the ski lift, I followed them. When I stepped out I fell. They helped me up. Very nice people, I thought. They sat on the chairlift and I did the same. The chair pulled me up, higher and higher and I looked down. Everything was beautiful and people moved fast on the snow. I was excited. When I reached the top I saw them just standing up and sliding smoothly down the hill. I stood up but instead of sliding smoothly, I tumbled. The attendant at the chairlift came to me.

"Have you ever skied before?" he asked.

I thought he was thinking I was an idiot.

"No, this is the first time in my life," I said proudly. "Is there anything wrong?"

"No, no," he said. "Did you take any lessons down there before you came up here?" He gave me a friendly smile.

"Oh, no. I just watched and followed people."

"Oh!"

He helped me hold my skis parallel to each other and I pushed with my ski poles. I fell again. He came and helped me up again patiently. What is wrong with me, I wondered? Everyone is doing fine, even a little child who just passed me. I stood up again and the attendant took out a brochure to explain to me where to go.

"Follow this green slope," he pointed at the map. "This is the easiest way."

"Sure, thank you," I said.

"I have to go back to work now. I hope you have a good time," he said, and left me by myself.

I looked down the slope where he had pointed. It looked steep—yet he had said it was the easiest way. Was he kidding? He thought I was stupid or something. I stood up, pushed, and fell again. The boots felt strange on my feet. I stood up again and followed the martial arts steps I had learned when I was young. I didn't care about what he had instructed me to do. I pushed myself, went a little ways, and fell again. People kept passing me as if they were in the fast lane. I struggled with the skis and got about ten yards away from the chairlift.

"Hello."

I looked back and there was a beautiful girl with a charming smile.

"Hello," I said.

"Are you doing okay?" she asked.

"I think I'm in trouble, I guess."

"What trouble?"

"Skiing," I said. "I don't know what's wrong but I can't move these things on my feet."

"Look, it's easy. If you want to turn left, move your butt to the right and if you want to turn right, move your butt to the left. Got it?"

She demonstrated for me. I tried to do it the way she showed me.

"Yeah," I nodded my head.

"Bend your knees, keep your skis parallel, and move from side to side," she said. "Don't go straight because you'll move too fast and you'll lose control."

"Oh, I got it," I smiled at her.

She helped me for fifteen minutes and then left. I kept falling but not as much as before. The air was fresh and cold. I felt as if my body had turned numb and I looked down to see how far I had to go. The trail seemed to stretch out forever to the bottom of the mountain where I saw the resort. I pushed on. By the time I arrived at the bottom, the stores were closed and lights were coming on. My temporary host had finished her job, and sat on a bench waiting for me.

"How come it took you so long?" she asked.

"Because I walked all the way down the mountain and counted every one of my steps," I said.

I was proud that I had taken the challenge to count my steps from the top of the mountain all the way down. I smiled and she smiled. We went home.

The winter was hard, the cold wind chilling my bones. I forgot all about my college applications until I received a letter from Bennington College and Castleton College: I had been accepted to both. The month was dreary, cold, and depressing, but I felt light. Joan threw a party to celebrate the news. We were all happy and life rolled on. Minh, Nick, and Phong had a hard time at the beginning of the year with their work at school, but after a couple months they moved from being D students to the honor roll at Mt. Anthony High School. I was proud of them and for my parents in Vietnam. I watched my two brothers and nephew happily growing up. Bennington extended a full scholarship to me, so in the spring of 1984 I was able to move into the Wooley House dorm to begin my academic life and continued to look after my two brothers and nephew.

I sat on a platform up on the hill, surrounded by trees in their spring blossom, looking over the pond at Bennington College, listening to the gentle voice of Arturo Vivante blending with the morning air as he lectured on Tolstoy's great novel, *War and Peace*.

I felt like one of the characters in Tolstoy's story—in a different place, and a different time—victimized by the same destruction of life.

Birds flitted round a hollow in one of the trees. I heard the little ones calling to their parents for nourishment. Now and then, the mother and father flew in and out of the nest with some worms dangling from their mouths. Beneath the tree, squirrels scampered about, chattering to each other, some searching for a companion. They ran and stopped, lifting their heads as if they were listening to the sounds of spring. Across the platform stood the red admissions building—people called it the Barn. At the window, the bees danced on the flowers, making the petals quiver; the dusty pollen flew lightly in the air.

From the bushes, a family of ducks marched like a small squadron toward the pond, the father and mother ahead, their chicks following behind. When they reached the water, they swam slowly to a large pool among the reed bushes where they flapped their wings and splashed each other playfully, happy in their freedom.

Through the golden rays of sun, I noticed gossamer drifting out of nowhere into empty spaces. From the other side of the campus I could hear the noise of the lawn mower running, now loudly, and now quietly, the smell of freshly cut grass filling the air with fragrances of change—maybe the warmth, maybe the passion of spring fever beckoned me; maybe the sun shone exceedingly bright; maybe the hope for change, like life, was ignited again. All of a sudden, a light blue butterfly wandered in front of me, twittered around my book, and then flew towards the sky into the sun's warmth.

I left my mother, my family. I had a family—a father, a mother, brothers, and sisters. We had such a happy family: even though there was pain, we had each other and we shared the bitterness of life. Now, each of us had taken a different

path. Nine of us were refugees scattered around the U.S. trying to make a living and holding on to our lives. We left our
parents and two older brothers behind in Vietnam. I tried to
sponsor them after I came to the U.S. but I could not beat the
odds, the bureaucracy, the government, especially when I did
not have money and power. What have we done or completed?
Were we just a bunch of people who betrayed our parents, especially our mother? Am I the one who left in the middle of
the game? Am I the one who gave up?

I received a letter from my mother. She wrote: "Your uncle
and my two sisters have just died all at the same time and I attended the funeral. Everyone my age is gone now. My eyes are
blurry and I don't know when I'll become blind. After the war,
I'm left with only eleven children. I count on my fingers to
make sure how many of you are left—but where are you? What
has happened to you? I wish I could see you before I die. In
spite of my blindness, I could touch you and listen to your
voice . . ."

There was something stuck inside my throat, something
pressing heavily upon my chest—maybe because I hadn't had a
chance to cry.

I kept thinking of my mother. She never went to work—she
stayed home and took care of the family, but the household job
seemed to last a whole day. Every night, I heard her footsteps,
the flip-flopping of her sandals, walking into our room, listening to our breathing or restlessness. If my sister or brother
tossed and turned she would light the candle and go into our
net to search for mosquitoes until she assured herself that we
were comfortable enough to sleep. Sometimes she just sat at
the side of our bed and rubbed our backs or fanned us on a humid night.

After we were asleep, she checked us all again and again.
When I was sick, she brought me food and medicine. She held
us when we cried or yelled out—after a nightmare or a spanking from my father.

If the battle outside drew near, she would hide us in a corner of the house while my father and older brothers rushed to
gather provisions, ready to evacuate. Often, my mother walked
over and stood near the window, peering through the city's

darkness, listening to the shells drop here and there upon the city. With every shell explosion her heart went out to her children, wondering if they were safe, if the army had been attacked; then she sighed and stepped away from the window, wishing her children were still young and happy the way we were before the war. I heard my father sneezing and calling to my mother, asking for coffee. Then they comforted each other, telling themselves not to worry—"Who knows about life?" Their voices became softer and softer.

It was my old house, our family house—where we had grown up, bathed in the warmth of family love, listening to my mother's voice. The divan was there where mother used to sit. All those lively scenes from yesterday come back vividly.

Mama, what am I to say now? Perhaps the only pain we have is that pain of distance from family, far away from our homeland—the pain of your son who is still alive after that long war.

The roughness of her skin, dry with wrinkles showed the hardship she had to suffer, as she paid the duty of a daughter-in-law, the duty of a wife, and the duty of a mother. How can I describe that life in words?

ABOUT THE AUTHOR

Jade Ngọc Quang Huỳnh was born in 1957 in the Mekong Delta region of South Vietnam. He attended Saigon University in 1974 until the North Vietnamese Army took control of the south in 1975. After enduring a year of inhuman conditions and torture in a labor camp, he managed to escape and finally reached a refugee camp in Thailand. In 1978, Huỳnh flew to the United States. Since his arrival, he has worked in a series of factory and cleaning jobs, completed his B.A. at Bennington College in Vermont, and received an M.F.A. degree from Brown University.

The text was designed by Ellen Huber Scott.
It is set in Galliard type by The Typeworks and
manufactured by Edwards Brothers
on acid-free paper.

Jade Ngọc Quang Huỳnh was born in 1957, survived the war, and became a university student in 1974. Because the Hanoi government policy was to persecute writers, intellectuals, and any suspected "enemies of the state," Huỳnh was sent to labor camps for "education in communist ideology, psychological and physical retraining, and lessons on how to become a happy and productive member in their new society."

Escaping Vietnam in 1977, first to Thailand and then to the United States, Huỳnh spent six years working at fast food restaurants, cleaning bathrooms, washing dishes, and working in factories. He then decided that formal education would improve his situation, and he received a Bachelor of Arts degree from Bennington College in 1987. In 1992 he received a Master of Fine Arts degree from Brown University.